HO E

Explorations in Practical, Pastoral and Empirical Theology

Series Editors

Leslie J. Francis, University of Warwick, UK
Jeff Astley, North of England Institute for Christian Education, UK
Martyn Percy, Ripon College Cuddesdon and The Oxford Ministry Course, Oxford, UK

Theological reflection on the church's practice is now recognized as a significant element in theological studies in the academy and seminary. Ashgate's series in practical, pastoral and empirical theology seeks to foster this resurgence of interest and encourage new developments in practical and applied aspects of theology worldwide. This timely series draws together a wide range of disciplinary approaches and empirical studies to embrace contemporary developments including: the expansion of research in empirical theology, psychological theology, ministry studies, public theology, Christian education and faith development; key issues of contemporary society such as health, ethics and the environment; and more traditional areas of concern such as pastoral care and counselling.

Other titles in the series include:

Ordinary Christology
Who Do You Say I Am? Answers From The Pews
Ann Christie

The Ecclesial Canopy
Faith, Hope, Charity
Martyn Percy

Shaping the Church
The Promise of Implicit Theology
Martyn Percy

Engaging with Contemporary Culture
Christianity, Theology and the Concrete Church
Martyn Percy

Ordinary Theology
Looking, Listening and Learning in Theology
Jeff Astley

How Survivors of Abuse Relate to God

The Authentic Spirituality of the Annihilated Soul

SUSAN SHOOTER
Diocese of Truro, UK

Routledge
Taylor & Francis Group
LONDON AND NEW YORK

First published 2012 by Ashgate Publishing

Published 2016 by Routledge
2 Park Square, Milton Park, Abingdon, Oxfordshire OX14 4RN
711 Third Avenue, New York, NY 10017, USA

First issued in paperback 2016

Routledge is an imprint of the Taylor & Francis Group, an informa business

British Library Cataloguing in Publication Data
Shooter, Susan.
How survivors of abuse relate to God : the authentic spirituality of the annihilated soul. — (Explorations in practical, pastoral and empirical theology)
1. Abused women—Religious life. 2. Abused women—Attitudes.
3. Abused women—Pastoral counseling of. 4. Church and social problems.
5. Spirituality. 6. Theology, Practical.
I. Title II. Series
261.8'33153–dc23

Library of Congress Cataloging-in-Publication Data
Shooter, Susan.
How survivors of abuse relate to God : the authentic spirituality of the annihilated soul / Susan Shooter.
p. cm. — (Explorations in practical, pastoral, and empirical theology)
Includes bibliographical references (p.) and indexes.
ISBN 978-1-4094-4126-7 (hardcover : alk. paper)
1. Abused women—Religious life. 2. Adult child abuse victims—Religious life. 3. Sexual abuse victims—Religious life. 4. Child sexual abuse—Religious aspects—Christianity. I. Title.
BV4596.A2S56 2012
261.8'327082—dc23

2012005339

ISBN 13: 978-1-138-27963-6 (pbk)
ISBN 13: 978-1-4094-4126-7 (hbk)

Contents

List of Tables *vii*
Foreword *ix*
Preface *xi*
Abbreviations *xiii*

1 Introduction: What Lies Beneath 1

2 Knocking at the Door: Presenting Issues 9

3 Finding the Right Key: A Grounded Qualitative Design 29

4 Opening Up: How Survivors of Abuse Relate (to) God 51

5 Crossing the Threshold: Job the Survivor? 81

6 At Home with God: Marguerite Porete's *Mirror* 113

7 The Authentic Spirituality of the Annihilated Soul 151

8 What Lies Ahead: Conclusions and Implications 169

Epilogue *173*

Bibliography *175*
Author Index *191*
Scripture Index *195*
Subject Index *199*

List of Tables

2.1	Comparison of Sgroi's and Herman's stages of recovery	12
2.2	Penal substitution theory compared with experience of incest victim	20
2.3	Incarnational atonement compared with experience of clergy abuse	22
3.1	Range of different abuses experienced by nine interviewees	42
3.2	Range of denominations experienced by nine interviewees	43
3.3	Early coding of incidents in open code 'difficulty in forgiving'	47
4.1	Development of three main open codes into higher concepts	52
4.2	Open codes grouped under the higher category Transformation	59
4.3	Examples of how serving God and others became a concept	66
4.4	Informal ministries undertaken by nine interviewees	67
4.5	Formal ministries sought by eight respondents	72
4.6	Excerpt from MACSAS leaflet (2009)	73
4.7	Theoretical memo 'Obstacles to Ministry'	74
5.1	Comparison of Joanna and Job about being heard	89
5.2	Comparison of Joanna and Job about suicidal thoughts	90
6.1	How the Mirror's various schemes and stages fit together	122

Foreword

by Ann Loades[1]

Dr Shooter has a distinguished track record as a teacher and ordained minister in the Church of England, and has harnessed her resources in scripture (the Book of Job), tradition (Marguerite Porete's *Mirror of Simple Souls*), reason (appropriate research design) and experience (those of Christian women survivors of abuse) to produce a remarkable book. She has needed her own tenacious kind of spirituality to find a way of grappling with 'survivor spirituality' so as to 'voice' it.

Dr Shooter rightly attends to aspects of supposed 'pastoral care' which veer between the inept and the positively abusive, whether in respect of premature and bullying injunctions about 'forgiveness' or a 'point' of deep personal suffering. Offered by ordained representatives (not themselves 'abusers') of precisely the ecclesiastical institutions that have fostered and protected 'abusers', the harm done can be deepened and not merely perpetuated. The implications for ministerial 'training' and 'formation' are all too obviously very serious.

Astonishingly, Dr Shooter found that whilst those being abused may have prayed for some form of 'divine intervention', they found rather that they experienced 'God's timeless presence' transforming them over time. Ambiguities may abound, but as the possibilities of self-deception are plumbed to the limit, illumination and blessing may also abound. The problem is then to avoid offering this as yet another abusive 'justification' for the suffering of abuse, as a survivor both moves into a kind of unbounded relationship with God which at the same time enables them to establish proper boundaries with others. Not only do those in positions of authority have to come to appreciate the limits of their own capacities for pastoral care, perhaps for the first time, but they should also find themselves positively learning from those who have endured abuse, to whom they need most profoundly to listen.

Extraordinarily, survivors may become informal and 'unauthorized' agents of transformation for others in their turn, no longer living merely as 'survivors'. Not the least important facet of their agency may be in generating a community's capacity to 'attend' to the presence of God in some apparently God-denying circumstances.

---

[1] Ann Loades CBE is Professor Emerita of Divinity in the University of Durham, England, and Honorary Professor in the School of Divinity, University of St Andrews, Scotland.

Dr Shooter's combination of resources both past and present is unique to her personally, as is her capacity to think her way through to an appropriate comprehension of what she has learned so that she can transmit it to her readers – of which, one may hope, there will be many.

Preface

The authenticity of a natural pearl can be detected by an x-ray which reveals its multiple layers of iridescence. These layers are developed following an injury or attack on soft tissue within the organism, from which emerges a beauty beyond price. For this book I feel I have had the privilege of uncovering some genuine, rare pearls and have held them up to the light so that we might appreciate their singularity. It has at times been a dark voyage, yet the faith and commitment of the women I interviewed kept me afloat. For the spine-tinglingly exquisite moments of grace experienced in the darkness, I will be eternally grateful to them.

The impetus for my doctoral thesis, on which this book is based, lies much further back in my personal life story than in the conception of a social scientific research design. The lack in material on the spirituality of the abused was the presenting problem, but this scarcity struck a deep resonance with my experiences from parish ministry, my church background, my faith journey and my hunt for scriptural and spiritual sustenance. Serendipity also played her part when during the early stages of the DMin course at King's College London, I came across the *Mirror of Simple Souls* written by obscure medieval mystic Marguerite Porete. Marguerite, which means 'pearl' in her native French, reached down the centuries like a beacon, her spiritual insights holding up a mirror which helped me view more clearly so many diverse strands of experience. Alongside her, and the nine women I interviewed, I have been aided in this task by many colleagues, friends, advisors and family members, to whom I owe debts of gratitude and whom I now wish to acknowledge and thank.

The Women's CME Trust and the Diocese of Rochester both generously provided some of the funding towards my doctorate. The academic support which my supervisor Dr Susannah Ticciati gave me, by thoroughly reviewing early drafts of each chapter, stretched me intellectually and on numerous occasions she helped me to 'see the wood for the trees'. Dr Yvonne Warren, Christian psychotherapist, and Andrea Blows, Bishop's Advisor for Child Protection in the Diocese of Rochester, gave me excellent professional advice for elucidating the criteria for canvassing and interviewing participants. I must also mention MACSAS for their willingness to place an advertisement for volunteers on their website, and who continue to do excellent work in supporting survivors of clergy abuse.

I am so grateful to my external examiners, Professor Ann Loades and Dr Nicola Slee, who gave me strong encouragement to seek publication. I deeply appreciate Ann's unhesitating agreement to write the foreword for this book, and for reading and commenting on the final draft. Nicola, who showed me generous hospitality after the viva, has continued to encourage me in my research and has given me lots of helpful advice on publishing work. I must also mention Dr Anne Phillips who has advised me on production of the manuscript, and Sarah Lloyd and David Shervington at Ashgate who have provided ongoing support throughout the process. My cell group friends, Revd. Canon Ruth Oates, Revd. Paul Hunt and Revd. Adam Carlill, have also encouraged me in my writing; I am grateful to Adam for his help in transliterating the Hebrew for the chapter on Job.

For spiritual sustenance and priestly ministry during the rigorous times of analysis and theological exploration I am eternally thankful for my friends and colleagues Revd. Susan Twynam and Revd. Canon Gordon Oliver. They were at the end of a phone line when I needed to talk and, with their families, have generously opened their homes to me. The daily office was never a favourite spiritual practice of mine, but sharing evening prayer with Revd. Deryn Roberts and Sheila Cooper in our village church has been a 'godsend'.

My family is the greatest support of all. My parents have helped me in practical ways with the Porete material: my Mum (Nancy) put her typing skills to good use, and my Dad (Árpád Kásás) translated two academic articles from the original Hungarian. Adrian, Matt and Tom, my three lovely sons, have constantly encouraged me and helped me in lots of little practical ways, from searching out stray references to supplying me with food and drinks to keep me going.

I am absolutely delighted with the cover design which was created by my daughter-in-law, Catherine Kásás. She grasped immediately the essence of the book's themes and has produced a stunning image that encapsulates the spiritual story of 'survivors'.

Ben, our dog, has been a faithful companion; he has kept me grounded, healthy and sane with our daily walks in the beautiful setting of north Cornwall, where we moved in order for me to work on this project. It is the willingness of my husband Ian to travel long distances and work extra hours that has been the key to making this book a reality. He has provided me with time and space to think and write; only he knows how costly the research journey has been, because he has shared the storms. Yet he has remained my best friend. Thank you.

Susan Shooter
Advent 2011

Abbreviations

The following abbreviations are used in the text:

AV	King James Authorized Version
CSSA	Christian Survivors of Sexual Abuse
ESV	English Standard Version
JB	Jerusalem Bible
MACSAS	Ministry And Clergy Sexual Abuse Survivors
NIV	New International Version
NRSV	New Revised Standard Version

Unless otherwise stated all scriptural quotations are from the New Revised Standard Version (Oxford: Oxford University Press, 1995).

For the Posse

Chapter 1
Introduction: What Lies Beneath

By the age of 18 around 25 per cent of girls and 10 per cent of boys have been victims of sexual abuse, so most available statistics tell us.[1] Some authors suggest even higher percentages[2] and it is clear that in the first decades of the twenty-first century we have been gripped by panic about such abuse, not to mention the furore about the sexualization of children in our culture. The alarming statistics and the daily dose of abuse stories in the media highlight the silence which shrouded this issue before the 1970s, when Child Sexual Abuse was considered extremely rare, a mere footnote in textbooks on child psychology.[3] It was the women's movement, or 'second-wave feminism', that provided the political context which was so crucial in exposing the extent of the sexual and other wide-ranging abuses suffered in secret and in silence by women and children, particularly in the private and personal 'sanctuary' of the home.[4] Helena Kennedy QC reminds us in this respect that not until 1991 was it deemed possible for a man to rape his wife, and consequently such abuse made illegal.[5]

In the sanctuary of the church silence has been even more obdurate,[6] where ecclesiastical authorities have been slow to defend the abused, particularly when perpetrators are clergy.[7] Abusing priests have often been sided with in order to avert scandal, or more recently disassociated from the institution of the Church in an attempt to avoid punitive financial damages. For instance, in the case brought by 'JGE', who was sexually abused as a six-year-old resident of a children's home, the Catholic Church claimed that the culpable priest should not be considered legally as an employee, and therefore the Church was not 'vicariously liable' for the priest's actions, thus shirking any responsibility.[8] Even churches with robust child protection policies can still mishandle clergy exploitation of adults who,

---

1 Finkelhor et al. (1989), p. 381; Hall (1995), p. 129; Gosney (2002), p. 3; Hedges-Goettl (2004), p. 12.

2 Loades (2001), p. 154.

3 Valentine and Feinauer (1993), p. 216; Cooper-White (1995), pp. 152–3; Rosetti (1995), pp. 1469–70.

4 Herman (1994), p. 32; Loades (2001), p. 142.

5 Kennedy, H. (2005), p. 119.

6 Hedges-Goettl (2004), p. 14.

7 Poling (2005), p. 63.

8 Doward (2011).

seeking spiritual support during a life crisis which often can be precipitated by experiences of abuses in childhood, are drawn instead by predatory clergy into an unwanted and damaging sexual relationship. Subsequently these victims are forced to keep silent to protect ministers' reputations and the sensibilities of their congregations, and if the abuse should be reported, it is regularly referred to by the authorities as an 'affair'. Researchers into such exploitative relationships insist this is a complete misnomer and that these liaisons should always be more appropriately labelled an abuse of professional ethics.[9]

The title of this chapter makes reference to a film[10] in which an apparently respectable research scientist has killed the student with whom he had an adulterous, and unethical, sexual relationship. Having dumped her corpse in the lake, his amnesiac wife becomes his next quarry after she recovers her memory and uncovers his deadly secret. With supernatural help from the murdered girl, we learn that behind the face of the outwardly loving husband there is violence and lust; in the murky waters of the past there is a body to be discovered. This book, with the help of those who have been victims of abuse and 'soul murder',[11] seeks to answer the question, what *does* lie rotting beneath the surface of the Christian Church and its theology that must be dragged into the open? For if we are to find some way of swimming through the mire of damaged and damaging relationships, of opening wounds to the air for healing, then those who have had their voices drowned out are the people we need urgently to listen to, and more importantly, hear clearly. The driving force behind the doctoral thesis on which this book is based began as a hunch and grew into the full conviction, that those who have held the secret of their victimization might understand most about the corrosive subtlety of abusive power relations. We need to know what is at the heart of the abused and their continuing relationship with the God, whom as Christians we declare is Love. A slither of hope is proffered by this study, but it is discovered in the deepest oceans of despair and damage through which we must wade. For hope cannot be conjured up by the will; we must not 'rush to resurrection'[12] without first facing the reality of destruction, for some never do find their way to Easter morning.

Having met with many vulnerable and abused people on my own journey, and reflecting on these encounters during the course of this study, I have come to realize that, not only have I experienced specific assaults on my own person of which I was aware, I have also been part of a web of distorted and distorting relationships in systems that are themselves warped; of this I was not so aware. Therefore what now follows in this introduction will first place the dynamics of

---

[9] Ormerod and Ormerod (1995); Fortune (1999); Kennedy, M. (2003).

[10] *What Lies Beneath*, directed by Robert Zemeckis (Dreamworks and 20th Century Fox, 2000).

[11] 'Soul murder' is a term for child abuse and deprivation coined by Leonard Shengold, quoted in Cooper-White (1995), p. 152.

[12] Cashman (1993), p. 74.

power abuse within the context of patriarchal values, looking beneath the 'secular' context and suggesting that these values have been supported by distorted Christian theology at its bedrock. Subsequently an outline of each chapter will set out the parameters of the book and the empirical research at its core, which pays close attention to the spiritual experience and faith of nine Christian survivors of abuse. This work shares an underlying hermeneutical principle with that of James Poling, who writes that 'those with the least power can reveal the most about the nature of the good and unmask the abuse of power'.[13] My assertion is that those who have made the arduous journey to recovery from abuse have along the way acquired an authentic spirituality. This spirituality turns out to be theologically challenging, deconstructs traditional doctrines and practices, and insists on the intimate and empowering presence of God.

Abuse, Patriarchal Values and Theology

Witnessing a *SlutWalk* might on the surface give the onlooker the impression that liberated female self-expression has finally, in 2012, been realized. On the contrary, *SlutWalk*[14] is a new global demonstration of female solidarity that aims to expose age-old rape myths, particularly the myth that rapists can be excused their violent behaviour because of what women wear. Such movements show that despite twentieth-century legislation addressing equality for women, patriarchal values appear intransigent. Power inequalities are seen obviously in pay and promotion differentials,[15] and Poling's argument still holds true that the family is idealized in our culture as the basic social unit. This 'ideal' is, according to him, a location where children are not listened to, especially if they come from a 'good family'; moreover, females are socialized into accommodating behaviours while males are socialized into a sense of entitlement to control the family and to be served.[16] According to him this combination of attitudes results in 'sanctioned forms of social control of women and other marginal groups' expressed explicitly through sexual violence and in socially sanctioned protection for men in their abusive conduct.[17] That Western society is an unsafe place for women and children is supported by Judith Herman's analysis of her clinical experience with victims of rape and battery, whose symptoms of post-traumatic stress were indistinguishable from those suffered by soldiers exposed to extreme combat. She concludes that the trauma of the public warzone for men is comparable to the private social environment to which women and children are exposed in the home *as a rule*.[18]

---

13 Poling (1991), p. 14.

14 See SlutWalk London! (2011).

15 For statistics see Fawcettsociety (2012). See also Banyard (2010), p. 2.

16 Poling (1991), pp. 29, 54.

17 Poling (1991), p. 12.

18 Herman (1994), pp. 2–3, 20ff.

Nearly 20 years on, Angela McRobbie, in a resounding echo of Poling, writes about 'resurgent patriarchies and gender retrenchment' played out particularly on girls' and women's bodies, not only in a 'post-feminist masquerade' of endless beautifying regimes aimed at pleasing the onlooker,[19] but also in pornographic violence.[20] Furthermore, while there has been no let-up in the incidence of sexual and domestic violence, young women without any history of specific abuses are now arriving traumatized in Susie Orbach's consulting room, suffering from a bodily anxiety, terror even, which she believes is transmitted 'transgenerationally' and dictated by global consumerism.[21] The added complication of the present situation, which all these feminist writers identify, is that women and girls are supposedly making an empowered 'choice' to go under the knife, starve their bodies and become sexual objects. Abuse, then, has a wide and complex definition, although the survivors I interviewed in this study reported specific traumatic events and relationships rather than any perceived social malaise.

Reluctance in our culture to relinquish stereotyped gender roles and traditional family relationships is reflected in the Church's corresponding reluctance to relinquish dominant masculine imagery in liturgy, in academic theology, and in ecclesiological representation. For instance, Jim Cotter points out that the Anglican Common Worship Baptism service which was introduced in 2000, includes the promise required of candidates that they 'submit to Christ as Lord', despite the extremely negative effect this would have on those who have been forced to submit to abuse. The response of a member of the Liturgical Commission to Cotter's critique was that 'the connection simply had not been made'.[22] Regarding academic theology, in response to the feminist challenge to the all-male Trinity, still worshipped as Father, Son and Holy Spirit who is 'Lord of life', Colin Gunton argues that the only self-relatedness of God to us is as Father of Jesus and therefore God is necessarily patriarchal and should remain so.[23] Furthermore, the theological arguments for excluding women from positions of authority, namely that they cannot represent the paternal Father or be an icon of the masculine Son, are set out clearly in the report *Women Bishops in the Church of England?*[24] Such convictions are still held by many Christians. These examples may seem less damaging, even benign manifestations of die-hard or, if McRobbie is to be believed, retrenching social values. But when it is observed that in Australia in the Diocese of Sydney the subordination of women to men is still taught under the guise of 'complementarity', and the single biggest cause of death in New South

19 McRobbie (2009), pp. 54, 59ff.

20 On the massive growth of the 'sex industry' and the abuse of women in it, see Maguire (2008) and Banyard (2010).

21 Orbach (2010), p. 10.

22 Cotter (2000), p. 55.

23 Gunton (1992).

24 House of Bishops (2004), pp. 136–82. See Shooter (2013) on the pastoral and ecclesiological effects of challenging the exclusively male Trinity.

Wales for women under the age of 45 is domestic violence,[25] questions must be asked. Poling has argued that the most intransigent sex offenders (sexual abusers of children and clergy sexual abusers of parishioners who fail to recognize their culpability even when confronted) give extreme expression to the patriarchal theologies of domination that lie at the base of our Western culture.[26] With its intrinsic code of adult male entitlement to the submission of women and children, onto whom sinfulness and weakness are projected, the underlying adult male identification is with 'Father-God' who gives those in power rights and privileges, creating a society which refuses to identify with the vulnerable and abused. Thus the abuse of power is a *theological* problem.[27]

It is not extraneous that for centuries women have been silenced in theology. It is also in the wake of the women's movement that feminist theologians have emerged and, as Gunton's essay shows, begun to challenge the fundamentally masculine values on which the male God was modelled. Many feminists have argued that this God is idolatrous, reflecting a narcissistic self-aggrandizement of male theologians[28] with notions of unilateral autonomy signified by disembodied transcendence; familial headship by omnipotent fatherhood; and entitlement to service from lesser beings by the omnipresent demand for obedience. Worship of such divine masculine attributes have left women, children and 'lesser men', that is, anyone without political or social clout, in a powerless and vulnerable location, with no voice. Furthermore, the silence that occludes violence against women and children and reinforces patriarchal dominance is found throughout Scripture, such as in the stories of Hagar, Tamar, Jephthah's daughter and the concubine in Judges, all highlighted in Phyllis Trible's literary-feminist readings.[29] Pamela Cooper-White recreates the story of 14-year-old virgin princess Tamar (2 Samuel 13) and shows how she is betrayed by all the men in her household.[30] Raped and thereby socially destroyed by her half-brother, ignored and cut off as 'spoiled' property by her father, then silenced and used as a pretext by another brother in his quest for political power, Tamar's voice is quashed. The focus of the text is on the men's political relationships, the male God of Israel appearing, silently, to sanction this social structure, deaf to her cries for justice. Tamar is left desolate.

Opening Up the Silence

Digging beneath the layers of silence, this book focuses first and foremost on the voices of women like Tamar. The qualitative study at its core is concerned

25 I am indebted to Professor Ann Loades for this insight.

26 Poling (1991), p. 155; (2005), p. 62.

27 Poling (1991).

28 See McFague (1987); Burrus (2000).

29 Trible (2002).

30 Cooper-White (1995), pp. 1–14.

fundamentally with the following question: What do abused people reveal about God that can be brought to bear on theology? In order to produce a study on such a sensitive subject which is ethically sound, I pioneer a practical theological method which not only uses social scientific research to inform theology, but rigorously applies a social scientific method to the raw material of scriptural and spiritual texts. Any discussion of systematic theology that arises as a result is directed by the voices we have heard, and not by imposing pre-conceived theological frameworks on those voices.

The literature review in Chapter 2 serves primarily to contextualize the location of survivors so that we can gain an understanding of their situation. Referring first to non-theological literature, I outline the healing process necessary for recovery from abuse. Second, I evaluate literature from the field of pastoral theology and show that while theological and ministerial implications of abuse are being addressed, analysis of the direct testimony of Christian survivors is sparse. I highlight the dangers of patriarchal theologies that distort the nature of God and raise several pertinent themes for discussion, such as traditional theories of atonement and simplistic concepts of forgiveness. Along the way, awareness of the pitfalls of failing to listen attentively to survivors becomes crucial for the methodological decisions I took in carrying out the empirical research. Consequently my research design will be explained in Chapter 3 in which, given the dearth of qualitative studies on spirituality and abuse, I highlight the danger of academia losing touch with the experience of those without the power to make themselves heard. I attend to underlying epistemological and feminist principles of ethical research undertaken with the vulnerable and 'voiceless', and these considerations support my choice of Glaserian grounded theory as appropriate social scientific research method to create theory emergent from the 'grass roots'. Barney Glaser, one of the co-founders of this method, has observed that 'the research problem is as much discovered as the process that continues to resolve it and indeed resolving process usually indicates the problem. They are integrated'.[31] Indeed the problem of how to ensure the voices of survivors were at the centre of theological discussion was resolved by taking the risk of abandoning pre-conceived concepts and trusting that new ones would emerge from the data; this was the breakthrough which allowed the words of the survivors to take precedence over all else. Thus in the subsequent chapters I hope to show how theological theory can be integrated with the substance of people's lives.

Chapter 4 is, then, the heart of the book in that it presents the interviews given by nine Christian women survivors. The stories they tell about their relationship with God and how their faith has been affected by their experiences of abuse allow three main concepts to emerge from the process of analysis: *God's timeless presence*, *Transformation*, and *Knowing ministry*.[32] I describe this evolving

---

[31] Glaser (1992), p. 21.

[32] For the purpose of clarity, all major concepts formed from the interviews will appear in italic type.

process in detail with reference to the interviews and to grounded theory method to show how ever more sophisticated concepts were formed. Finally I show how these concepts combined to develop the 'core category' that encapsulates the underlying process of the women's spirituality: *knowing God's timeless presence transforms*. This central theoretical concept holds a double meaning because it shows on the one hand that the survivors know that God's constant presence has transformed them, and on the other that this knowing allows them to become agents of transformation for others.

Chapters 5 and 6 proceed by virtue of an original, experimental step. The analytical stage known in grounded theory as 'theoretical sampling' is usually carried out in order to achieve 'theoretical saturation', which means that the developing core concept can evolve no longer; that is, it cannot be modified by any further information.[33] In this stage, I apply the concepts developed from the interviews to two theological texts in order to add this further depth to the emergent theory. That is to say, the three main concepts which arose from the interviews, *God's timeless presence*, *Transformation*, and *Knowing ministry*, are used as the lenses through which I read scripture and mystical spirituality. So in Chapter 5 I consider how the archetypal sufferer, Job, struggles to keep his faith in the face of extreme abuse. Although there is ambiguity whether this paragon of patriarchal virtue in the Prologue becomes recovered victim or rehabilitated perpetrator of abuse in the Epilogue, I argue that by reading the text as an integrated whole, his journey is nevertheless one that is transformative. Job's final role as silent community intercessor reflects the experience of his profound encounter with the paradoxical God of the Theophany, as a result of which he becomes hospitable, attentive and radically aware of just boundaries. In Chapter 6 I explore the spiritual writing of the relatively unknown mystic, Marguerite Porete, who perished at the hands of the Parisian Inquisition at the beginning of the fourteenth century. I present Porete's subtle and complex work *The Mirror of Simple Souls*[34] as a prophetic struggle for theological integrity within an extreme patriarchal church and society. Her account of spiritual transformation through the process of 'annihilation' raises pertinent questions about the ambiguity of agency and surrender to God, particularly in relation to the role of free will.

Having paid close attention to the stories of the survivors' spirituality, the comparison with the book of Job and with Porete's treatise sharpens the focus of certain theological issues that lie beneath the surface of Christian theology. In Chapter 7 I bring these issues, which pivot around vulnerability and autonomy, into dialogue with contemporary theological debate in a final attempt to 'saturate' the grounded theory. I suggest that the three main concepts integrated into the spiritual process of *knowing God's timeless presence transforms* correspond to three theological ideas. First, the paradoxical idea of 'surrendering agency' describes our cooperation with God in *Knowing ministry*. Second, the retrieval of the practice

33 Glaser and Strauss (2009), ch. 3.

34 Porete (1993), trans. Ellen L. Babinsky.

of 'listening with the Other' is advocated as active spiritual praxis for community *Transformation.* Third, *God's timeless presence* is portrayed as 'God's holding company', locus of the generous 'Other' who lies beneath the nothingness of human destructiveness, on whom we can rest, and in whom we may be re-created.

Finally, in Chapter 8 I conclude with some implications about ministry in view of the principal value of autonomous personal power in Western society, which through globalized capitalism is seeping into the whole world. I consider whether those who have made the arduous journey of faith from enforced powerlessness to empowered relationship with God's silent and timeless presence may be the authentic prophets and priests we need: prophets to speak of the pain of being made powerless by others' grasping of power, and priests to provide attentive and hospitable healing ministry for the world's casualties. We are left still with questions, such as where can authentic spirituality be found in the ministry of our churches? Are we prepared to look beneath the surface of our certainties? Can we take the risk of being guided by those who have walked with God at the edges of the abyss?[35]

35 Reference to Job 38.16.

Chapter 2
Knocking at the Door: Presenting Issues

> They laugh 'cause they know they're untouchable, not because what I said was wrong.[1]

Introduction

She collapsed in front of the door. Beyond lay hospitality and security. But finding herself locked out, her hand merely brushed the threshold. It was not granted to the concubine of Judges 19 to utter one word in the narrative of her life, her abuse and her death. Yet all who were in that land were invited to view her tortured and dismembered body. Biblical women have often been visible, yet largely mute about their own lives. Like porn-stars and prostitutes in the burgeoning 'sex industry' of the early twenty-first century, they are acted upon with violence but given no opportunity to express a word, let alone complain about what is happening to them.[2] Rarely do we hear the full story of female victims of abuse. Even Hagar, the abused slave who is given one precious sentence of dialogue, is sent back by the male God of Israel for more of the same treatment from those who own her.[3]

Silent submission to sexual violence and a role as cultural symbol of blame have been a regular feature for women throughout the ages. For instance, although as a girl she was sexually abused by her teacher, possibly raped, more assuredly pimped as a political object by her family and definitely murdered as a young woman by the powerful men around her,[4] Katharine Howard has been recorded in the annals of British history as little more than a strumpet. At the turn of the nineteenth century the slither of hope appearing on the horizon, that the real truth about girls' lives might finally be exposed, evaporated like a mirage when Sigmund Freud stopped listening to victims of incest and proceeded to construct his Oedipal theory. In denial about the shocking truth of the extent of sexual abuse in that 'civilized' society, he chose the trumpeting of his own professional status

---

1 From 'The Emperor's New Clothes', on the album *I Do Not Want What I Haven't Got* by Sinead O'Connor (Chrysalis, 1990).

2 See Banyard (2010), pp. 135–77.

3 Gen 16.8–9.

4 See Wheeler (2008).

over acting on what he was hearing in his consulting rooms,[5] thereby exonerating the patriarchs of Vienna. Judith Herman laments Freud's disavowal of his female patients and his reinforcing of patriarchal prejudices about women:

> Though he continued to focus on his patients' sexual lives, he no longer acknowledged the exploitative nature of women's real experiences ... he insisted that women imagined and longed for the abusive sexual encounters of which they complained.[6]

It may then be unsurprising that, despite its presence throughout history and even after the intense campaigning of social reformers in the Victorian era,[7] the myth of rarity about Child Sexual Abuse remained unchallenged, and its effects uncharted, until the sea-change of the 1970s when women were enabled to speak about their personal lives and the devastating effects of domestic and sexual violence.[8] Once the door was open, a proliferation of research studies followed, leading to greater knowledge of the effects of such abuses and of the statistics as quoted in the introduction. However, the place of spirituality in the consulting room and in psychotherapy, due on the one hand to mistrust of religion from many in the field of psychology,[9] and on the other to the impossibility of applying the scientific method to 'God',[10] has meant that research on the relationship between spirituality and abuse has been limited. Nevertheless, although still sparse, since the 1980s there has been a trickle of studies,[11] and interest is growing. In Chapter 3 I will assess some of the existing social scientific studies to contextualize the empirical research, but here I first address literature from the field of psychology that will help us understand the impact of the trauma faced by those reporting their stories in Chapter 4. I will proceed with an evaluation of the stages in the recovery process that survivors must negotiate. Next, acknowledging a concurrently steady increase in material about abuse in the field of pastoral theology, the literature reviewed in the second part of this chapter raises some of the implications of abuse specifically for Christians. Noting at the outset that only a minority of the literature clearly foregrounds the survivors' voices, I highlight some of the major problems they experience in their search for authentic spirituality, particularly concerning traditional attitudes to forgiveness, the doctrine of atonement, the nature of God and humanity, and the body. As a result of the review, I will argue that approaches which epitomize the

---

5 Cooper-White (1995), p. 153.

6 Herman (1994), pp. 18–19.

7 See Jackson (2000); also Loades (2001), pp. 143–4.

8 Cooper-White (1995), pp. 152–3.

9 On scepticism amongst psychologists about spiritual ideas, see Schermer (2003), pp. 24–5. His book *Spirit and Psyche* is a pioneering vision of a new paradigm for combining psychological treatment and spiritual healing.

10 Kliewer (2004), p. 617.

11 Sargent (1989); Hall (1995); Ganje-Fling and McCarthy (1996).

theology of domination that undergirds Western Christian civilization, and tries 'to convince a suffering people that they have sinned',[12] is more thoroughly challenged the more clearly survivors' voices are heard. It is time to listen.

Long and Winding Road: The Process of Recovery

The material reviewed in the following analysis is non-theological and has no specific emphasis on spirituality. Nevertheless, the content which addresses Child Sexual Abuse and wider forms of abuse will prove relevant for understanding the context of the survivors I interviewed in the empirical study, and also raises important implications for Christian doctrine and practice. At first sight my approach appears to resemble that of Alistair McFadyen, who employs 'secular' discourses from research on victims of Child Sexual Abuse and the Holocaust to establish the contours of concrete pathologies of relational dynamics.[13] He goes on to use the pathological dynamics of abuse to test the Christian doctrine of original sin and applies the resulting theological framework to worship in order to delineate the pathological dynamics of idolatry. While a comparison with pathological relational dynamics will prove helpful in Chapter 7 as one key to understanding the interviewees' spirituality, there are two major differences in my approach from the outset. First, my study will focus on the concrete situation of *healing* rather than pathology, and second, the voices of survivors will be clearly included at the heart of the text. For on the one hand, McFadyen analyses the pathology discovered in concrete research on abuse, but offers no concrete grounding for the healthy, joyous dynamics of worship which he describes; rather he bases his definition on Augustine's concept of God as good. I am not at this point arguing with Augustinian theology or criticizing McFadyen's conclusions, merely highlighting the need for concrete empirical study of positive dynamics. On the other hand, in his acknowledgements McFadyen expresses the hope that survivors of Child Sexual Abuse who have shared their stories with him 'might feel that this work has not done them a disservice'.[14] The implication is that their opinion was not sought before publishing the text. In contrast, by opening the door wide to them, my research seeks to expose theological debate primarily to survivors' voices and also to contribute to a concrete theology of hope for victims. So we turn now to the stages of healing from abuse.

According to the literature there is broad agreement that the path to healing from any type of victimization encompasses different stages that survivors must negotiate. In this journey, two particular factors for survivors in recovering from the effects of abuse prove significant: an awareness of their own agency and the ability to reframe experience. In her clinical work with victims of rape

12 Dussell (1983), p. 65.

13 McFadyen (2000).

14 McFadyen (2000), p. xiii.

and other forms of violence, Judith Herman suggests there are three fundamental stages of recovery, each subdividing to include several tasks which have to be accomplished.[15] Similarly, Suzanne Sgroi's observation of survivors of Child Sexual Abuse suggests a fairly predictable pattern for those who are able to persevere with therapy, but in five stages.[16] While the following analysis uses Sgroi's five-stage scheme, it draws on the work of both authors and Table 2.1 shows how the two theories correlate.

Table 2.1 Comparison of Sgroi's and Herman's stages of recovery

<table>
<tr><th colspan="2">Stages of recovery according to Sgroi</th><th colspan="2">Stages of recovery according to Herman</th></tr>
<tr><td>1</td><td>[Safety is assumed in the therapeutic environment]
Acknowledging the reality of the abuse</td><td>*Establishing safety*
Naming the problem</td><td>1</td></tr>
<tr><td>2</td><td>*Overcoming secondary responses to the abuse*</td><td rowspan="2">*Reconstructing the story*
Transforming traumatic memory
Mourning traumatic loss

Reconciling with oneself</td><td rowspan="2">2</td></tr>
<tr><td>3</td><td>*Forgiving oneself (ending self-punishment)*</td></tr>
<tr><td>4</td><td>*Adopting positive coping behaviours*</td><td rowspan="2">*Restoring the connection between survivors and their community*
Learning to fight
Reconnecting with others

Finding a survivor mission
Resolving the trauma</td><td rowspan="2">3</td></tr>
<tr><td>5</td><td>*Relinquishing survivor identity*</td></tr>
</table>

Sources: Sgroi (1989), p. 111; Herman (1994), pp. 133–213.

In the first stage, the protective denial adopted by the powerless victim as a defence against anger and fear, typified by dissociation and emotional detachment, must be overcome. Such denial results in dysfunctional behaviour, shown by a distancing of the person from pain and emptiness. Symptoms include non-reciprocal, pathological care-taking and extreme busyness, generated by a learnt need to keep the abuser happy. Self-mutilation and eating disorders are common, as well as holding oneself responsible for the abuse. These symptoms are all coping mechanisms designed to give survivors an (imagined) measure of control

[15] Herman (1994).

[16] Sgroi (1989).

over events, past and present. Protective denial requires a vast amount of energy to sustain and along with coupling (the fear of being overwhelmed by reliving the emotions when remembering the event), denial must be resolved in order to retrieve and verbalize memories. A major complication is that victims already lack power in relationship to the perpetrator, who usually compounds the feeling of being trapped by enforcing secrecy. In the context of Child Sexual Abuse, secrecy comes to include victims hiding the abuse even from themselves, by repressing memory as a survival strategy. For adult victims of rape or clergy exploitation, secrecy and silence demanded by perpetrators are reinforced by the victim's fear of losing reputation, of reprisals or of not being believed. For all survivors in therapy, the deconstruction of protective barriers and conscious *re-membering* of events is extremely painful since exposure of their woundedness and vulnerability is excruciating, but it is necessary. Suicidal thoughts, depression and anxiety are common at this stage.

Second, there is a kind of contemporary denial. Anger and fear have been felt in remembering and *naming* the abuse, but guilt and shame remain, the survivor experiencing a 'pervading sense of damage'. These secondary responses cause victims to further minimize and trivialize what happened, even repeating the past blame-shifting by the abuser onto themselves in the present. A survivor negotiates this stage by coming to recognize these distortions of reality, and group therapy can be particularly helpful in reconstructing the story more realistically. Group members challenge each others' distortions, helping to recreate the healthy sense of self which the abuser destroyed. The following account comes from a survivor whom I will call Abigail:[17] Abigail attended a group therapy session and was telling her story. She began to berate herself because she believed that having entered her abuser's house 'voluntarily', she had caused the sexual assault he had perpetrated on her. Another member of the group, who so far had been unable to say much about her own childhood experiences of incest, responded by giving Abigail very strong reassurances that she could not possibly have known at seven years old what was going to happen to her. Both women were helped in their recovery by this session. The persistent sense of shame that Abigail related about her childhood abuse can be just as real for sexually violated adults in a culture that encourages the blaming of victims who must have 'asked for it', by somehow provoking abusive behaviour.[18]

The third stage, reconciling with oneself, which has major implications for the theological material addressed later in the book, is a turning point and is 'an immensely freeing process' in which a survivor 'gives permission to [the] self to end self-punishment'.[19] Paradoxically, even though victims have no objective need to be forgiven for an offence which was not theirs, this stage is crucial. The coping

[17] Abigail is not one of the nine women I interviewed in this study.

[18] On our victim-blaming legal system and culture see Kennedy, H. (2005) and Banyard (2010).

[19] Sgroi (1989), p. 123.

mechanism which helped victims manage the anxiety of having had no control by mentally framing *themselves* as evil, contaminated and damaged is now being relinquished. Survivors invariably become 'self-punishers' and Sgroi suggests that this stage of self-forgiveness brings the termination of behaviours which punish the self for being fallible and weak.

The fourth stage, which will also prove significant in correlation with the results of the empirical study, requires the relinquishment of redundant dysfunctional behaviours, such as compulsive secret-keeping and the redirection of energy to coping with emotions in the *present*. This involves practising the art of sharing by communicating to others 'who I am', 'what I feel' and 'what I want'. It also entails practising limit-setting, and establishing the intimacy that is mutual and has appropriate boundaries, which requires exposing the self to another, as well as being receptive without being passive. For victims of abuse, it is the shattering of their boundaries that causes great difficulties, particularly within intimate relationships. So this more healthy from of relating is difficult to maintain, particularly within a social environment that largely does not support equality, mutuality and openness, since what is required from a survivor is vulnerability in the same culture that sustained the victimization in the first place. Thus a healthy supporting community becomes vital.

The final stage of recovery, Sgroi's 'relinquishing a survivor identity', necessitates moving beyond the view of oneself as victim *or* survivor. Notably the unattainable desire for a 'benevolent caretaker' must be relinquished, hence the need in the previous stage to practise skills for developing successful relationships, so that the person will 'have their needs for affection, affiliation and nurturance met in a milieu of mutuality and reciprocity'.[20] In Herman's corresponding task 'resolving the trauma', referring to psychologist Mary Harvey's work about this stage, she observes that 'the person has reconstructed a coherent system of meaning and belief that encompasses the story of the trauma'.[21]

Some writers have a less systematic approach to the stages of recovery, for example Ainscough and Toon in *Breaking Free*,[22] perhaps because their material is aimed at survivors rather than at clinicians. However, both Herman and Sgroi do stress that the process of healing is neither static nor linear, although the stages are interconnected. Sgroi suggests that the process works in 'a three-dimensional spiral format'[23] while Herman notes that

> no single course of recovery follows these stages through a straightforward linear sequence. Oscillating and dialectical in nature, the traumatic syndromes defy any attempt to impose such simpleminded order.[24]

---

20 Sgroi (1989), p. 129.

21 Herman (1994), pp. 212–13.

22 Ainscough and Toon (1993).

23 Sgroi (1989), p. 121.

24 Herman (1994), p. 155.

Furthermore, Sgroi admits that many clients stay at the second stage. The process gets 'stuck'. In the first stage, Sgroi stressed the importance of the client *self-initiating* memory retrieval, of 'choosing to remember',[25] since the loss of control that was central to the abusive experience must not be repeated by coercion in therapy. Therefore the difficulty of moving to the third stage is that survivors must experience once again their lack of power and initiating agency in the past event in order to forgive themselves for their 'weakness' (even though they *are* now initiating forgiveness of the self for self-abuse). Marie-Nathalie Beaudoin suggests that such impasses are due to the negative evaluation made by clients of themselves which then become embedded in their 'problem saturated' stories, and she advocates a real commitment to *attentive listening* by therapists. In standing back from the problem saturated narrative in order to recover pieces of story which have been forgotten by the conscious mind or unnoticed at the time, the therapist is enabled to ask appropriate questions without forcing. The questioning should allow the client's positive 'non-actions' and/or forgotten actions during the traumatic event to be noticed, and in the process retrieved. These observations, for example recollecting one's determination to get away at the time of the abuse, or perhaps noticing one's resisting body, are then connected consciously in the present with the client's positive values and some degree of agency can be recovered. This re-authoring of the story brings breakthrough for 'if clients are able to understand their experience in context, then they are less vulnerable to pathologizing their identity'.[26] Beaudoin's insights will be valuable when considered alongside the interviewees' experiences of healing.

In sum, the journey to recovery from abuse is a long, arduous and somewhat repetitious one of re-framing experience, relinquishing dysfunctional belief systems about the self and those in power, and actively forming relationships of mutuality. This evaluation of the psychological material has highlighted the issues for survivors against which pastoral theology might be assessed, and will have a bearing on the interview analysis.

Waiting on the Threshold: Pressing Themes in Pastoral Theology

Within the field of pastoral theology the material on abuse, particularly Child Sexual Abuse, is growing. Official documents on child protection policies[27] that can be seen on ministerial bookshelves reflect, thankfully, the much greater awareness that now exists of this issue in churches. Furthermore, guidance for pastors

25 Sgroi (1989), pp. 114–15.

26 Beaudoin (2005), p. 43.

27 See for example the recent House of Bishops' official guidance *Responding Well to Those Who Have Been Sexually Abused* (London: Church House Publishing, 2011).

on ministry to the abused[28] and some resources for survivors[29] have appeared alongside feminist theological analysis of the implications of patriarchal theology for the abused.[30] While some of this material is authored by survivor-theologians, there is, however, only a minority of the theological material that gives direct testimony from survivors about their experiences and spiritual struggles.[31] It is not my aim to plough through all the literature systematically here. Rather I will take a thematic approach which evaluates the key interrelated themes of forgiveness and atonement, the nature of God and creation, and individual and communal bodies. These themes are, according to the literature, theologically weighty for survivors, and after all, survivors and their faith are the focus of this book, which seeks to add the new dimension of social scientific research to the practical theological material. A significant outcome of this thematic approach will demonstrate that the greater the emphasis given in the literature to the perspective of survivors, the greater the challenge to patriarchal theologies. An exclusion of survivors' own voices reveals an under-examined, traditional theology, whereas when survivors are given the opportunity to tell their story, a grappling with *their* issues necessitates a radically deconstructed and re-envisioned theology which profoundly questions received Christian doctrine and praxis. This will prove entirely relevant for the empirical study, and shows that it is time to open the door wide to those who stand on the threshold, knocking.

Forgiveness

The vast majority of the literature argues that although forgiveness is necessary in recovery, it is *self*-forgiveness that is crucial, which correlates with the third stage of recovery as explained above. Under no circumstances should survivors be pressurized into forgiving their abuser. Sadly, however, survivors in church contexts are frequently encouraged by pastors, and expected by fellow Christians, to 'forgive and forget'.[32] Marie Fortune, who has pioneered work on domestic violence and sexual abuse within Christianity, maintains that many Christians mistakenly think that their 'forgive and forget' theology comes from the Bible, when in reality it comes from *King Lear*. She argues that this simplistic formula allows Christians to ignore the difficulty of grappling with the complex power

---

28 For example, Hedges-Goettl (2004); Gosney (2002); Meyer (2005); Griffin and Griffin (2007).

29 For example, Fortune (1987); Flaherty (1992); MACSAS (2010).

30 For example, Poling (1991); Cooper-White (1995, 2000); Fortune (1999, 2002); Brock and Parker (2001); Crisp (2001, 2004, 2007); Kennedy, M. (2003).

31 See Cashman (1993), and the anthology edited by Kennedy, M. (1999). One survivor, Karen, is given a central voice in Poling (1991).

32 Cooper-White (1995); Kennedy, M. (1999); Loades (2001); Arms (2002); MACSAS (2010).

dynamics involved in forgiveness.[33] Furthermore, Margaret Kennedy, founder of the organizations MACSAS and CSSA,[34] stresses that it is almost impossible to forgive some abuses, yet blame is often poured on survivors who find that they cannot forgive their abuser. They are held responsible for their own lack of healing because many Christians do not want to stay with the difficult and messy issues involved; on the contrary, they want a 'quick fix'. Thus, exhorting forgiveness becomes a tool of social control, because getting forgiveness over with quickly restores silence about abuse.[35]

Most authors discern the critical distinction between the *self*-forgiveness necessary for recovery and forgiveness of the perpetrator, which requires a comprehensive reconciliation process. Reconciliation is a relational, social and public issue and to be valid perpetrators must be fully involved in the process. This is an eventuality which sadly is unlikely to happen since perpetrators rarely acknowledge their accountability, even when confronted with the evidence of their offence(s).[36] Drawing parallels with the reconciliation process in post-apartheid South Africa, Margaret Arms maintains that forgiveness needs to have both private and *public* integrity and that 'truth-telling' is an indispensible part of this process, with victims' safety being paramount. Privatized, unilateral forgiveness has limits because power dynamics are always central to the act of forgiveness, therefore forgiveness must be embedded in social ethics and satisfy moral law.[37] If there is no public engagement, then institutions are complicit in abuse because privatization shields the abuser, ignoring the issues of justice and restitution which are necessary for the victim's healing. Thus Arms maintains that church leaderships are highly blame-worthy in their handling of forgiveness when they misuse institutional power by exhorting victims to forgive, even as part of private devotion.[38] Such exhortation is tantamount to spiritual abuse, for once again the victim becomes enclosed with their pain in a hermetically sealed space labelled 'prayer'. According to Fortune, never in Christian scripture are the less powerful expected to forgive the more powerful, signifying a balance of responsibility that protects the vulnerable from coercion.[39] She also suggests that the Church might take on responsibility for justice-making for victims of violence when perpetrators do not or cannot repent and/or offer restitution.[40]

Unfortunately there is some material available in mainstream Christian circles which fails to recognize these complexities about forgiveness. At a Diocesan

33 Fortune (2002), pp. 109–10.

34 Ministry and Clergy Sexual Abuse Survivors and Christian Survivors of Sexual Abuse, respectively.

35 Kennedy, M. (1999), pp. 68–70.

36 Poling (1991); Cooper-White (1995); Fortune (1999); Kennedy, M. (1999).

37 Barnes (2002); Fortune (2002), pp. 105–8.

38 Arms (2002), p. 110.

39 Fortune (2002), p. 111.

40 Fortune (1999), p. 71.

Conference I attended I chanced upon a promising title at the bookstall, *Hope and Healing for the Abused* by Paul and Liz Griffin. This book describes the Griffins' ministry with survivors of Child Sexual Abuse, and in my opinion highlights some of the worst kind of ministerial practice with survivors. It advocates, amongst other things, 'willing submission' to leaders[41] and the strategy of victims being physically held by a male minister who is called a 'Daddy substitute', in order to teach them the right sort of father love.[42] This contrasts starkly with the more enlightened ministry received by Karen, survivor of incest, rape and clergy abuse, about whom we will shortly hear more; Karen was promised by the two male pastors who supported her that they would not touch her in any way.[43] Furthermore, Griffin and Griffin's eight-step path to recovery begins upfront with 'Forgive those who have abused you in any way', which as we have seen evades the issue of accountability, manoeuvring survivors into a powerless position, and even more manipulatively, demands they forgive 'because it is what Jesus asks us to do'.[44] In contrast, Sandra Flaherty reaches a different conclusion about this biblical exhortation to forgive. As a child Flaherty was habitually raped by her father, a man who remained unrepentant when as an adult seeking healing, she courageously confronted him. She concluded that in order to move on in her recovery, the best she could do was to leave forgiveness to God, for it is 'a grace we receive as a gift'.[45] While Griffin and Griffin maintain that forgiveness is an act beginning in the victim's will,[46] Flaherty stresses the need to let go of a false sense of responsibility to forgive what is unforgiveable. She also gives a fuller assessment of Christ's teaching on forgiveness in Luke 17.3–4, which demands that the offence is not forgotten but acknowledged; that the offender accepts his responsibility in relationship to the offence; and that the offender must have asked for forgiveness and reconciliation.[47] Fortune echoes this interpretation and insists that forgiveness is never the first step in the process, but always the last.[48] Griffin and Griffin have not taken into account what is made explicit by Kennedy, that survivors need their communities to grasp the very complex nature of forgiveness and that simplistic theology can be harmful and hurtful.[49] The problem with their ministry is that it is supported by a conservative theology which perpetuates abuse, as we will see even more clearly as we now turn to theologies of 'atonement'.

41 Griffin and Griffin (2007), pp. 39, 73.
42 Griffin and Griffin (2007), p. 108.
43 Poling (1991), p. 45.
44 Griffin and Griffin (2007), p. 98.
45 Flaherty (1992), p. 142.
46 Griffin and Griffin (2007), p. 100.
47 Flaherty (1992), p. 141.
48 Fortune (2002), pp. 109–11.
49 Kennedy, M. (1999), p. 72.

Atonement

While many scriptural victims of abuse such as those in Trible's volume[50] are passed over, it is the passion of Jesus of Nazareth that is central to Christian doctrine and meaning. Theologies of the atonement have long been controversial in feminist theology, yet Margaret Arms asserts that, along with notions of privatized forgiveness, traditional understandings of the doctrine of atonement which are detrimental to victims continue to be taught in mainstream churches.[51] For instance, the penal substitution theory of atonement has been critiqued as an endorsement of 'divine child abuse',[52] with its relational structure played out in the patriarchal family unit of Father, Son and silent mother.[53] Parallels can easily be drawn between the crime of incest and the submission of the worshipper to a wrathful, almighty Father-God in this understanding, for in incest

> the child is forced to submit to the will of the father, take on the guilt for any sin involved, and sacrifice her life for the sake of the relationship. Her father has put himself in the role of God who is all-powerful, all-knowing and all-loving, and whose decisions and values cannot be questioned.[54]

Table 2.2 illustrates further the implications of penal substitution theory as delineated by Poling, when set alongside the experiences of an incest victim. Furthermore, on the basis that only God can deliver the person because 'the redemption price had to be paid' and 'Jesus has taken the punishment for our sins',[55] the outcome is that survivors' need for agency in their own healing is disregarded. Uncritically embraced, the damaging effects of this atonement theology are played out in the 'ministry of deliverance', which Griffin and Griffin believe is a necessary part of healing for survivors over whose lives 'demonic rights [have] become established'.[56] On the damage done by deliverance ministry, Margaret Kennedy is uncompromising.[57]

50 Trible (2002).
51 Arms (2002), pp. 116–18.
52 See Carlson Brown and Bohn (1989).
53 Poling (2005), p. 64.
54 Poling (2005), p. 66.
55 Griffin and Griffin (2007), pp. 85, 99.
56 Griffin and Griffin (2007), pp. 72–3.
57 Kennedy, M. (1999), pp. 64–5.

Table 2.2 Penal substitution theory compared with experience of incest victim

Substitutionary atonement	Point of view of incest victim
God the Father is all-loving and all-powerful and demands to be loved	Child loves father (and continues to do so)
There is nothing the child can do to earn mercy, for the Father who created us and gave us everything, is wrathful	Child is too small to escape the adult, and has nowhere to run in a domain provided and owned by the intimidating adult
There is no basis on which to appeal to the love of the Father because child's sin is overwhelming	Appeals like 'Daddy please don't do it because it hurts' do not work. Child's sin is in tempting adult
Father's rage is justified	Sexual violence is an act of rage condoned by scape-goating women/children (weak/sinful)
No matter how the Father treats the child, it's her fault	Abuser makes projections like: 'She wanted it really' or 'She was leading me on' (even though she was only seven years old)
Child must be submissive to the omniscient Father or risk hell	Child may be threatened with murder or injury to mother/sibling if she does not comply
The guilt is made worse by the existence of a perfect sibling who obediently gave his life for the child, proving that the Father is just after all	Child feels 'it's my fault Jesus had to die therefore I must be bad and that's why this is happening to me'
Child must repent of sins and pledge obedience to Son in order to avoid death	Child feels 'different', marked out and bad, so must need forgiveness and must forgive

Sources: Poling's summary of substitutionary atonement (2005), pp. 64ff.; incest victim's view gleaned from Flaherty (1992).

These alarming issues are discerned by Lutheran Pastor Rick Meyer in his ministry with survivors. Meyer wishes instead to impress survivors with the 'credibility' of Jesus through his experience of suffering on the cross.[58] However, comparing the suffering of a survivor with the suffering of Jesus has also been shown to be dangerous. Images of Jesus, the chosen and beloved child of God who suffers in silence, are internalized by worshippers, and this internalization renders Christian survivors vulnerable to further exploitation by encouraging them to sacrifice themselves on behalf of others. The important question to ask of Meyer

[58] Meyer (2005), pp. 154–5.

is whether solidarity, in the sense that God 'knows what it's like to suffer', is in reality helpful. Accordingly Poling raises the unresolved problem of the inequality of power intrinsic to such 'incarnational' theories of atonement:

> While a benevolent parent is preferable to one who is abusive, the patriarchal structure of the relationship is fully intact. God is the perfect parent ... God unilaterally decides to institute the incarnation as the revelation of divine reality. The [morally corrupt] children are helpless until they are rescued by the omnipotent [perfect] God ... The unilateral power relationship between God and humans is maintained.[59]

It was noted earlier that in the fifth stage of recovery the survivor's wish for a 'benevolent caretaker' must be relinquished and future relationships built on mutuality and reciprocity. Thus, while it is vital to have supporters alongside survivors in their healing, the agency for their recovery must be theirs. Cooper-White's suggestion of regarding the cross not as submission, nor as passive gesture, rather as a choice of Jesus to surrender himself on behalf of victims of injustice, appears to incorporate the concept of agency:

> Christ's surrender to the cross is not redemptive because of his suffering, but because of his choice to remain faithful in the face of death. And it was that choice, and not the suffering that was vindicated by the resurrection.[60]

It does not, however, address the victim who had *no choice* but to surrender and suffer. Indeed Poling argues there is something amiss with an omnipotent God who encourages a victim to suffer in silence for the evil of the leaders of his society, and with whom we cannot have a mutual relationship because of the power differential. This scenario mirrors abuse. Thus 'incarnational' theologies of atonement are equally problematic and accordingly, Kennedy's research shows how abusive clergy, as representatives of God working within this framework of atonement, can make sexual demands on those (mostly women) whose self-esteem is already low, by grooming them as 'special' and 'chosen' to receive their love.[61] In illustration, Table 2.3 shows how vulnerable parishioners can become like 'lambs to the slaughter'. Hidden violence in such theologies is, according to MACSAS,[62] fundamental to the present Child Sexual Abuse crisis in the Church and these dangers are most deeply expressed by theologian survivors Rebecca Ann Parker and Rita Nakashima Brock in their book *Proverbs of Ashes*, which will resonate clearly with the results of the empirical study. Interwoven with the autobiographical accounts of their own abuse is a radical deconstruction of traditional, liberal and liberation theologies of

59 Poling (2005), p. 66.

60 Cooper-White (1995), p. 152.

61 See summary of Kennedy's research in MACSAS (2010), pp. 29–32.

62 MACSAS (2010), p. 5.

atonement. They conclude that the self-sacrificial love which is sanctified at the heart of these theologies is distorted and downright dangerous because they teach a lesson of subordination through terror, for

> atonement theology takes an act of state violence and redefines it as intimate violence, a private spiritual transaction between Father and Son … then says this intimate violence saves life … behind the holy mask of intimate violence, state violence disappears.[63]

Table 2.3 Incarnational atonement compared with experience of clergy abuse

Incarnational atonement	**Viewpoint of victim of clergy sexual abuse**
God the Father is all-loving and all-powerful	Fr./Pastor knows best
God is merciful towards sinners	Fr./Pastor will help me with my problems
God voluntarily suffers on behalf of his children/creation	Fr./Pastor gives me a lot of his time and risks his career to show me love
God loves the outcast	I feel bad about myself but Fr. is showing me I am special (women in life crisis have low self-esteem and might be survivors of abuse)
Crucifixion means redemption because love is more powerful than hatred and violence	Fr./Pastor tells me our love is sacred and pure in an evil world
God is the perfect parent who intervenes to save disobedient children	Fr./Pastor will heal me of my problems and was put here for that purpose: it is God's will
Jesus freely chooses to suffer abuse in silence	I cannot tell anyone what I am feeling, or endanger Fr./Pastor's ministry which is part of God's plan of salvation
We must love God	I have to comply with sexual relationship

Sources: Poling (2005), pp. 65ff.; Fortune (1999); MACSAS leaflet (2009).

The intimate violence of the cross preached down the centuries has, according to Brock and Parker, wrought damage on bodies, women's and children's privately, and men's in the public field of warfare, by its model of self-sacrifice promoted by patriarchal, imperial and religious systems seeking to maintain political, territorial

63 Brock and Parker (2001), p. 49.

and social control.[64] They eschew valorizing violence for any reason, even as a moral strategy for calling unjust systems to account, because this damages victims for the sake of perpetrators who are unlikely to repent anyway. 'Mysticism of the cross,' which has spiritualized the crucifixion and resurrection as a way through death to life, is exposed by them as a veiling of the torture and murder of Jesus. Consequently they argue that suffering cannot be salvific or illuminating. This begs the question whether abuse has *any* spiritual meaning, and Kennedy remarks that any theology that suggests abuse has a *purpose* and produces 'useful spiritual by-products', is 'anathema' to survivors. While the experience of sexual abuse might make for mature Christians, because difficult questions about God have to be faced within the healing process and authentic and honest Christianity is often the *result*, in no way is it a rationale.[65] This issue will become important in the empirical study, as survivors grapple with the issue of 'God's will'. When survivor Flaherty writes that 'for Christians, recovery and the Christian journey are one and the same ... It is a reliving of the paschal mystery of Jesus',[66] it may appear that she is contradicting Brock and Parker. But one could say that she is describing what the journey to healing is like with the God who suffers *with* us, not *for* us, and not in order to prove something as Meyer's theology appears to suggest.[67]

Finally, I was struck by how Meyer's *Through the Fire* is an account of *his* ministry with survivors, which presents case studies in *his* words and witnesses to *his* own painful theological struggle. Survivors are not heard from directly and little reference is made to wider theological viewpoints. Similarly Griffin and Griffin's book alludes to no other theologians or pastors, and while some quotes from survivors are used, these are generally appreciative anecdotes about the ministry they received from the authors. We might say that survivor authors like Brock and Parker and Kennedy have a clearer grasp of the issues, because we are hearing it from the 'horse's mouth', so to speak.

The Nature of God and Humanity

Flaherty, having experienced incest and recovery, describes the breaking down of 'God-images' that accompanied her journey of healing.[68] As a child she learnt that God was synonymous with unconditional love and with maleness, but explains that for incest victims the image of God as an all-powerful male and as father is problematic, as is the maleness of Jesus.[69] 'Mother-God' alternatives are no

64 In a later book which explores early Christian artefacts, Brock and Parker (2008) note that emphasis on crucifixion appeared in artwork around the time of Charlemagne's enforced imperial baptismal policy, whereas earlier art had emphasized paradise on earth.

65 Kennedy, M. (1999), pp. 64, 66.

66 Flaherty (1992), p. 154.

67 Meyer (2005), p. 14.

68 Flaherty (1992), p. 54.

69 Flaherty (1992), p. 29.

easier, since mothers might be complicit in abuse, fail to protect the child or even perpetrate abuse themselves.[70] Furthermore, to a dysfunctional family the idea of unconditional love is 'foreign'.[71] Flaherty maintains that the crumbling of 'God-images' has an upside in that 'we will formulate healthier images which promote more authentic communications between ourselves and God'.[72] This is echoed by Poling's appraisal of the distorted nature of a theology and a society in which women and children are sacrificed to male propriety, and he asserts that 'in the presence of such human destructiveness it is impossible to retain a *naïve* doctrine of the goodness of God'.[73]

As pastor and psychotherapist, Poling's work reveals for me the most profound theological transformation in the literature written by non-survivors. His well-referenced reflections begin with the witness of Karen, a survivor of incest, rape and clergy abuse. Her story, told in her words, is the driving force behind *The Abuse of Power*.[74] Furthermore, in order to understand abuse from within, Poling has worked with sex offenders, a deeply challenging experience through which he has faced his own propensities to abuse power in the context of his inherited sense of adult male entitlement. Impressed by the resilience and hope that some survivors retain,[75] Poling develops his theology from their testimony to a resilient God who has been revealed in Christ, an inspiring figure of hope in the midst of evil. He suggests that this God has an ambiguous approach to good and evil, and that God relates to both transformatively. This is not to claim that God is good and evil, as in dualistic creation myths, but that God is fully aware of the ambiguities of createdness, its goods and its evils, yet is fully committed to including all of creation in divine experience:

> Through the suffering of such inclusiveness, the contradictions of good and evil are transformed into compatible contrasts and the relational web moves beyond self-destruction to re-creation.[76]

The logical conclusion is that God's commitment to our full humanity requires that we are in a free, mutual relationship with God. The antithesis of such a

---

[70] The majority of sexual abuse is by men, estimated at 81–95 per cent according to Cooper-White (1995), p. 152. However, women do abuse. While I was working on the original draft of this chapter, Veronica George was convicted of many counts of Child Sexual Abuse perpetrated by her in the nursery school where she worked.

[71] Flaherty (1992), p. 29.

[72] Flaherty (1992), p. 54.

[73] Poling (1991), p. 51, emphasis added.

[74] Poling (1991), pp. 35–49.

[75] On the importance and nature of resilience in adult survivors, see Gina Higgins (1994). This is a non-theological text and Higgins contends that resilience is mainly contingent on hope, and having had a surrogate carer's support.

[76] Poling (1991), p. 175.

relationship is symbiosis, when differentiation between self and other is so weak that any strong relationship can result in a loss of the self and this is a fundamental problem for perpetrators, themselves often victims of a terror that left them feeling abandoned, isolated and outraged in the past:[77]

> [A perpetrator of sexual abuse] cannot see the child as separate from himself. He lacks empathy, if he wants something, he distorts his perception until he thinks it is something the child wants also.[78]

He then dumps his own rage on the 'most helpless, defenceless persons in society',[79] whose fragile boundaries are in turn damaged by his need.

The inability of abusers to differentiate their own wilful act from the victim's lack of agency is related to the inability to call evil, evil. Arms notes that one way in which church hierarchies betray the abused is by sanitizing language used to describe perpetrators. She argues that in identifying abusers only as 'sinful', the Church confuses sin and evil. For survivors will readily agree that they themselves are 'sinners' like everyone else, but would deny that they are 'evil-doers'. Perpetrators on the other hand are very definitely described by survivors as evil-doers, yet the Church robs them of this language, calling both perpetrator and victim 'sinful', thus equating their behaviour.[80] Furthermore, this is compounded for the victim by the consequences of abuse. For instance, Poling explains that children who are sexually violated have had to absorb the un-neutralized sexual aggression of the perpetrator, and so the consequences of abuse bring a deep ambiguity borne out by the experience of love and hate, good and evil, life and death, at the very base of the survivor's selfhood. Thus, Poling argues, survivors are seeking 'a spiritual stature that is greater than the abuser's' because in order to find wholeness the adult in recovery must 'attain enough moral strength to reconcile the contradictions of love and hate absorbed from the abuser'.[81] While this seems to come uncomfortably close to Griffin and Griffin's rather unpleasant idea that survivors have 'something of the enemy attached to them'[82] which they perceive needs removing by deliverance, Poling's focus is instead on the value of survivors as pioneers in facing the depths of the human condition. He suggests that survivors can become revealers of Jesus because the healing process leads them to the edge of chaos and fragmentation 'where the awareness of death and nothingness is fully present'.[83]

---

77 Poling (1991), p. 104. It must be stressed that the majority of victims of abuse do *not* become perpetrators, but that perpetrators have frequently been victims.

78 Poling (1991), p. 66.

79 Poling (1991), p. 67.

80 Arms (2002), pp. 116–17.

81 Poling (1991), pp. 119–20.

82 Griffin and Griffin (2007), p. 54.

83 Poling (1991), p. 120.

Rebecca Parker witnesses to how she realized that along with the awareness of death at such a terrible moment as this, also fully present was God's 'Presence'. When as a child she was being raped, a Presence that she now knows was the holy power of God was with her; this Presence was unable to stop the perpetrator from his evil act because he was not aware of it, but it is a Presence who she maintains is available all the time if we notice it.[84] Not to pre-empt the results of the empirical study for which the concept of 'God's presence' proved crucial, we will return to Parker's experience in Chapter 7 in the theological discussion prompted by the grounded theory, but here we note that awareness of the presence of God is important to recovery for Christian survivors. The paradox of surrender to God as healing is also significant, and Karen's story illustrates this when she relates that an important moment of transformation for her resembled the Genesis story:

> Creation occurred following the time of nothingness. Out of chaos came the new, the fresh. I also had my 'genesis moment' a time of being in the dark, surrounded by chaos. It was at that point that death looked inviting.[85]

The difficulty for Karen was in letting go of control and she notes that rebirth, painful as it was, began simultaneously with surrendering to her illness. Each time a survivor comes to the point of practising trust during the process of recovery and beyond, it feels like a death. Surrender is for them an existential nightmare as it recalls the experience of being overwhelmed by another. However, the paradox lies in the fact that it is with surrender that healing begins. Facing this terror is the subject of this book.

Bodies

Many Christian writers suggest that the availability of a community that offers meaningful liturgy[86] and a safe place to process recovery[87] are vital for the Christian survivor. We have seen that victims of abuse commonly suffer symptoms of depression, presenting with negative body- and self-image expressed in eating disorders and self-harm, and the literature on recovery from abuse stresses the need to care for the body that has been violated. Accordingly, for the individual survivor's spiritual nurture Flaherty offers gentle and sensual spiritual exercises that survivors can instigate for their own healing. These include a meditation on Creation which ritualizes the re-creation that happens with recovery.[88]

Within the communal body of the Church, Beth Crisp argues that the post-resurrection flesh of Jesus Christ in the Eucharist represents the possibility of

---

84 Brock and Parker (2001), pp. 211–12.

85 Poling (1991), p. 44.

86 For example, Kennedy, M. (1999); Gosney (2002).

87 For example, Poling (1991); Brock and Parker (2001).

88 Flaherty (1992), pp. 145–52.

healing to Christian survivors as the re-membering of a broken body which was freely given, not forced, which echoes Cooper-White's approach to atonement theology. Crisp's argument that regular participation in the Eucharist 'reflects a desire for life in the face of adversity' is a note of hope.[89] However, in view of traditional understandings of the atonement embedded in Eucharistic liturgy, ministers and theologians should perhaps heed Hilary Cashman's admonishment not to 'rush to resurrection' too quickly, for 'how can the survivor be convinced that God accepts and loves him, if God's Church distances itself from him and refuses to understand the reality of his pain?'[90] Indeed Kennedy stresses that any attempt to silence the pain of abuse victims in our churches avoids the work of grief which needs to be shared; what survivors need, as well as receiving well thought-out liturgy, is to hear that the Church is standing up and condemning Child Sexual Abuse for what it is, an evil and criminal offence.[91] I would add other abuses to that condemnation, since the hostile environment of the culture in which we live and move and have our being centres around misogynistic and sexual violence. The pornographic depiction of intimate violence and the harsh judgment and degradation of particularly female flesh within our society continue to terrorize, and to obstruct healing for survivors. Bringing actual broken bodies into the heart of a Christian community that is naïve about issues such as the content and availability even of 'soft porn'[92] does not bode well for the possibility of seeing clearly the damage of abuse. For the acquiring of such insight would entail exposure to the very violence that survivors are forced to contend with at the heart of their lives. How, then, can Christianity offer any help if it is blind to what goes on beyond its threshold?

Above I stressed the importance of group support to enable survivors to reframe damaged perceptions of themselves. Spiritually, the collective body of the Church needs to be that place. Brock and Parker assert that comrades are needed who do not 'flee in horror to hide their eyes', or console the abused with sweet words such as: 'It isn't all that bad. Something good is intended by this.' They assert that

> violence is illuminated by insistent exposure. Steady witnesses end the hidden life of violence by bringing it to public attention. They help to restore souls fragmented by violence. They accompany the journey to healing.[93]

Can we risk that exposure? For if the most significant role the church community as a body has to play is to hear the witness of survivors, certainly for their benefit, it may also turn out to be crucial for its own survival. This is not to suggest there is a *purpose* in abuse, but it is to offer a challenge to Christian theologies, for

89 Crisp (2007), pp. 310–11.

90 Cashman (1993), p. 74.

91 Kennedy, M. (1999).

92 Cooper-White (1995), pp. 56ff.

93 Brock and Parker (2001), p. 250.

> in the midst of the worst evil, God's resilient hope is ceaselessly at work. This is why the witness of slaves, holocaust survivors and victims of child abuse is so important. They know the truth about good and evil.[94]

This chapter began with the scriptural degradation of female flesh left to perish, unprotected, in a hostile environment and progressed through to the intimate violence and tortured male body lying, well-defended, in the inner sanctum of Christian doctrine and liturgy. I have plotted the survivor's journey to recovery, and drawn on a range of theological authors, suggesting that theology which includes the survivor's perspective radically challenges traditional theology and practice. I have noted the subtle and problematic features for survivor spirituality of theological concepts such as atonement and forgiveness, which are intrinsically linked to violent, patriarchal power dynamics. I have also raised issues about the nature of God and humanity, and how the Church might represent the body where the two meet. It is time to open wide the door, welcome in survivors and listen to their voices. Only then will we really see.

---

[94] Poling (1991), p. 191.

Chapter 3
Finding the Right Key: A Grounded Qualitative Design

Making a Noise: Introduction and Aims

'I never spoke up to you because I could never get a word in.'[1]

Laura Hoff, aka Little Voice, yells these words at Mari, her vicious bully of a mother, who had been completely unaware that her shy young daughter had an amazing gift. Little Voice, LV for short, is able to mimic superbly every female diva from Marlene Dietrich to Judy Garland, yet has spent her adolescence cooped up in her room trying to avoid the abuse her mother dishes out. The trigger that releases LV's tirade against Mari is the loss of her most precious possession, the record collection with which she has identified her own voice, burnt in the house-fire caused by her mother's negligence. Having finally made Mari listen to her, she reclaims her real name, Laura, and is able to fly the nest.

Getting a word in edgeways is very difficult for the quietly spoken, since it is invariably the loudest voice that commands the floor. For someone vulnerable like Laura who has been damaged by a powerful individual in a commanding position, it is virtually impossible to make oneself heard clearly, let alone understood. When the eminent Doctor Freud projected onto young abused girls his psychological theories, in what position were they to challenge his conclusions about their stories? In a rare qualitative study on the spirituality of adolescent girls, Patricia Davis questions Professor Mark Edmondson's theory (based on his analysis of his own enthralment) that in Western culture obsession with the gothic horror genre is due to loss of belief in God. From her empirical research, Davis has found that in the case of girls, who in truth see a great deal of horror in their lives in the form of sexual violence, commodification of their bodies and distortion of their sexuality, horror is not so far away from their real experiences. She asserts that girls have not stopped believing, but that they do have a problem with the divine. Their problem is that the God with whom they are presented in church is the God of *Forrest Gump*. This is a God who is in the world but only capable of innocuous goodness, essentially unaware of evil, offering no answers to life's hard questions.[2] Davis stresses the urgent need for girls to find God in the midst of the horrors they see

1 From *Little Voice*, directed by Mark Herman (Miramax Films and Scala Productions, 1998).

2 Davis (2000), p. 108.

around them, and to find adult role models who have 'wrestled with God' and refused to turn away from the horrible questions of faith. These adults must be willing to 'face up to the reality and horror of violence in their lives – and not try to cover it over' because for girls 'who are just developing their voices and just beginning to understand the realities of their world, a God who smells like honeysuckle may be more of a horror than an absent one'.[3]

The 'wrestlers' Davis may refer to, however, are often those who have had no power to influence mainstream theology because they have been at best sidelined, and at worst demonized by dominant cultural and theological narratives about family and gender. Their voices have not counted and those in command have not listened. Pamela Cooper-White insists that as the first move in changing the 'social, political, and ecclesiastical contexts that sponsor abuse through denial and inertia', sexual abuse and trauma must be made visible.[4] Accordingly, this empirical study explores the relationship between Christian survivors of abuse and the God they worship. How is it possible that despite experiencing abuse, some survivors still have a profound faith? The aims of my study give expression to Christie Neuger's assertion that paying theological attention solely to pastoral responses to suffering (as important as these are) is inadequate for safeguarding the vulnerable and supporting healthy relationships. Rather, fundamental core narratives that are the seedbed for abusive behaviour, concealed by screens of honeysuckle godliness, must be deconstructed and actively resisted. Giving the abused a voice necessarily means challenging the status quo of the 'narratives of harm'[5] which have been constructed by patriarchal theologies. Hence, it is to the theological academy and the ecclesiastical system that I seek to direct the voices of survivors, and my aim is to 'hear into speech'[6] those who have been silenced and had least access to the levers of power; those who have been through dark experience and yet may offer us some enlightenment about the nature of God and the issues raised in the previous chapter. This means creating a bit of a noise.

Chapters on methodology can be tedious. However, I need to present the rationale underlying the development of my methodology, especially since my research design utilizes a social scientific method in a way that is unprecedented in practical theology. I take this risky step because I believe that without using the tools of social science in a rigorous fashion, we run the greater risk of closing our ears to the voices we are supposedly attending to, before we have truly understood. So in this chapter, as well as outlining the context for the empirical research, locating it in the field of feminist pastoral theology, I also discuss my underlying feminist principles and the process of data collection and analysis. I make particular reference to the principles of grounded theory method, and the internal controversies between its founders, in order to commend Glaserian grounded

[3] Davis (2000), p. 113.

[4] Cooper-White (2000), p. 101.

[5] Neuger (2000).

[6] Nelle Morton's phrase, quoted in Harrison (1990), p. 204.

theory in particular as an experimental tool theologically. The controversy I refer to and the appraisal of academic theology I offer are in my opinion connected. For social scientific methods have been used in recent years to inform practical theology, particularly missiology and pastoral care, but I develop grounded theory to be used as a rigorous theological method in itself that allows theory to emerge. This is one way of exposing theology to the voices of the participants, rather than expecting them to leap over patriarchal hurdles. It permits them to get their word in first and the result is an integrated study that addresses their real issues, not questions that are merely academic or imposed.

Echoes: Context for the Research

Because research material is sparse both on spirituality and abuse[7] and on qualitative theological studies of women's faith,[8] I make comparisons in this section with research projects which use social scientific method across the three disciplines of clinical psychology, feminist pastoral theology and congregational studies.

In clinical psychology the relevant studies to mention first are those in the quantitative paradigm which test specific hypotheses[9] and so have no methodological comparison with my study, but which show that there is a connection between healing from abuse and spirituality.[10] For instance, Ganje-Fling and McCarthy's analysis of the impact of Child Sexual Abuse suggests that psychological and spiritual development is arrested around the age the abuse happened,[11] and it is a spiritual relationship of some sort that helps many survivors endure the difficult process of therapy.[12] However, they argue that it is not unusual for survivors to embrace a set of beliefs in order to reduce anxiety and build their self-esteem, an observation also reported by Janice Humphreys in her research on the spirituality of battered women.[13] Embracing faith may give survivors the sense of belonging

[7] Sargent (1989); Hall (1995); Ganje-Fling and McCarthy (1996).

[8] Davis (2000), p. 107; Slee (2004), p. 10. Such studies are beginning to appear, and the reader is referred to the forthcoming collection edited by Anne Phillips, Fran Porter and Nicola Slee, *The Faith Lives of Women and Girls: Qualitative Research Perspectives* (Ashgate).

[9] Quantitative research, which generally uses statistical analysis, is given a simplified definition as 'empirical research where the data are in the form of numbers' by Keith Punch (2005), p. 3. For a more complex comparison of qualitative and quantitative paradigms see Punch (2005), pp. 236–9.

[10] Some studies exist about the use of spiritual intervention in therapy for survivors which have produced contradictory results according to Murray-Swank and Pargament (2005). However, the focus of my study is not on therapeutic techniques.

[11] Ganje-Fling and McCarthy (1996), p. 257.

[12] Ganje-Fling and McCarthy (1996), p. 253.

[13] Humphreys (2000).

to a community, but Ganje-Fling and McCarthy judge that their spiritual growth 'may not be authentic' if 'they have not struggled to personalise these beliefs, that is, [if] their spirituality lacks complexity and meaning'.[14] Accordingly, Valentine and Feinauer who researched resilience in female victims of Child Sexual Abuse named several factors influencing successful healing: *active* participation in a church was a turning point for many, accompanied by the ability of the women to 'reframe their situation'.[15] Finding meaning through the active process of reframing one's outlook resonates with Sgroi and Herman's recovery processes outlined in the previous chapter, and my study seeks from a theological perspective to add to the sparse research on the reciprocal relationship between spirituality and abuse, hinting that healing from abuse may necessitate a spiritual solution by its nature. Support for this suggestion can be found in Victor Schermer's original attempt at delineating a new 'psycho-spiritual paradigm' for the field of psychology. This concept grew out of his clinical experience of seeing 'hopeless' addicts, some with histories of abuse, recovering through the AA's 12-step spiritual path.[16]

Second, there is a major qualitative study of survivors which is not specifically about spirituality, but which covers faith as one underlying factor in resilience and healing. Over a period of 20 years Gina Higgins studied a group of resilient adults with a horrendously cruel and traumatic past. Higgins calls them 'thrivers' rather than survivors, and understands faith as undergirding not just religious beliefs but also secular beliefs.[17] She has observed that the courageous faith that these 'thrivers' demonstrate includes a combination of factors: they have the conviction that they can choose their own path in life; they have found sustenance outside conventional religious communities which have generally not provided an 'adequate spiritual tool kit'; they prize human relationships above all things, for it is human relationships that have been integral to their overcoming; and they exhibit a pride in being 'chosen' to beat the odds. Higgins emphasizes that feeling 'chosen' to survive is not to condone in anyway the abuse they have received. Neither is this an elitism based on some kind of triumph in overcoming suffering, for they could not choose their childhood, but what they *can* do is influence what they do with their pain.[18] This last factor has led each of the 'thrivers' to a deep ethical commitment to helping others do the same, and this was a central finding of Higgins' qualitative research along with the fundamental importance for them of 'loving well'. In these two points Higgins' conclusions find some resonance with my own findings.

In pastoral theology there are no rigorous qualitative studies of survivor spirituality to compare with my study, but most relevant is Nicola Slee's ground-breaking work on women's faith development. Her research design is similarly

14 Ganje-Fling and McCarthy (1996), p. 256.

15 Valentine and Feinauer (1993), p. 216.

16 Schermer (2003), pp. 4, 35.

17 Higgins (1994), ch. 5.

18 Higgins (1994), pp. 219–20.

rooted in feminist methodology, which I address shortly, and moreover as an example of feminist pastoral theology she is concerned with 'feminist theological analysis, critique and transformation of the life and practice of the Christian community'.[19] Slee analyses the convergence of the qualitative research paradigm and the praxis model of theology, since both begin with story and lived experience, for the researcher/theologian explores the area of study by immersing herself in the 'field'. Analytical reflection is the next stage, so that theoretical concepts are created from the ground upwards.[20] Key to the praxis model is that theology is understood as a corporate act of the whole Church rather than as the domain of the professional elite,[21] which we will see echoed by wider feminist concerns regarding academia. Slee's contextualized approach gives value primarily to 'hearing' and therefore shares the methodological aims of my study, which requires listening closely to the survivors. However, I then proceed differently, using the survivors' viewpoint as the lens through which we view scripture and academic theology. Slee's objective is clearly to inform pastoral and educational responses and although not one I share, there are some practical implications which do arise. While our aims may differ and our research questions are distinct, the results of Slee's analysis nonetheless have some resonance with this study. These resonances are the interviewees' emphasis on concrete and mundane experience as the locus of spiritual awakening,[22] the connectedness of empathy,[23] and most striking, how experiences of alienation might become generating forces for transformation.[24]

The participants in my project belong to different denominations, congregations and geographical areas, but *Changing the Subject* is an ethnographic study which is of further relevance.[25] Mary McClintock Fulkerson's congregational study of Presbyterian women and female Pentecostal preachers differs in method from mine in that she uses discourse analysis rather than grounded theory, and this produces a dissonance with my research alongside its resonance. Fulkerson interviewed women in traditionally patriarchal church environments about their relationship with God, and the echoes with my study include the women's experience of the 'intersection of divine and ordinary life'[26] and the Pentecostal preachers' testimonies about their vocation in traditional congregations. However, there is dissonance in that Fulkerson makes the judgement that the women's vocations were based on a contradictory discourse of self-abasement on the one hand, and divinely sanctioned, but unacknowledged rebellion on the other. I query whether this negatively critical judgment is an imposition of her own interpretation on the women's motives without

19 Slee (2004), p. 5.
20 Slee (2004), p. 10.
21 Slee (2004), p. 8.
22 Slee (2004), p. 133.
23 Slee (2004), pp. 149–54.
24 Slee (2004), p. 107.
25 Fulkerson (1994).
26 Fulkerson (1994), pp. 256ff.

checking more deeply within the interviews for verification or incongruity. Indeed she has been criticized by Marian Ronan for 'burying her insightful explorations behind nearly two hundred pages of convoluted methodological analysis'[27] and thereby reinforcing Christian reluctance to engage with the real *substance* of empirical research. Ronan's critique was influenced by her attendance at a seminar on Fulkerson's work where there was no discussion of the interview material.[28] This highlights the importance of carefully choosing one's method if the participants' voices are to be clearly heard in the analysis and raises the methodological issue about subjective analysis, or 'reflexivity', and the imposition of the analyst's perspective. Indeed Fulkerson's own point about feminist academic endeavour through qualitative research is proven, for she notes that

> however well-intentioned the scholar, the power dynamics of relations [between researcher and researched] negate the innocence of the academic as representer of women who have no access to the discourses of certification.[29]

This ethical dilemma lies at the heart of my choice of emergent grounded theory and my decision to extend use of this method in relation to the theological material. Perhaps it is unsurprising that the issue of power dynamics and the balance of submission and agency in relationship to God become significant for the theological discussion later. Content and method are integrated.

In sum, notwithstanding the 'absence in the existing theological frameworks of abuse survivors' experience of God',[30] and the complications of spanning the disciplines of social scientific research and theology, my project can be located in the field of feminist pastoral theology. As Nicola Slee asserts, the interdisciplinary nature of the praxis model of theology as reflected in this type of research is a strength, affirming 'God's truth as one'.[31] However, the use of social scientific method in this particular study is, I believe, unprecedented in feminist pastoral theology on two counts: first, there are no published qualitative studies on the theological perspective of Christian survivors of abuse; second, I have used grounded theory method not only for data collection and analysis, but as will be explained, I systematically 'saturate' the emergent theory with biblical and mystical theology. This breaks relatively new ground and my aim is not to provide answers or add to techniques on 'how to' minister to the abused, although pastoral implications may emerge. Nor is it to report on abuse descriptively, since enabling Christians and ministers to know *about* abuse, yet not insist they engage *with* the experience of abuse, merely papers over the cracks of suffering and encourages

---

27 Ronan (1998).

28 Ronan (1998).

29 Fulkerson (1994), p. 379.

30 Unpublished dissertation, Grovijahn, J. (1997), quoted in Cooper-White (2000), p. 97.

31 Slee (2004), p. 7.

uncritical complicity with its systemic causes, the 'narratives of harm'. That would mirror oppression of survivors; it would not reflect the God who is 'with us, in it'.[32]

In a Different Key: Methodology

When a clarinet player arrives in church ten minutes before Sunday worship is due to begin with her B-flat instrument and no music, a frantic moment ensues. Transposing sheet music which was written for instruments in the key of C at the drop of a hat is not easy, especially when music theory is not one's forte. Nevertheless, transposition is necessary in order that all musicians can take part and contribute to the musical ensemble. These technical issues can be tiresome, but need to be grasped if good, harmonious music is to be made. So having drawn attention in the last section to the importance of 'reflexivity', a technical term which refers to social researchers as subjective participants of the social world they study,[33] I should now locate myself and the timbre of my voice in this project before explaining its methodological underpinnings.

I was ordained 15 years ago in the traditional institution of the Anglican Church, although as a child I was brought up as Baptist. From these two influences I derive my love of meaningful liturgy and of biblical study. I bring to this project my own experiences of abuse, both inside and outside the Church, and have ministered within patriarchal structures to, and with, survivors of various traumata. The dearth of material by feminist theologians on the core syllabuses of two post-graduate theological courses over the last two decades represents for me a disconnection from what ought to be my historical faith roots. The joy of reading contemporary women theologians has been matched for me by the excitement of discovering many female theological voices through the ages that I had never heard of, women throughout the history of Christendom who have tried to contribute to the Christian project, only to find themselves rebuffed or censored, and sometimes brutally so. There is something about the spirituality and theology of specifically women's faith that strikes a deep chord. Thus I admit my bias towards repairing the ruptures caused by female exclusion from Church history and theology. Male voice choirs are wonderful, but do sopranos and contraltos not also have important contributions to make to our musical heritage?

Women's issues certainly bring a different tone, indeed a challenge to the patriarchal norm of academic research, and a crucial factor for the empirical study was the monitoring of the power dynamics of my relationship as researcher with the people researched, particularly in view of the sensitive subject matter. Feminist challenges to traditional patriarchal assumptions from a position of marginalization has in many academic disciplines exposed sexist gender bias in both the production of knowledge, and therefore also in social scientific research. Consequently I

32 Quote from interviewee, Lydia. See below regarding anonymity of participants.

33 Punch 2005, p. 165.

argue in the following section that relevant to my choice of research design were feminist epistemological concerns. I will first outline the implications of feminist epistemology for a research design aimed at empowering the marginalized, and then I will address the treatment of these issues within the discipline of social science. I will acknowledge the unsatisfactory polarization of gender norms that has resulted from feminist endeavour to redress gender disparity in research, since this may account for the absence of men in my interview sample, an absence which was entirely unintentional.

Feminist Epistemology

Reflecting on the collective nature of knowledge production and its role in sustaining the status quo, Kathryn Pyne Addelson argues that, rather than individuals creating the knowledge that becomes 'dominant', it is social and political organizations that lie at the root of epistemological constructs or philosophical doctrine. Thus deconstruction of the processes of knowledge production is crucial if we are to understand how epistemological work can either undermine or support a 'dominant elite'.[34] For feminists, this entails demonstrating how male epistemological dominance has succeeded in supporting patriarchal society. Addelson shows that moral epistemology, the dynamic process of making knowledge, should properly take place in public debate.[35] That is to say, although it is through the process of making moral problems public that dominance might be maintained, there is simultaneously exposure of this process to the possibility of change. Thus feminists are provided with the chance to make a difference in this way to the lives of the subordinated. A different type of moral reasoning would see philosophers more 'fully engaged with the social worlds they serve', and face-to-face interchange would make this work more politically useful as it has been 'tested in the heat of conflict within important arenas'.[36] Addelson advocates a 'dissolving of the walls' of the academy in order that knowledge is made *with* the women that feminist philosophers serve rather than keeping them on the outside, and this would have the reciprocal effect of critiquing the process of knowledge production. Here we can discern a feminist emphasis on working from the 'grass roots' in the making of theory, which we will see reflected in the development of feminist social scientific research method.

It is the 'grass roots' of women's lived experience that feminist 'standpoint epistemology' recognized as the location from which dominant philosophical discourse can be opposed, and which offers an alternative and less distorted view of reality. Grounded in Hegel's perceptions about the master/slave relationship and developed further in Marxist theory to highlight a proletarian oppositional 'standpoint' to those in power, it focuses on the gender differences that have

[34] Addelson (1993), p. 268.

[35] Addelson (1993), p. 276.

[36] Addelson (1993), p. 286.

accrued from the opposing situations of men and women's lived experience. Sandra Harding offers a set of eight grounds for valuing a feminist standpoint.[37] These include the maximizing of objectivity because women are 'strangers' to the prevailing social order; the sense that shaping knowledge is an achievement rather than a privilege, because for women there is a real struggle involved; the notion that women are 'outsiders within', hence they notice the gap between their lived experience and dominant conceptual schemes; and they have knowledge of 'women's work' (for example through childbirth and childcare) which enables the transformation of natural objects into cultural ones. This transformative role has remained largely invisible as a social activity to male eyes since, Harding points out, the real effect women have had in trying to improve the quality of daily life and preserve a cultural heritage has gone unrecorded in history. Postmodern feminist critique of standpoint feminism, however, pivots around the issue of gender essentialism, based on the premise that there is no concrete 'women's experience' from which to construct knowledge, and that it is important to view sexism in relation to other systems of domination.[38] Furthermore, it is important not to lose sight of the intrinsic value of 'women's work', of care and relatedness, which is not an innately gendered activity, but only made so by the elite having devalued it and abstracted themselves from it.

Slee observes that such criticism has been levelled at Carol Gilligan for her potential essentialism.[39] *In a Different Voice*, Gilligan's seminal work in the field of developmental psychology, laid the foundations of feminist epistemological critique. Her research on women's development was a reaction to previously skewed developmental theory, due to its reliance on experimental data from the lives of men as normative. The (patriarchal) viewpoint that attachment is a less mature state than the 'ideal' separated, individuated self inferred that women are less developed morally than men.[40] According to Gilligan, for women, attachment and connectedness are the most important values and their sophisticated moral reasoning functions in terms of relationships. Female reasoning tends to be based in a complex ethic of 'care', rather than on abstract reasoning which uses pre-formulated 'rules'. Criticism of Gilligan seems unfair, since she defines moral maturity as an ability to hold both approaches to moral questions in tension, neither being superior, but being dependent on context.[41] Elaine Graham maintains that despite the perception of an enormous difference between the two poles of maleness and femaleness, the biological difference is actually quite small: socialization exacerbates the differences, and women and men have identical

---

37 Harding (1991), pp. 121–33.

38 On the latter point see Poling (1991), p. 12; also Brock and Parker (2001).

39 Slee (2004), p. 24.

40 Gilligan (1993). On men's spirituality as normative, and on the solitary withdrawal from community and human intimacy as exemplar of advanced faith in James Fowler's faith development theory, see Slee (2004), pp. 35f.

41 Gilligan (1993), p. 173.

capacity for rationality and irrationality, for thinking and feeling, for abstracted and embodied thought. She suggests that the way forward is to deconstruct 'androcentric defences of objectivity, by challenging notions of fixed, rational and unitary accounts of language, knowledge and science'.[42] Working from the 'grass roots' of the marginalized and holding to the importance of relationship may do just that, and the following outline of the history of feminist development of social scientific research will demonstrate the significance of these values for my choice of method.

Feminism and Social Scientific Research

With the post-war advent of women into higher education there emerged a critical awareness of the sexist bias built into traditional academic research methods.[43] Ann Oakley highlighted the exclusion of women's experience from the results of research and observed the unsuitability of positivist, and largely quantitative methods of data collection with their *a priori* questions that disadvantaged women and covered topics of little importance to their lives. Traditionally prescribed ethics of interviewing curtailed what women said about themselves, making the interview paradigm clinical and unyielding of women's voices.[44] Oakley advocated an approach that fosters intimacy, responding to the interviewee's own questions and providing a non-hierarchical relationship between researcher and researched, reflecting more closely the nature of women's lived experience and the way they usually share information about themselves. She exposed as mythology traditional masculine claims to 'hygienic' research that 'mystifies' the researcher and the researched as 'objective instruments of data production', and argued that 'personal involvement is more than dangerous bias – it is the condition under which people come to know each other and to admit others into their lives'.[45]

In any case, the presence of the data collector within the research process affects the situation under scrutiny, no matter how objective the design claims to be, a truth of which even natural scientists have long been aware. In the social sciences, it is the social location of the researcher that is crucial and Marjorie DeVault highlights the place of listening as an aspect of communication research, wholly neglected in favour of excessive research on speech. Dale Spender claims that 'those who control knowledge production are more concerned with airing their views than with hearing those of others',[46] which is a variation on one theme that runs throughout this project. Accordingly, DeVault and women's oral history researchers concur that developing interview technique may be exclusively

42 Graham (1995), p. 206.

43 Slee (2004), p. 44.

44 Oakley (1981).

45 Oakley (1981), p. 58.

46 DeVault (1999), p. 93. This is reflected later in the theological discussion of silence in spirituality.

a female task since women are used to listening to others – and being unheard themselves. Oral history interviewing requires a change in methodology from a focus on the right questions, to interaction where the focus is on process, 'on the dynamic unfolding of the subject's viewpoint'.[47] Significantly, Anne Opie proposed three ways in which participants from marginalized groups might be empowered by the experience of being interviewed in this way. First, they are given the opportunity to reflect on their experience which offers an inbuilt therapeutic dimension; second, there is the potential for them to be subversive of power structures; and finally, their important issues are listened to and taken seriously.[48]

A problem that arose in the course of time with such qualitative approaches was their tendency to become over-emphasized in feminist research and the result was a false polarization of qualitative/subjectifying methods over against quantitative/objectifying methods.[49] Jayaratne and Stewart connect this polarization with epistemological issues of what counts as valid knowledge, so that one way of knowing was again becoming subsumed by another. The salient point, however, is practical: that methods best suited to answering a particular research question should be used, but in ways 'consistent with broad feminist goals and ideology'.[50] Weaknesses of a positivist approach and its unsuitability for exploring the experience of women or the marginalized, can be avoided without losing the systematic nature of quantitative research for which feminist qualitative approaches had been criticized (for example, by the rigorous selection of samples with the least bias possible). A healthy compromise is illustrated by G.A. Hornstein's research in which she analysed a recorded account in three stages: first she uncovered the structure of experience, followed by the constructing of 'analytic categories', and finally she described how these elements combined to create a unified whole.[51] This process made for a rigorously systematic study without having imposed a prior agenda on the interview procedure, a method akin to grounded theory which had its foundations in quantitative method[52] and to which we turn shortly.

In summary, with reference to the feminist critique of inequitable power in the production of knowledge, I have noted the need for connection with the 'grass roots' of lived experience for creating theory that challenges unjust dominant structures; I have suggested the significance of relatedness for women; I have also highlighted the importance of rigorous qualitative research and of the listening, interactive, but non-directive role of the researcher for interviewing women who have been marginalized in social scientific study. I suggest that such a methodology is most apt for survivors who are victims of power abuse and who remain the

47 Anderson and Jack (1991), p. 23.

48 Opie (1992).

49 Jayaratne and Stewart (1991), pp. 86ff.

50 Jayaratne and Stewart (1991), p. 91. Also Bryman (1999), pp. 62–4.

51 Jayaratne and Stewart (1991), pp. 92–3.

52 Glaser (1992), p. 7.

excluded voice marginal to dominant knowledge. Finally, having flagged up the epistemological issue of gender essentialism and imbalance, and in view of the lack of men offering for interview, it may be that further research is needed on a design that truly hears men into speech. There may be a 'different voice' which needs to be heard that is made neither in the image of, nor in the shadow of patriarchy.

Using the Right Instrument: Glaserian Grounded Theory Method

> In the best of feminist research, the purposes of research and analysis are not separable from the origins of research problems.[53]

In order to embody in a qualitative research design the feminist methodological principles which I have briefly sketched out above, I used grounded theory, an inductive mode of analysis, and drew on oral life history ethnography to inform the interview process. In addition to 'reflexivity', the hallmark of feminist research methodology that requires locating one's own voice in the project as researcher, another important feature is to own up when mistakes have been made in carrying out the research.[54] Thus it is incumbent on me to admit at this point that I believe I hit all the right notes, but not necessarily in the right order! Namely, the problem which arose as a consequence of the first stage of analysis proved fortuitous, since resolving issues of order and emphasis revealed the divergence that existed in the approaches of the two co-founders of grounded theory, Barney Glaser and Anselm Strauss. I was to discover that this controversy correlated directly to the methodological issues surrounding the opening of theological debate to new voices. As I outline each stage of my research with reference to these social scientific methodological issues, I will show why I deemed Glaser's freer approach the more appropriate for this venture.

Sample

Considerations of power dynamics, as already intimated, needed inevitably to be at the heart of the criteria for sampling. Crucially, participants had to be self-selecting volunteers since asking for referrals by clergy or other professionals might have engendered manipulation of survivors, who could feel pressurized to comply with a request from a person in authority. Thus volunteers were invited to participate by advertisement in local church publications and self-help websites. Openness and honesty, as well as the importance of proper boundaries, required that volunteers know that the researcher was a female priest, and I needed to stress clearly that the interview would be for research purposes only and not of a pastoral

53 Harding (1987), p. 8.

54 Traditionally such mistakes and wrong turnings would be rendered invisible. See Slee (2004), p. 52.

nature.[55] Nevertheless, the content of the research and the duration of some of the interviews in which two of the women wanted to speak at length indicated that the interviews were clearly therapeutic, which proves Opie's point about the benefit for the marginalized of participation in such research. I repeated throughout the process that confidentiality was of utmost priority, and I reassured participants that personal details, such as geographical information, would be eliminated from the original thesis report and from this book, so that their identity could not be traced. Consequently I gave each interviewee a biblical pseudonym to preserve anonymity, and also to signify female presence throughout faith history, a decision which was met with appreciation by participants.

In order to develop my aim of creating theology from the 'grass roots' by finding out how Christian survivors relate to God having retained their faith despite abusive experience, I need now to comment on the definition of abuse used in this study. I wanted to keep the basic research question quite loose, as in grounded theory it is 'the concern of the people in the substantive area' of research that is important.[56] Furthermore, I did not want to 'close down' the field, since it is what the subjects themselves are saying that should open up the ways of coding and analysing the data, as assumptions from the researcher's experience and knowledge can prevent theory from being truly grounded.[57] Therefore I allowed 'abuse' a relatively broad meaning, including spiritual, physical, emotional or sexual abuse. I stated this clearly in the advertisements and again in the information sheet which I sent out to respondents containing details about the recorded interview, with assurances of anonymity, to aid them in making a decision about participation. The volunteers who self-selected as 'survivors', brought with them a wide range of experiences of abuse. Some were individual instances, for example rape or assault, and some were experiences of long-term exposure to abusive environments, for example domestic violence or systematic physical abuse in an institution. Some participants had suffered a combination of both, as illustrated by Table 3.1. The table records only those incidents of abuse reported by the participants, for there were some experiences mentioned that I would have counted as abusive but were not named as such by the interviewee. On ethical grounds and in order not to influence the data, I felt it was important to accept their interpretation, so did not record them. Furthermore, I did not press for details about experiences of abuse, so the data represents what these survivors wanted to disclose.

---

55 The latter was a stipulation made by the Research Ethics Committee of King's College London, who endorsed the project.

56 Glaser (1992), p. 4.

57 Glaser (1992), p. 50; Douglas (2003), p. 48.

Table 3.1 Range of different abuses experienced by nine interviewees

Abuse as reported by survivor	**D**	**E**	**J**	**L**	**M**	**N**	**P**	**S**	**T**	**Total**
Child neglect by parent/guardian	1					1				**2**
Clergy/minister exploitation			1		1					**2**
Child Sexual Abuse:										
Incest			1	1		1	1		1	**5**
Clergy			1						1	**2**
Other						1				**1**
Physical violence:										
Domestic	1	1	1							**3**
School						1				**1**
Political violence		1								**1**
Rape			2							**2**
Psychological abuse:										
Clergy					1	1		1		**3**
Other	1	1								**2**
Sexual assault						1				**1**
Unspecified*	1		1	1	1					**4**
Total	**4**	**3**	**7**	**2**	**3**	**6**	**1**	**1**	**2**	**29**

* *Unspecified abuse* denotes any comment made by an interviewee about having been abused in some way, on which they did not elaborate. I did not probe these comments further as I felt this would be prying.

It was necessary that respondents had the ability to articulate their spirituality, and naturally memories of painful experiences might resurface, so the only delimitations I felt necessary were that volunteers should be established, regularly worshipping Christians, not recent converts, and also that they had already disclosed their experience(s) of abuse in order to allow for sufficient distance. In this same regard, I felt participants should not be too young; a lower age limit of 30 was suggested in order to fulfil a general need for maturity of years in respondents.[58] The majority of the interviewees had experience of church

[58] I did not ask for specific details about age, as this had no significance for answering the research question (Glaser 1992, p. 52), but when contacted by one person who was six months short of her thirtieth birthday, I did not turn down her contribution.

Table 3.2 Range of denominations experienced by nine interviewees

Denomination/ adherence[a]	**D**	**E**	**J**	**L**	**M**	**N**	**P**	**S**	**T**
Atheist								*	
Anglican (High)	*		*		*				
Anglican (other)		*		*	*	*	*		*
Baptist					*		*		
House Church								*	
Methodist								*	
Pentecostal			*						
Protestant		*							
Quaker					*				
Roman Catholic	*		*		*				
URC								*	

[a] Esther, Miriam, Naomi and Sarah explicitly reported that they did not think belonging to a specific denomination was important.

membership across the denominations, including evangelical and High Anglican, Roman Catholic, Baptist, Quaker, URC and Methodist, and Table 3.2 illustrates this range of church affiliation. Several reported that they did not see themselves currently as belonging to any particular denomination, worshipping at the church that best fitted their own spirituality.

There were 17 respondents to the advertisements, 16 women and one man, but after considering the information sheet, the 11 who agreed to an interview were all women. A drawing of lines on the variable of gender was not my intention, rather an approach that allowed the marginalized their voices. However, as I intimated above, the feminist methodological underpinning of the study may have created an inherent gender bias, striking a note which did not resonate with male survivors and reminding us of the complex issues of different voices and the key to releasing them. For although statistics show that far more women have been victims of Child Sexual Abuse and domestic violence, a considerable minority of men have been victims, and many more have suffered other forms of violence. Taking into account the sexual abuse statistics alone as quoted in Chapter 1,[59] one might expect that out of ten interviewees, four would be male. However, we might factor in two gender-based considerations: first, many more women are regular Christian

[59] See p. 1, n. 1.

worshippers,[60] which was one of the criteria for participation; and second, men face the extra oppression of the patriarchal expectation that violence is a part of the male experience and requires 'masculine' containment, a consideration which requires further research beyond the scope of this project.

Interviews

I used a non-directive and open-ended style of interview,[61] beginning each time with an open-ended cue, similar to, 'What I'd like you to do is to tell me about your journey of faith.' This allowed the participant freedom to take the 'telling' in any direction she wished, interview length depending entirely on the interviewee.[62] Two of the women related their whole story from start to finish and so time ran well over the suggested hour. Both women gladly and generously agreed to give me a second interview at a later date to complete their contribution. Most of the women were happy talking about their story and faith without any contribution from me, and indeed one participant commented on this and thanked me for not butting in; she said that no-one had ever listened to her story before without interrupting and asking 'silly' questions.[63] A common remark made by participants about the process was that it had been very valuable, because it was a rare opportunity for them to talk about this important issue, specifically in relation to their faith. The reasons given for this were one of the following, or a combination of the three: no-one was interested in listening to their story; the subject of abuse had been seen by others, particularly in church, as taboo; or the respondent herself felt she had not had enough courage to share her story before. The women invariably reported that their motivation for giving the interview was to aid research, but more resolutely to help other victims of abuse.[64] I was happy to answer any questions the interviewee asked,[65] which were usually about what had motivated me to study this subject.

In all, 17 hours of material were recorded, the shortest interview lasting 43 minutes and the longest comprising two recordings which ran over five hours; the median was 75 minutes. I used a Samson C01U USB 2.0 microphone so that all the interviews were recorded directly into a laptop as .wav files, considerably easing transcription into MS Word documents, for I could type freely, stop the recording at a click of the mouse and move forwards or backwards to any point in the recording very quickly.[66] Although one interviewee declined to have her interview recorded,

---

60 See Davie (1994).

61 Slee (2004), p. 54; Lawless (1991), pp. 39–40; Punch (2005), p. 172.

62 Lawless (1991), p. 40.

63 I have since received the same comment from another of the participants.

64 This echoes Karen's motivation for her contribution to the work of Poling (1991), p. 48.

65 Oakley (1981), pp. 35–7; Minister (1991), p. 36; DeVault (1999), p. 93.

66 I used the Creative Media Source Software, manufactured by Creative Technology Limited.

I carried out and transcribed ten interviews and sent them to the participants for their comments and/or correction.[67] I offered a final opportunity at this stage to the interviewees to withdraw their contribution from the project before I began analysis and nine responded with full permission to use their interviews.

After receiving approval from the participants, I imported the transcripts into NVivo 8 software for analysis,[68] but before writing up the results for the original thesis, I sent a copy of all the quotes I planned to use to the interviewees, with an explanation of the emergent theory, for their permission and comments. All nine responses were positive. Before preparing this book for publication I contacted all the participants again, asking their permission to use their stories. Generously they all agreed and most expressed great enthusiasm that the research would be made known.

Data Analysis

> The research problem is as much discovered as the process that continues to resolve it and indeed resolving process usually indicates the problem. They are integrated.[69]

This evaluation of grounded theory by one of its founders, Barney Glaser, bears repeating, for the use of this social scientific method in my research proved his point. The meaning of the title of Glaser's monograph *Emergence versus Forcing*[70] will become clear in this section, for scrutiny of the problem that sparked controversy between the co-founders of grounded theory ensured that as far as possible the interview data was free from pre-conceptual control. In explanation, I will first give an overview of the method, followed by a more detailed account of the data analysis stage, highlighting the discrepancy between Glaser and Anselm Strauss. My rationale for choosing the Glaserian approach as the most appropriate for this study will emerge and lay the groundwork for subsequent chapters.

Integration is the byword of grounded theory, in which an overarching theory is created by constant comparison of data for their differences and similarities. Constant comparison is one method which reduces researcher bias when conceptualizing raw data because it prevents the analyst from following only one track exclusively; that is to say, all the data has to be taken into account.[71] Conceptual

---

67 Lawless (1991); Slee (2004).

68 NVivo 8 software is developed and marketed by QSR International. It enables text documents, as well as photos, audio and video files, to be imported and analysed with a variety of tools. Codes (called nodes) can be created and set in a hierarchy called 'tree nodes' with sections of text entered under each heading. 'Memos' can be created and linked to the nodes, and relationships between nodes and memos stored and annotated.

69 Glaser (1992), p. 21.

70 Glaser (1992).

71 Glaser (1992), p. 14.

'codes' are assigned to units of interview text, which could be a word, phrase or whole paragraph, provided it represents a stand-alone incident that encapsulates the meaning of the concept. Further creative conceptualization is added through the writing of 'theoretical memos' when connections begin to emerge between the different coded meanings. Finally, as the relationships between codes develop, ever higher-level concepts become indicative of a 'core category', an explanation that accounts for what is central in the data;[72] that is, what is really going on for the participants. Thus the foundation of a grounded theory is good coding which ensures that concepts fit well with the recorded incidents they represent, producing research that has relevance to the real concerns of participants. Glaser calls this 'grab', and maintains that results are not only of academic interest, for although social processes are being conceptualized, there are practical implications. A grounded theory explains how problems are processed with wide variation, and therefore meets 'the two prime criteria of good scientific inductive theory: parsimony and scope'.[73] Moreover, it is modifiable because it can be adjusted when new, relevant data are compared with existing data.

Although there is some encouragement to begin transcribing and analysing data while fieldwork is still progressing, allowing researchers to check the 'fit' of emergent concepts in the field with new participants,[74] I carried out all the interviews for this project before transcribing and coding. This was due to time pressures and the nature of the emotionally taxing material, which required that I waited until I had time and space away from full-time ministry. However, following Strauss and Corbin, I began reading the material for the literature review as an 'analytic tool' that 'fosters conceptualization'.[75] Now, coding has three distinct stages, the first stage of which is called 'open' coding. Open codes are the foundational building blocks, involving close scrutiny of the data, breaking it 'open' line-by-line to discover abstract concepts that connect together the incidents related by the respondents. Table 3.3 illustrates how an early open code named '*difficulty in forgiving*' fits with four 'incidents'. During this stage many more concepts emerged from the data than were suggested by the literature review, so by the second stage of analysis, named 'axial coding' by Strauss and Corbin,[76] I was faced with two sets of codes, one set pre-chosen from the literature, and one emergent set. I felt stuck, as there seemed to be a choice of which set I should conceptualize further. Which were the most important codes? It was when I returned to assess the literature on grounded theory to address this query that the subtle but major differences between Strauss and Glaser's methodology became clear.

---

72 Punch (2005), p. 205. On terminology, there is inter-changeability in the literature between 'category' and 'variable', the latter originating in quantitative methods. There is also correlation between 'properties' and 'incidents'.

73 Glaser (1992), p. 18.

74 Miles and Huberman (1994); Punch (2005); Strauss and Corbin (1998).

75 Strauss and Corbin (1998), p. 53.

76 Strauss and Corbin (1998), pp. 123–42.

Table 3.3 Early coding of incidents in open code 'difficulty in forgiving'

Incident 1	I've had to forgive my husband much more than that and forgiveness is not the sort of thing you do, a one-off thing. It's something you have to work at all the time. On a nice day forgiveness is easy. It comes with the sun. But on a nasty [day] all your things come out of the woodwork and you have to do your forgiveness all over again. *Esther*
Incident 2	I can make a decision to forgive those people and let them go away from me for God to redeem them, but that doesn't mean that I'll forget what they've done and it doesn't open up the way for me to have a relationship again, unless they can honestly say what they've done to me and I can accept what they've done and believe in what they're saying. So that's really helpful to me, because you feel guilty that you're not forgiving but you can't pretend to forgive. *Miriam*
Incident 3	That's where it gets difficult because I know in my heart that Jesus died for me and I know that he's taken all my sin, forgiven me every last bit of it, and yet I am holding on to this sin of my Grandfather's. *Priscilla*
Incident 4	I think it's quite difficult really because during most things in my life, if something happens, whatever it be, I'm fairly willing to forgive and move on but I think it's when it comes down to that, it's just that one issue, one event, two people, I have the issue with forgiving. *Tamar*

Glaser argues there are significant divergences in Strauss and Corbin's book *Basics of Qualitative Research*[77] from the method he and Strauss developed and originally published together in 1967. Two of these differences are pertinent here. First, the premature use of literature in Strauss and Corbin's approach advocates verification of categories found in the academic literature, leading to subsequent directive questioning of respondents in the field and 'forcing' concepts rather than allowing them to emerge naturally. This did not affect the data collection in my study since, as already mentioned, I did not carry out any further interviews after coding. However, the lack of 'fit' between the two sets of codes, one set 'forced' from the theological literature, and one set 'emerging' from the interviews, was explained. Second, while Strauss and Corbin's second phase of 'axial coding' appears identical in meaning to Glaser's term 'theoretical coding', there is a discrepancy.[78] In this stage of coding, the analyst examines relationships between the abstract concepts that have been formed in 'open coding'. However, in 'axial coding' Strauss and Corbin prescribe the use of only *one* pre-selected set of six relationships between codes and concepts. Glaser, on the other hand, identifies *eighteen* sets of relationship types, each with six variants[79] and argues that these should not be pre-determined in the second stage

77 Strauss and Corbin (1988 edition).

78 Glaser (1992), p. 29; Punch (2005), p. 210.

79 Glaser (1978), pp. 74–82.

of coding, otherwise the theory is 'forced' too narrowly into specific criteria, rather than allowed to emerge. This becomes crucial when determining the 'core category' which is not explicit in the data, because it is through the constant comparative method, noticing and following up numerous connections and testing out variables, that grounded theory is created from *implicit* themes. Significantly Strauss wrote that, 'in the analysis, it is the phenomenon focused upon [by the analyst] that is the researcher's core category'.[80] Glaser argues the contrary; that for the grounded theorist the opposite is true, because the researcher's core category is 'that which emergence from data forces upon *him*'.[81] This is a humbling task because it requires that the data, that is the participants' words, must be in control, not the analyst.

Although I had not begun coding with Strauss and Corbin's single set of six relational types,[82] my attention had been drawn to a pivotal issue: that is, moving away too quickly from the basic principle of allowing the respondents' words to determine the coding had led to premature conceptualizing, because I had begun by using themes from the literature. The Glaserian principle of 'What concerns *them*?' (that is, the participants) became crucial, underscoring my main aim of allowing the survivors to be heard, not theologians and pastors, even the feminist ones. Thus, despite having chosen some phenomena from the literature, I now gave priority to the emerging codes, following Glaser more closely.[83] So I proceeded with free 'theoretical coding' which further conceptualized the data to a 'higher level of abstraction'[84] by forming a plethora of relationships between codes. When a 'core category' emerged, I ceased all 'open coding'. Further systematic coding was then delimited to relating the concepts I had already discovered to that core idea in a third round of coding known as 'selective coding';[85] the result of this stage is that the theory becomes integrated by elaborating as far as possible the 'core category' in terms of all its properties. The analyst must check continually for alternative explanations of relationships by going back to the data

80 Strauss and Corbin (1988 edition), quoted in Glaser (1992), p. 82.

81 Glaser (1992), p. 82, emphasis added.

82 Strauss and Corbin's set is called the 6 Cs by Glaser (1978), p. 74: Causes, Context, Contingencies, Consequences, Co-variances and Conditions.

83 Judy Kendall (1999) had similar analytical problems: Strauss and Corbin's 'axial coding' had changed the focus of her study from the concern of her respondents, which was 'doing well with ADHD children', to the code 'disruption'. This provided her with vast descriptive detail about how disruptive ADHD is for families, but did not answer her research question about how they coped; this underscores Glaser's view that description of a problem is not the aim of grounded theory, but to conceptualize social processes. Kendall concluded that both Glaser and Strauss's methods are viable, but the goal of the study had to be the deciding factor for which to use. See also Allan (2003) for analysis problems resolved by the Glaserian method.

84 Punch (2005), p. 205.

85 Glaser (1992), p. 75.

and not speculating. This validates and strengthens the core category, although it might in the process be modified in order to harmonize all the incidents and concepts where there is discord. How this process works will become clearer in the next chapter.

'Selective coding' is usually followed by 'theoretical sampling' which further 'saturates' the developing grounded theory by carrying out more field work to fill out the aspects where it is less dense. The aim is to achieve theoretical 'saturation' which means that no further data produce any modifications to the theory, so that it is conceptually complete.[86] In my study there were no further field samples, but my aim was to carry out this wider comparison of the theory by relating it to the book of Job and to Marguerite Porete's *Mirror*. Glaser and Strauss in their earlier partnership encourage researchers to 'use any material bearing in the area' at this point, including writings of other authors.[87] Neither pioneer changed his mind about this, and I will comment on my choice of theological dialogue partners in the relevant chapters ahead.

One final aspect of grounded theory method that should be mentioned about the analytical process is the writing of 'theoretical memos' which continues apace throughout all stages of the research. The analyst writes down any ideas about the emerging theory immediately as they occur to her. Glaser calls these memos 'the frontier of the analyst's thinking'.[88] At the end of analysis, these stored ideas are sorted and ordered, a process which helps construct the full theory.

In sum, I have presented grounded theory according to Glaser as the method most appropriate for my study because it is designed to create theory from a new field of research, and puts the respondents' concerns at the centre. Rather than beginning with a theory or hypothesis and then verifying or disproving it, the analysis should produce a relevant theory grounded faithfully in the interviews. It provides the key that will open the door to a new set of voices, to truly listen, so that we can discover what 'processes the main problem that makes life viable for' the participants.[89] For survivors this is a spiritual process, but it has complex nuances and needs teasing out. Finding the right conceptual codes at the beginning is like finding the right riffs or themes for a grand composition; the memos are sketches, and the grounded theory is the final orchestrated symphony which includes all the variations on each theme. We need to be silent and receptive, a good audience, so that we can hear all the soft tones in which survivors speak.

86 Punch (2005), pp. 214–15.

87 Glaser and Strauss (2009), p. 169.

88 Glaser (1978), p. 83.

89 Glaser (1978), p. 51.

Chapter 4
Opening Up: How Survivors of Abuse Relate (to) God

A bruised reed he will not break, and a dimly burning wick he will not quench.[1]

Introduction

On the shelf in my study stands the copy of a fifteenth-century Russian icon from the Novgorod School that was gifted to me by a parishioner on my ordination to the priesthood. Appropriately it depicts the Presentation of Christ in the Temple,[2] since I was ordained on 1 February, the Eve of Candlemas. What is striking about the icon is that at its very heart is the figure of the Christ-child clothed in white, a minuscule dab of humanity, surrounded by the immense grandeur of the stone temple buildings and four disproportionately sized adults. Mary, dressed in red, holds the babe closely to her, appearing reluctant to hand him over to the waiting Simeon who is bending forward from the door of the sanctuary, eager to receive the Messiah into his hands. I think I understand Mary's hesitation. For some time I have nursed the stories of nine Christian women survivors, and it is with trepidation that I am now about to deliver them to the traditions of theology. I am unwilling to allow any harm to come to them, reluctant to put them into the hands of those who do not know them. It is, however, as people who are witnesses of God's presence that I now expose their words to scrutiny. As with all disclosures of abuse, it is incumbent upon us to listen to, and believe, the words of the discloser.[3] As Mary was to see the threads that ran through the whole of her child's life, sharing his traumatic and liberating history, I hope that we will see the common threads that run through the spiritual stories of these survivors and share in liberating their meaning.

Developing a Core Category

This research began with the desire to explore the authenticity of the spirituality of Christian survivors who have had to struggle with intense traumatic experience. Why do they keep faith, despite not being 'saved' from exposure to terror and

1 Isaiah 42.2.

2 See Luke 2.22–35.

3 Kennedy, M. (1999), p. 60.

chaos? What might spiritual authenticity consist of, and how might it be shown in survivors' lives? In this chapter I show how the core category *knowing God's timeless presence transforms*[4] came to describe how these questions were illuminated by the volunteers. Because the core category that emerges is not explicit in the data, but created from implicit themes by the constant comparative method as outlined in Chapter 3, I will explain how it was developed theoretically through the different stages of coding.

In the first stage of 'open coding', three significant concepts came into view that were eventually to integrate into this core category. These three were: *Presence of God*, *Life/faith process* and *Service of God and others*. The second stage of 'theoretical coding' modified these concepts as numerous relationships were made between them and other codes and incidents, so that when I began the third stage, 'selective coding', the three had developed into the 'higher concepts' shown in Table 4.1. In what follows, I will explain each of these higher concepts, showing conceptual inter-relationships, and after summarizing the developing grounded theory as encapsulated by the emergent core category, I will also give attention to the concept of *boundaries*. This concept will become significant in relation to the literature used to 'saturate' the theory, particularly the Book of Job, as will be shown in the next chapter. The concept *free will*, discussed in this chapter in relation to the higher concept *Transformation*, will also gain greater significance when I evaluate Porete's *Mirror* in Chapter 6.

Limited space and the very great risk of boring the reader prevent demonstration of how every concept was formed since there were dozens of open codes, each containing anything from one to over a hundred incidents. However, to help explain the dynamic and rigorous process of analysis, I will allude to features of grounded theory method as they impinged on the development of the core category. The most important illustrations are, however, the participants' own words which will be used to intensify the essential principle of this project, that it is their voices which need to be heard.

Table 4.1 Development of three main open codes into higher concepts

Concept ***after*** **'open coding'**	became	**Higher concept** ***after*** **'theoretical coding'**
Presence of God	⟶	God's timeless presence
Life/faith process	⟶	Transformation
Service of God and others	⟶	Knowing ministry

[4] For clarity, 'categories' or 'codes' formed throughout the stages of analysis will appear in italics.

Higher Concept: God's Timeless Presence

From the early stages the overwhelming message which was constant throughout the analysis was the sense participants had of God's presence. This concept appeared in a wide variety of incidents reported, and phrases used by the interviewees. Consequently, the following nine original open codes formed the main concept *Presence of God* early on:

1. *God is in everything*
2. *God has always been there*
3. *knowing God is there*
4. *only having God*
5. *God is there/in it for me*
6. *God is within*
7. *God holding my hand*
8. *feeling close to God*
9. *special experience of God*

For example, the open code *God is there/in it for me* had 64 references spread across all nine interviews, and eight of the nine participants reported at least one *special experience of God*. In this section I will first demonstrate how 'timelessness' was added to this earlier concept *Presence of God*, illustrating concurrently how variables were checked for 'fit'. Second, I will show how this modification helped reveal the key to understanding how the survivors dealt with the dilemma of accounting for the loving God who did not intervene at the time of their abuse.

Esther was in a concentration camp as a child and later suffered severe domestic violence in her marriage. I coded the following incident from Esther's interview under *Presence of God*:

> That's why that sentence we say in church nearly every week, when we were far off, God was there. When I really didn't know anything about God, he was there, I was his child. I was precious to him even then, and gradually I've seen glimpses of him. And you see glimpses particularly when you go through the valleys in life. I've had some fantastic mountain top experiences, but it's in the valley that you really meet God, isn't it?[5]

This excerpt exhibits two important properties of this category: the significance of special moments of God's presence ('in the valley'), and the acknowledgement of the presence of God throughout life, even when the respondent was unaware of it. This second aspect indicated recognition of the timelessness of God's presence which became significant in two ways: for the healing of past memories of abuse,

[5] I have not tidied up all the grammar since this is conversational English, but I have omitted turns of phrase such as 'you know' in order to help the text flow.

and for preparing the survivor for a difficult experience to come.[6] For instance, in prayer ministry some respondents have been able to return to specific acts of abuse, experiencing the trauma again, but this time with the knowledge of God's loving presence. God's presence now heals the memory of abandonment and fear because God experiences the hurt and pain *with* the survivor, but not *for* her, as Lydia relates:

> In this ministry time, the person in ministry asked the Holy Spirit to show me where Jesus was. And I was taken back to the very first moment that I remembered being abused and it was just the beginning; and it was the most horrific for me in that I was only little; and Jesus was stood on the stairs with me, and it was healing because it was just that sense of knowing that he was with me even if my mother wasn't taking any notice or not protecting me.

Here Lydia is recalling her sexual abuse by an uncle. She associated her experiences of healing with the scripture that God is 'the same yesterday, today and forever'.[7] Because God had been there then, when the abuse happened, God could heal that past in the present. Thus the use of the word 'timeless' to develop the concept of *Presence of God* explains the survivors' experience of God being present throughout time, though not just on a linear, historical continuum: God has constant access to the past, present and future and can interact with any moment, making it present. This is the context for healing.

Another participant Joanna, however, had found this type of ministry helpful only to a point, reporting that she had baulked at one healing session. This 'variable' (Joanna's negative experience of what was positive for other interviewees) had to be checked out. Going back to the interview data, four incidents in Joanna's story proved relevant. At the age of 13 she was sexually abused by a priest (Incident 1); later in life, when she was encouraged by a minister to return to this traumatic memory and imagine that Jesus was 'holding her hand' while the abuse was happening, Joanna became extremely upset (Incident 2); this upset seemed incongruous, since elsewhere in the interview she described the *Presence of God* at a different traumatic moment in her life as God 'holding my hand' and 'being there with me' (Incident 3); however, later in the interview she related the story of how she had protected her little brother from the sight of a tragic accident by 'holding his hand' and guiding him away (Incident 4). The apparent contradiction was thus resolved by scrutinizing what Joanna meant by the phrase 'holding my hand'. For her, holding the hand of someone trustworthy signified being actively protected, a sign of caring intervention even, rather than denoting presence. This interpretation corresponded with Incident 3, which conveyed Joanna's belief that 'the Lord' had protected her, giving her an image from scripture, in a situation where she had felt totally alone and vulnerable. Thus, to imagine being abused

---

6 Joanna, Lydia, Naomi and Sarah recounted such a preparatory event.

7 Hebrews 13.8.

while Jesus 'held her hand' (Incident 2) was tantamount to saying that God had refused to protect her and therefore condoned the sexual assault (Incident 1). The issue of unhelpful ministry and the dilemma concerning God's non-intervention in abusive experiences will resurface, but here it is important to show how I have accounted for contradictions when coding the data and integrated variation into the grounded theory.

Another variable appeared when some respondents spoke of times when God had seemed absent rather than present. When checked out across the interviews, these same respondents spoke of later acquiring the more developed understanding that God had 'been there' in reality, they just had not felt so at the time. In illustration here is Miriam's account of a major house move which took her away from the church community where her faith had been nurtured:

> I felt like God wasn't there. Then I remember buying that book by Gerard Hughes called *God Where Are You?* Because I just thought well, I haven't lost my feeling that God is there. I feel that God is there but I can't feel God, if you see what I mean?

Overall there were very few references to *God's absence* – only nine over six interviews, in comparison to the all-pervading sense of God's presence for which there were over 150 references in early coding. Besides, the significance was not in the absence itself, rather that these incidents were all located in past spiritual struggles. Many of these struggles involved the survivors' anger about the abuse, anger that was aimed at God for *allowing* the abuse to happen. If God is understood as having been present at the time and scene of abuse, but did nothing to prevent it, how can survivors square this with a loving God? The resolution of this question lay in acquiring a new understanding and awareness of the God whose timeless presence is closely connected to the divine nature, and in turn whose nature is bound up with divine action. When talking about God, descriptions were often connected with God's action rather than specific imagery. To illustrate this, we first examine God's attribute of *love*, then the category of God *allowing*, and finally how the two are related.

The women saw God unanimously as loving and accepting, *love/loving* being the most frequently referenced attribute of God's nature. Any negative attributes associated with God such as 'punishing', 'remote' or 'angry' had been relinquished during their long spiritual struggle, 'angry' referring here to negative anger, since some of the interviewees commented that righteous anger is positive and creative. Connected with the idea of God as *loving* were attributes such as *comforter*, *friend* and *caring*. It would fit with the data to say that God is loving because God loves me, and also that God loves me so God is love, there being a certain interchangeability of verb/noun/adjective as Priscilla's interview will demonstrate. Priscilla often referred to God as '*loving* father' and said that she always felt:

> God's love is constant, Christ's love is constant, the Holy Spirit is constant, always constant and always there, and no matter what I've been through, and no matter how I've handled it, or not handled it, that has never changed. That's always been the same and always will be the same.

Thus since God is always present and God is always love, God is always loving in every moment. God's presence is not static but dynamic and active, and the quality of the connection that exists between the respondent and God, their personal relationship, is vital. In her struggle with God about the incest she suffered from her grandfather over the course of several years, Priscilla observed: 'as time went on, the more I got it off my chest, the more I felt [God's] love. I thought, he really does love me, he really does care.'

The ongoing sense of a connection to God's love is the key to solving the problem of God's non-intervention, for although in the past it seemed that God *allowed* bad things to happen, this appraisal was made when there was no real personal connection or knowledge of who God really was. Connection with God developed and deepened through the process of pain-sharing with God, as the last excerpt shows. When there is this connection, things are done in the world and crucially, bad things are put right. It is therefore no longer about God *allowing* things to happen, but about facing the world together, no matter what. God's presence, experienced with the survivor, means that they now go through things together, past, present and future. The implications of this joint action will resurface later in the section on *Knowing ministry*, but it must be noted here that the survivor is not always at one with this joint experience of the world; the struggle goes on, but what is vital is the connection to God, as Lydia explains:

> The pain is [still] intense, but I choose to believe that whatever happens in it, that Jesus is in it, and to praise God in all circumstances for whatever is happening. It's hard to do that, and we have subsequently had dark and difficult things, but I say thank you God for permitting this to happen because I know that you will use this for something good to come out of this. I wouldn't want you [*interviewer*] to think that it doesn't still hurt and that I float over the top. No. Things hurt and hurt and hurt and hurt, but they hurt with him and not without him.

This shows that for Lydia, seeing good come out of bad things is crucial, a concept developed in the next section on *Transformation*. It also demonstrates that it is mutuality that counts: God still *allows* bad things to happen, but struggle and pain are survived *with* God, and transformed because of God's active presence.

The use of the verb *allow*, as attributed to God, is also crucial for understanding the solution to the problem of non-intervention: God not only *allow*s abuse to happen but also *allow*s the survivor to be angry and have negative feelings. This was key to the change in understanding of God's identity, acquired through the faith struggle. If God had been seen before as remote and punishing of human weakness, it was a relief to know now that it was okay to feel angry and yet still be loved by God.

Freedom to be oneself without the loss of being loved, moreover with a deepening of the faith relationship, is the other side of the coin to *allow*ing bad things to happen in the world. God's evident lack of intervention at the time of the abuse, which brought anger to the surface for the survivors, can be seen not as abandonment, but as God's commitment to humanity's freedom. This permissiveness of God is then a double-edged sword: God's nature and action are constant, therefore God's *allow*ance of the survivor's freedom to be (angry or whatever) also *allow*s perpetrators to exercise their freedom to abuse. Some respondents commented on this conundrum. Tamar, who in childhood was sexually abused by her vicar and by her stepfather who were in collusion with each other, said:

> If [God] was to control our actions, of everybody on the earth, I'm not sure I'd want to live here. So it's very awkward and it's very difficult. I guess the conclusion is that everyone has their own mind and their own actions, and if I wanted to get up now and walk across the room, I'd get up and walk across the room. And [the vicar] obviously decided, for whatever reasons his reasons were, that he was going to do that to me and he did.

This implies a view shared more explicitly by other respondents that human choices to do evil are not God's fault. In their struggle with this issue, some have been able to discover that our human freedom, which is exactly the same freedom that abusers have, is the freedom to choose to be like God, or rather a co-worker with God, who is present even in the hard things: precisely here *we* can *allow* love to work. Then transformation happens and bad things are used for good, a dynamic we now consider in the next category.

Higher Concept: Transformation

In this section I show how codes were developed, interrelated in hierarchies and then theoretically across categories to form the higher concept of *Transformation*. A picture begins to emerge of how interviewees have been transformed, of how God transforms, and of how situations are transformed. Consequently, a further key issue is raised which I then go on to address: the reason for this transforming struggle.

Since one of the indicative questions sent to the interviewees concerned how their view of God had changed over the course of their faith journey, 'open coding' was bound to highlight this change as a theme. However, further coding suggested transformation in a wider sense was significant, and Table 4.2 shows how six open codes were grouped under the heading of *Transformation*, with examples of an incident for each. Out of these six, three specific codes came into focus after I had systematically inter-related them with other codes:

- *transformation of self*
- *spiritual awakening/conversion*
- *transformation of evil/pain into good*

Taking these three in order, I will highlight certain relationships with other important codes to show how each developed.

First, two of the relationships between *transformation of self* and other codes would be classed as 'consequences'[8] and the terms I use for these consequences are 'leads to' and 'revises view of'. We have already seen how *God's timeless presence* might effect change in the survivor's ability to heal from past abuse and view a positive side to God's non-intervention as *allow*ing. Here, *God acts positively* in relation to the survivor, *allow*ing her to be angry or upset, which as a consequence 'leads to' *transformation of herself*; this in turn 'revises her view' of *God's nature*. Accordingly, Esther recalled how being *allow*ed by God to be depressed proved to be the beginning of healing for her, which in effect disconnected God from the emotional cruelty she had suffered from her husband, who had been 'furious' at her depression in the past. She recalled how she had had to be a 'perfect woman' or else encounter her husband's wrath, and here she relates her contrasting experience with God:

> I can remember once being very angry with God and it was the first time. I was so angry. I can't even remember what it was but I can remember being angry. I'm not an angry kind of person. I don't easily anger, but afterwards I thought, maybe if you love somebody really very much, you're allowed to be angry, and it's the one continuous thing I have learned about God, that however I am, God will accept me the way I am, and if I do feel occasionally angry, he will understand.

This shows how healing from past abusive ties and a transformed view of God for the future seemingly go hand in hand.

Recognizing the difference between the human choice to abuse and God's will is also crucial: responsibility for abuse is laid at the door of perpetrators, as is shown by Joanna's transition from anger to renewed faith:

> I was just screaming at God, saying – I don't want you in my life; I don't want you anywhere near me. You're supposed to look after me. I'm told you're my father. If you were my father you wouldn't stand there and watch somebody rape me and I was really, really angry with God. That happened, I think for the rest of that day. But by that evening I was just in floods of tears, asking and pleading with God to come back in my life. I didn't want to be without him, and then I realized that it wasn't God's fault, it was this man and not God.

Joanna has been able to rediscover God's presence:

> I feel with Jesus – he's like my constant companion. My feelings now, even if they've been up and down, my feelings now are that Jesus is with me all the time.

---

[8] One of the 6 Cs family of relationships noted in Chapter 2, p. 48.

Table 4.2 Open codes grouped under the higher category Transformation

Open code	Example of incident
Change for worse, going away from God	I suppose for some people, they fall off the edge don't they? They feel so let down that they don't turn back to God again.
Change in view about abuse	I've found that if you think about things you always look, and think, that was horrendous. But it's not until you've started writing things down that you begin to see there's some really lovely things, in horrible situations, either to do with people, or whatever. Once I started remembering things, I actually started remembering far more lovely things about the camps than the horrendous things about the camps. Life is not made just out of horrible things.
External change in life	It's completely changed now. My whole lifestyle is completely different. When I was first left on my own, because he did walk out on me, after that time when he beat me so badly, when I came home from the hospital, he'd gone, packed his bags and gone. I suddenly realized that was it, that was my escape route. I went straight to the solicitor's and filed for a divorce. Looking back I don't know how I had the guts to do it, but I did and it's then my relationship has changed so completely. Because all I had then was God.
Spiritual awakening, conversion	I can't ever turn back, I don't have any plans at all – you know that song, *All I once held dear, built my life upon*? It says to know you in your suffering, to be like you in your death, O Lord? I think at some level, that I've experienced that and I suppose in a way then it's a privilege. So my relationship with God, I'm in a completely different place.
Transformation of self/ behaviour	He's worked with me all this time and helped me, like he's been nurturing me. For so many years I've felt like a child and wouldn't have been able to do this interview because I just would have sat here crying and crying.
Transforming evil/pain into good	Through all of it I realize that humanity has choices and people make choices and God uses what you're in for good to come out of it. I don't know but if it hadn't been for all of that I wouldn't know in my – we know things with our heads, but it's a difference when we feel them, when it moves from here to here.

So the second important code *spiritual awakening/conversion* shows how a particular traumatic experience, such as a humiliating court case or the death of a loved one, or a life struggle such as coping with depression, can 'precipitate' or 'accompany'[9] a spiritual transition. Again this process can lead to a reassessment of *God's nature* and to renewed spiritual commitment. Some respondents related that they had had a particular *spiritual awakening* before they were to face a very difficult time, rather than after it.[10] Once more God's action is not seen in preventing the bad experience or struggle from happening, but in providing the spiritual resources to endure it. The following experience of Naomi's came in advance of a deep period of suffering, and assured her that God is committed to her even when she has to enter the darkest of places:

> There was just this overwhelming feeling of being loved. I can't explain it any better than that, but if I had stayed there any longer, I just felt that my heart would burst. Somehow I knew that was God telling me how much he loved me and that was quite amazing. But I have to be careful who I say it to because a lot of people would say stuff and nonsense; but I really believe that was God saying to me, this is how much I love you. But that was before I attempted suicide; that was maybe, well he did, he knew all that was coming.

Naomi has experienced multiple forms of serious abuse, as has Joanna,[11] and they are the only two out of the nine interviewees who reported attempted suicide. Naomi (who I would guess was in her late sixties at the time of the interview) realized later on in her faith journey, that although her life had been very tough and cruel, it is purely because of her connection with God that she has survived:

> I know I wouldn't have got this far without God. Because I think that's where I get my self-worth from – that I know God loves me. I'm worth loving. So I get my self-esteem and my self-worth from knowing God, which is great.

That is not to say that Naomi or any of the respondents do not still have struggles, but now they have the spiritual resource of knowing better who God really is, and the assurance of God's loving presence which positively transforms the self. This is illustrated in the following comment from Lydia whose ongoing struggle we have already noted:

> I know at the depths of the situation, particularly in the trial and the newspapers, TV and other stuff, was that – I'd written [in my journal] that, OK God you're not going to bail us out then. And I remember I wrote, 'I'm sure you'll still be

---

9 'Precipitate' would be a relationship of Cause, 'accompany' would be a relationship of the Interactive family of mutual effects and interdependence; see Glaser (1978), p. 76.

10 See n. 6 above.

11 See Table 3.1, p. 42.

> there for me when it's over.' *When it's over*. But I didn't say to him, be with me *in it*, because I hadn't learnt that. I remember saying right, I'll drown, that's it, I'll give up, the waters will go over my head, and that will be it, and if I'm still alive at the end of all this you can have what's left. But I did learn that he was walking along the bottom of the river with me holding my hand. But I wouldn't have known that before.[12]

Lydia is relating how she survived a devastating period when she was healing from painful memories of her own sexual abuse in childhood, while simultaneously supporting her husband through a legal process in which he was eventually imprisoned for sexually inappropriate behaviour with children. This was a double-edged sword, razor-sharp, requiring Lydia to confront immense loss:

> When you lose something you thought you had control over, your reputation, your significance, your status, when you lose something like that, I think you then realize that you're not controlling anything.

Lydia had suffered other losses, including the loss of a child, but it was this latter experience that brought her to a point of no return:

> I can't ever turn back, and I don't have any plans at all because, you know that song, 'All I once held dear, built my life upon'? It says 'to know you in your suffering, to be like you in your death, O Lord'? I think at some level, that I've experienced that and I suppose in a way then it's a privilege. So my relationship with God then, I'm in a completely different place.

Lydia's comment about 'privilege' and in an earlier quote about thanking God for 'permitting' awful events to happen, are not for her some form of masochism, or a lack of hold on reality. She did not choose to suffer in this way, and some of the survivors said explicitly that they wished the abuse had never happened, an admission I suspect that went without saying for the rest. But what Lydia and the rest of these survivors are not denying is the reality of what has happened, and there seems to be agreement that since they are in this dreadful place, the only hope they have found is in God who becomes their raison d'être, as illustrated by these three excerpts:

> Lydia: When you lose something like that, I think you then realize that you're not controlling anything, and I've learnt that. So I only live for God.
>
> Esther: My relationship has changed so completely. Because all I had then was God.

---

[12] The italics reflect Lydia's emphasis.

> Priscilla: If somebody said to me, you can go back and have that not happen, but not have that relationship with God, I would go through all of that again for that relationship. I wouldn't want to change that. If it was either or, there's nothing that would make me not want to have that relationship. Although it was awful and it was horrible, I'd rather that than not have God.

Thus spiritual transformation via the place where there is nothing but God is painful, but appears irreplaceable for them. There is only one way out of it and that is through it, with God who brings good out of the evil and pain. This will be one of the important focuses for discussion in Chapter 7 and now brings us to the important third aspect of *Transformation.*

Apart from an incomparable and vital relationship with God, seeing evil and pain transformed for good is the one positive that participants gleaned from their difficult journey. This has in turn led to service as an aspect of this transforming action in the world and illustrates the growing complexity in the coding relationships between *God's action*, the survivor's *Transformation* and the survivor's subsequent vocation. The impetus and initiative for their *Transformation* is placed squarely with God and Lydia sees this as an undoing of bad human choices (not necessarily her own):

> Through all of it I realize that humanity has choices and people make choices and God uses what you're in for good to come out of it.

Accordingly she perceived that for her family some of the good that had come out of the terrible ordeal of her husband's trial and prison sentence was the deepening of their family relationships and love. She connected these family blessings with a message from scripture that someone had spontaneously given her years before, which she had now come to understand, showing once again the timelessness of God's active presence in her life:

> 'And I will show you treasures in dark places so that you will know that I am the Lord your God.'[13] Hadn't got a clue what that meant at all. I kept [the text] and didn't really do anything with it, but then, I now know what God does – he gives treasures in dark places and the treasures are the healing and the goodness that's come out of all of this in the way that our kids love and support each other, and the way that they respect their father and the way as a family – I know that we've got so many blessings that other families that are fragmented and don't speak [don't have]. So I've found loads of treasures in dark places.

One problem that was raised about the issue of good things coming out of evil was the question of God's part in it. While being the author of this *Transformation* is seen as God's positive purpose and role in their lives, the implication that the experience of abuse was *worth* something raised a dilemma about God, supposedly

[13] Isaiah 45.3.

loving, planning such a 'learning' experience. However, the interviews show that this is to view the issue from the wrong angle. Healing and learning may come through the transformative struggle of facing the abuse, but these are not the *reason* for it: life and its traumata are not a 'test'. Miriam insists that 'it's never God's will for you to suffer, even though God can make good things out of bad things, it's never God's will for people to suffer and God doesn't test us'. Priscilla said this on the matter:

> I think over the years, I've struggled with the idea that some Christians have that God allows things to happen to make you a better person. I actually find that quite insulting to God really. I cannot imagine that any loving father would allow a child to go through what I went through in order for them to be something when they grew up. I can't get my head round that. That's not my Father. He wouldn't do that. The fact that he's used it, that it hasn't been wasted, that's a different thing, but you do hear this kind of talk that oh, well, it's part of God's plan. I don't believe it was ever part of God's plan. I don't think it's part of his plan for anybody to hurt, or to go through that kind of pain, whether it's physical abuse or mental abuse or sexual or whatever it is. I don't believe that that's part of his plan at all.

I was quite surprised that the metaphysical question of why evil exists was not raised by any of the participants. What they did share, however, was a concern to stress that God does not *will* evil and pain, a view which was 'accompanied' by the conviction that God does not *do* any evil; he does not even punish bad choices. The issue of *God's will* was reflected on with reference to atonement theology by two of the women, Miriam and Sarah, both of whom had undertaken some formal study of theology. As one of my indicative questions, sent with the information letter, had asked about the significance of Jesus, understandings of the atonement were likely to be mentioned and it was touched on by three of the other respondents using general doctrinal or devotional formulae:

> I know in my heart that Jesus died for me.

> When I think what he did for me, how he died for me, boy was some of my behaviour – I drove the nails in, we sinners do.

> Jesus is God's son who died on the cross so that I might have life.

Miriam, however, had been reading about a theology of abuse,[14] trying to make sense of what had happened to her and God's puzzling presence within it:

> It's saying in that book, it wasn't God's will for Jesus to die on the cross – this cannot be said often enough or loud enough. And I just thought thank you, hurray

[14] A chapter from Ormerod and Ormerod (1995).

> that's so brilliant. Because it says if you believe that, then you can justify all sorts of bad things in the name of God and in the name of religion, this is all part of God's will. What kind of God is he then? You just think, no it's not the way God is.

This suggests that for Miriam *God's will* is not about instigating suffering, even Christ's death on the cross, which recalls the debate in the literature review, a debate which will resurface in Chapter 7 in relation to Christ's 'kenosis'.[15]

Sarah also has reservations about traditional theology. Her metaphorical understanding of scripture had been severely criticized by ministers in her church, in a form of spiritual abuse, one part of a larger picture of her systematic bullying by church leaders. Her reflection on the atonement came in the context of considering how religious authorities continue to misconstrue scripture and rules, just like the Jewish authorities did in Jesus' day. Sarah put emphasis less on the significance of doctrinal formula and more on the purpose of Jesus' actions and words:

> The really powerful thing that I find in my mind I cannot grasp is 'to redeem us from our sins', 'to bear the sins of the world' on our behalf. I've never understood that, I never will, and I'm not going to try because I don't need to. Just accept it because if you're not going to understand it now at 47, I'm not going to understand it ever – and does it matter? I can see Jesus in my mind's eye, saying, 'No it doesn't matter, you're OK.'

Sarah argued that Jesus was sent not to overturn scripture but to overturn people's perception of scripture; that Christ's meaning was *Transformation*. Furthermore, she compared turning water into wine with changing bad things into good:

> If we turn hate into love, if we've turned disunity into harmony, if we've turned aggression into peace, haven't we turned water into wine? Haven't we turned something abundant, something common, something tasteless, something thin into something rich and meaningful that actually matures and you can share with people?

Sarah maintains that Jesus did this all through his life, that this was his purpose. Therefore transforming the damage and hurt of abuse into a force for good is purely an outworking of God's nature: it is what God does, it reveals who God is and the potential for newer, richer life that is always there. Sarah insisted that to serve God in ministry is to bring 'God's love into a hurting and broken world'. According to both Sarah and Miriam, some commonly held understandings of the atonement are either unimportant or wrong, and far more significant than the reason why the bad is there in the first place is the nature of God's love, bringing good out of bad, and how we then live in that love.

---

15 'Kenosis' meaning self-emptying.

The following reflection by Priscilla ends this section on *Transformation* and leads us neatly into the analysis of the higher concept *Knowing ministry*. It draws together the survivors' view that on the one hand God does not will evil, yet can and does transform it into good, and on the other that there is no ultimate purpose for abusive experiences, yet there is resolution:

> I don't think that [God] wanted it to happen. I don't think he let it happen, but when it did happen I think he was then able to change that, transform that into something that was good. So that out of that pain and out of that evil, good actually came, inasmuch as I was then able to talk to other people and get close to other people. Not necessarily in that situation but in any situation, so that was a good side of it. The older I get the more I see the good that's come out of it. It took me a long time. Yeah, but it wasn't all wasted.

Higher Concept: Knowing Ministry

In relation to ministry, the early concept *serving God and others* was formed from five open codes. An example of an incident for each of these open codes is given in Table 4.3. It became clear that the respondents had already served in a vast range of different informal ministries, some of which are recorded in Table 4.4. However, some had also pursued some kind of formal ministry in the church, yet notably none of the respondents had been successful in formal authorization, except one for whom this led to sexual exploitation by the minister who had in the first place encouraged her to become a pastoral assistant. In this section I will outline three complex relationships between codes which led to the development of the higher concept *Knowing ministry*.[16] This higher concept shows how the respondents are active in ministries which clearly reflect God's care of them. Additionally, the issue of criteria for success in formal ministry is raised by the exclusion of respondents from it, and this leads to a discussion of survivors' views on ecclesiology.

I discovered one complex relationship between the concept *serving God and others* and the higher concept *Transformation*. In order to make this connection it first has to be noted that there are various faith practices when participating in a Christian community which affect the life of its members. These effects I coded from the interview data as:

- *effects of scripture/spiritual writings*
- *effects of doctrine*
- *effects of other Christians*
- *effects of liturgy*
- *effects of questioning faith*

---

[16] There are many cross-category relationships, too numerous to show, so these are examples most pertinent to this section.

Table 4.3 Examples of how serving God and others became a concept

Serving God and others	**Example of incident**
Present service	I am very much a community worker. I am out there with the people. When I went and put myself forward to become a councillor, I wanted to bring the Christian faith to politics.
Sense of calling	I believe that when I was at the right point I was in the right place because I really wanted to be involved in ministry. I got into that church and started to work in the church; he asked me if I wanted to be a pastoral assistant, and I really wanted to do it. I thought what better life could it be than to be able to pray and do Bible study, teach and visit people, and always be constantly reminded of the presence of God in our lives, always be focusing on that and spirituality. It's what I love, it's my vocation.
Past service	As a nurse, I used to run hospice care here, and to me the healing was not necessarily physical healing. In fact it rarely was. The spiritual healing made all the difference to a patient's well-being right till the end – and the family.
Desire to serve	I've pleaded with him to please let me help other people. Let things come into my path where I can either talk to people or give a speech, or help. Just let me help people, to say that whatever you've gone through in your life, even if you've turned your back on Jesus, you can ask him to come back in your life.
Future service	That's the role I'm looking to do, because although I am not out in the workplace at the moment, who knows that that might not change? I won't depend on the church for my living. I can support myself.

Some respondents reported cases where these influences had been negative, for example in Tamar's case, liturgy and prayer had been the context of clergy sexual abuse. An example from Deborah's interview illustrates how doctrine had had a detrimental effect on her in her early years:

> Every time I wanted to escape, I was pulled back, because then the Catholic duty – it's your duty to be here! And so you had duty from your parents even though by that time you couldn't respect them; duty from the priests in the pulpit; and I thought, I don't like this God, I don't want to know him. And yet I was terrified of him.

On the other hand, some faith practices were seen as positive or motivating influences. In particular the positive influence of scripture can 'lead to' a survivor's sense of calling. For example, Deborah reported that she was pursuing ordained

Table 4.4 Informal ministries undertaken by nine interviewees

Interviewee	Service/ministries undertaken
Deborah	Community work as councillor
Esther	Led intercessions; hosted Cursillos; ran hospice care; gives talks in schools; leads house groups; theological study; gives prayer support
Joanna	Fostered children; serving at altar
Lydia	Sang in choir; plays guitar in worship group; helped in crèche; led Sunday school; co-ordinates and gives prayer ministry
Miriam	Theological study; visited sick and housebound; ran toddler group; financially supported small church; wrote/led Bible study; gave ministry to the dying; administering home communion; long-term fostering; delegate at national church event; chair of local justice and peace group
Naomi	Gave secretarial support to vicar; led house group; joined choir; leads prayer meetings; ministry team
Priscilla	Helped with Alpha and house groups, crèche and Sunday school; making tea and coffee
Sarah	Visiting sick; leading studies; theological study
Tamar	Counselling children; teaching in church school

ministry in order to 'defend the role of women'. She related an incident about a conversation she had recently had with her curate in which she was sharing her sense of calling and explaining the importance of Mary for her as a role-model:

> I did bring in Mary, who without her, the Church as we know it would not have developed. It was her consent. I mean if you believe in things are preordained, fine, she couldn't really get out of it, but I don't know. We still have free will. You can still choose and she chose to obey, so the Church really was based on Mary, I see, before Jesus was old enough to take over the ministry. So many people have difficulty in relating to Mary, but she is such an important woman and she's a marvellous role model for us.

This scriptural insight that Mary was fundamental to the foundation of the Church and its ministry was revealed to Deborah only through voicing her idea of Mary as her vocational role model. This idea really took her by surprise and she exclaimed that she did not know 'where that came from!' but it seemed to be very significant to her personal vocational motivation. A second example comes from Esther who had learnt, and inwardly digested, a text from scripture at a 'Cursillo' retreat which she had hosted in her home:

> One of the clergymen had brought a banner. It was the bit about John: 'you are a child of God'. Cursillos last four days, so for four days I looked at this banner and it says, 'you are a child of God' in huge letters. When you look at that for four days you don't forget it and it got into my heart somehow. So that's when I accepted that first bit.

Esther has written a prayer which she now uses when ministering to others with low self-esteem. It incorporates this scripture about being a child of God and therefore precious:

> Over the years I accepted bits of this [prayer] and this is what I've come to now and I send this to some people, and I say you are a very special person even if you don't think you are, or if you've been made to believe you're not. You are precious to God.

Thus *Transformation* brought about by *effects of scripture* 'enables' the survivors to become ministers to others.

Spiritual writings can also 'evoke' a *special experience* or a *spiritual awakening/conversion*. Miriam had what she believed was an experience of the Holy Spirit after she had been studying and praying with a book called *The Lover and Beloved* by John Michael Talbot, which encourages the reader to seek a relationship with Jesus 'as close as that between lovers'. She reported that she had once felt very disturbed by the image she had had of Jesus reaching out and lightly touching her cheek, followed by the experience of what felt like a rushing wind. Although several respondents reported special experiences of God that were of a supernatural kind, they all regarded themselves as sceptical of such events, Miriam in particular. So she confided in her vicar (not the minister who abused her), and he gave her the following verse from scripture:

> If you then, though you are evil, know how to give good gifts to your children, how much more will your Father in heaven give the Holy Spirit to those who ask him.[17]

Reassured, Miriam felt a renewed commitment to the practice of her faith. Although she does not herself connect this event and scripture specifically to vocation, it was soon afterwards that she was convinced of a calling to ministry and she connects this calling with other spiritual books she was reading:

[17] Luke 11.13 (NIV).

> I was always reading spiritual books. I can remember reading something by John Stott that was asking the question, do you have any sense of vocation, calling into ministry at all? So I started to think, well I think I should speak to my minister because I do feel like that, because I had this passion for it.

A second complex relationship concerns a connection I noticed between *God's timeless presence* in the survivor's life and *transforming evil/pain* [of abuse] *into good.* This *Transformation* inspires godly practice in the survivor's own ministry, that is to say, the survivor's pastoral relationship with others reflects God's healing relationship with her. For example, we noted earlier that Lydia found healing in knowing that God was the same yesterday, today, forever. She later reported the following about her own subsequent prayer ministry with others:

> In ministry with other people – that's when you can apply that truth to asking the Holy Spirit to take them back to that time, when they experience that pain that's now causing them so much trouble. The Holy Spirit gives them pictures and they have that deep sense of knowing where he was and that really does help them to let go of the past, or understand that he was there with them then, or that he cried with them then, or that he was experiencing the same physical pain maybe.

Furthermore, the passage from Priscilla's interview quoted above which suggests the formative effect of working through the pain of her abuse,[18] was preceded by her comment that her 'over-sensitivity' as an abused girl had now been transformed into a blessing by God: this sensitivity now enables her to 'pick up on what other people are feeling' and put herself 'into someone else's place', to empathize with them. Lydia sees her *Transformation* as helpful in her professional life too, where she regularly deals with people facing terminal illness:

> It's helpful for having compassion and I'll sit – because obviously in my job I'm interacting on a daily basis with people at the end of their life – young people at the end of their life, people who are having a real shit time. And I know what you don't say. I know what not to say, because the reality of it is, no-one can walk your path. No-one can do your experience. When you sit alongside someone, even if it's a similar journey, it's not your journey, it's theirs and how they experience it is different, but I think that if they know that you know, I think that they find it easier for you to sit alongside them. But I still don't think that it gives you the permission to say what it's like, what it's like for them. And you can't take it away either.

This is a profound reflection of what Lydia had experienced in God's healing for her. God did not take the pain away, for as she commented elsewhere, God does

[18] See p. 65.

not 'bail us out'; God does not 'answer prayer the way we want him to', but is 'in the business of being in it'.

Esther acknowledged that during her violent marriage, her faith had been her only 'secure place'. When the physical danger from her husband was over after her separation and divorce, there was a long process of healing from the psychological damage and the deep humiliation he had caused her. At this point, the support she received from members of the local church now became her secure place, where she was allowed to cry, being invited to stand between two ladies who produced a handkerchief for her whenever she needed it. For her, this was akin to the God who allowed her to be upset and angry, and in turn she now provides a safe place for others who need accompaniment. When she underwent a complex and frightening nine-hour operation on her spine, the result of many years of physical abuse, she had been upheld in prayer by others, and was given Julian of Norwich's prayer to use for reassurance.[19] On the day of the interview when Esther welcomed me into her home and showed me warm hospitality, she had that very morning given support over the telephone to a young mother who has spinal cancer. She passed Julian's prayer on to her:

> She's having her operation today – and I said can you remember that? And she said, Yes, I'll remember that. What a good idea she said. And she's not a Christian. I didn't tell her that was Julian of Norwich. I just didn't want to – there wasn't much point in talking about that. So hopefully she'll remember to say, all will be well, all will be well.

Knowing God's healing presence is, then, transformed into godly service of others.

A grateful *desire to serve* as 'consequence' of one's own *Transformation*, a healing of the personality or self-worth, is a third complex connection as I will now illustrate with Joanna's story. Joanna has a long history of sexual abuse and has suffered acute and chronic physical illnesses, including severe depression. She attempted suicide once, but reports that on two other occasions she had a *special experience* in which God saved her from attempting suicide: God had 'taken [her] to a place' where she was kept safe until the suicidal feelings had passed. Even though Joanna still suffers, she feels she has something to offer others who have been through abuse and have been turned against God by the terrible experience. She feels she is living proof that God does not abandon you:

> [God]'s worked with me all this time and helped me, like he's been nurturing me and for so many years I've felt like a child and wouldn't have been able to do this interview because I just would have sat here crying and crying. And yet now I've come to this strength and I would like to be able to give my testimonies again and again, they are just so strong.

---

19 'All shall be well, and all shall be well and all manner of things shall be well.'

For Joanna, giving testimony would be an important ministry. Although she was brought up Roman Catholic and now worships in a High Anglican church, she came to adult faith through a charismatic fellowship where testimony was crucial. Her *desire to serve* was repeated throughout her interview, but she feels she is side-lined by church leaders and communities. She thinks this is largely because of her propensity to ask awkward questions about scripture and theology. Indeed Joanna was banned from attending an Alpha Course in case she upset newcomers because she had asked how Adam and Eve's children populated the world without committing incest, which is a perfectly logical (and even pressing) question for someone who had been the victim of incest herself.

Naomi's story echoed Joanna's experience of being side-lined. She reported how the women's Bible study group she led was taken away from her by the vicar after Naomi had been absent for a time, due to a family tragedy. The only explanation given her by the vicar was that there had been complaints from some of the husbands of the women in the group (not the women themselves), that Naomi went 'too deeply' into things. Naomi expressed sadness that the Church discourages sharing and open discussion of difficulties, and believes it must become more 'real'. Throughout her life she has served the Church in many practical ways, supporting clergy with her secretarial skills, leading prayer groups and singing in the choir. Yet the ministry to which she feels drawn is one of spiritual leadership:

> I would love to lead quiet days. I would love to, but you never get any opportunities. That's what I'd like to do more than anything – leading people into a deeper knowledge of the Lord.

Clearly Naomi is extremely well-read in spiritual matters, yet her story suggests that Christians with spiritual depth who have been making a profound faith journey are being overlooked. She closed her interview with a lovely story she had read, which compares our relationship with God to a bird learning trust from someone who visits the park every day to feed it:

> First of all you start by just getting a few crumbs, but you can work your way so that you're eventually standing on God's hand, and I thought that that was so beautiful. There's so much further we can go.

Naomi and Joanna have both been as far as the brink of self-destruction and found God's love there, and they wish to share this knowledge with others; but they have been made very aware that they should keep quiet about their experiences. Joanna shared the following about her treatment by other Christians:

> People have said to me you didn't ought to tell people about things like that, they should be kept to yourself. You shouldn't share your experiences with somebody. Well how did Jesus spread the word then? He didn't keep it to himself, did he?

He didn't say I won't tell anybody else about this, I'll keep it to myself. So you do end up not telling people.

From these and many other similar connections, the higher concept *Knowing ministry* was developed, yet we have seen how these ministries are informal and even how sometimes the *desire to serve* has been obstructed.

Table 4.5 Formal ministries sought by eight respondents

Interviewee	Ministry sought	Succeeded?	Reason given
Deborah	Ordination (past)	No	Too old/female
	Ordination (present)	In process	*
Joanna	Counselling	No	Training incomplete
Lydia	Ordination	No	Husband's CRB status
Miriam	Ordination	No	Advised instead to be pastoral assistant
	Pastoral assistant	Yes but lost post	Sexually harassed by minister, so left
Naomi	Retreat leadership	No	No opportunity
Priscilla	Churchwarden	Yes	–
Sarah	Ordination	No	Bullied by leaders; theological differences
Tamar	Churchwarden	Yes	–

* Deborah has since informed me that she was turned down for Non-Stipendiary Ministry.

Table 4.5 shows how eight respondents have sought some type of formal or authorized ministry. Four respondents reported that they had met difficulties in their vocations to ordination due to structural discrimination (on grounds of age, gender or theological standpoint) and/or exploitation. In Miriam's case she found herself isolated and vulnerable, when the minister who had encouraged her to train as a pastoral assistant used his position to exploit her sexually, emotionally and spiritually. It was only when she realized that her sense of calling had come long before the abusive relationship began that she found the courage to report his behaviour, with the support of MACSAS, whose leaflet *Clergy or Minister Sexual*

Table 4.6 Excerpt from MACSAS leaflet (2009)

'Warning signs' given in the section: ***Why is sex within the pastoral relationship always wrong?***
Sexual comments about your appearance, body or private life.
Flirting.
Inappropriate interest in the details of your sex life.
Inappropriate touching, anything that makes you feel uncomfortable.
Requests/suggestions that the relationship be moved into a social context, such as going out for lunch.
Sexual jokes/innuendo.
Seeing you late at night when there is no-one around, or visiting you at home and more frequently.
Discussing his own problems.
Sexualizing the conversation.
Phoning you at home to chat.
Encouraging you to be dependent on him.
Sitting close to you, hugs become more frequent/intimate.
Touches which feel uncomfortable, confusing or upsetting.
Suggestions that sex will 'cure', 'heal' you of intimate problems.
Suggestions that God has put him in your life to heal you of sexual difficulties.
Suggestions that God has told him to become intimate in order to heal you.
Suggestions that sex is a 'holy' thing, therefore not wrong between you and him.
Any attempt to destabilize an already established relationship you may have with a partner.
He gives you personal gifts.
You are receiving unusual time and attention.

Exploitation of Adults in the Pastoral Relationship she found stunningly accurate (see Table 4.6).[20] The action she took was at great cost to herself, for not only did Miriam have to leave the church and lose the support of that community, she also lost her own strong pastoral and spiritual ministry. The minister was given a great deal of support by the authorities and church members; she was given none. While an appraisal of recruitment for ordained ministry and testing of attitudes towards power and status may be beyond the scope of this thesis, a deeper scrutiny of the processes and theology behind institutional structures might be appropriate. Accordingly, in the context of Tamar's reflection on the nature of God's power and apparent non-intervention, she pinpointed the deeper dimension of the Church's action, as represented by its spiritual leaders:

[20] MACSAS (2009). Of the 20 'warning signs' listed in Table 4.6, Miriam identified 12 in her minister's behaviour toward her.

> One of the people involved [in the abuse] was the vicar and I feel, if he was ordained and he went through the searching process and all that, and God was this almighty person, all knowing, all powerful, transcendent, etc., how did that happen? How did he let that happen? How did he let that person get ordained and be in that situation to do that? And almost, partly the reason why I feel so angry about that, is because that has caused me more damage I think, I feel, than what happened with my stepfather.

If it is the Church's calling to do God's work, not least in its selection of leaders, the following question might be extrapolated from Tamar's comments in the context of the preceding incidents discussed: When exploitative and abusive clergy are allowed through the net of selection, yet the abused can find themselves excluded from ministry, what ideology is supporting this incongruity? The theoretical memo entitled 'Obstacles to Ministry' in which I began to develop the idea that the side-lining of survivors' ministry might have something to do with power and *boundaries* is reproduced in Table 4.7, and this will prove illuminating as we approach the theological issues in Chapter 7.

Lastly then, in connection with the question of ministry are issues of ecclesiology: What do survivors see as a 'good church'? What sort of church has a sound ministry for the most vulnerable, the abused? We have seen how Esther had a good experience of ministry from her church community to help her through her healing. Lydia received prayer ministry, and she also received some very practical support. For example, members of her church, including the vicar, accompanied Lydia through the traumatic experience of her husband's nine-day trial. Furthermore, Tamar received good counselling and support from the church authorities and social services when her abusers were exposed, and as an adult has had encouragement and support from her present vicar in facing the hard questions. Notably, these three women are very much involved in ministry

Table 4.7 Theoretical memo 'Obstacles to Ministry'

Memo: Obstacles to Ministry
Some ministries seem to be open to all the women: – those they have been drawn into by involvement as parents/congregants etc.; – or those they have been asked to do by others/ministers. But there have been obstacles for particular ministries (especially authorized or ordained). Check out the obstacles to see if the issues are about gender, or about being labelled as 'depressive' or something else to do with effects of abuse. Is this normative for church? Is it to do with authority and nature of authority? Is it to do with vulnerability? Boundaries?

still: Tamar as Churchwarden, who now counsels children at the school where she works; Lydia in prayer and healing ministry; Esther in prayer support of others and in giving talks in schools about her war-time experiences, in which she discusses the issue of forgiveness with students.

However, positive response from the Church was not always the case. When Miriam confided in the appropriate authorities about what was happening to her, she was left uncared for and unsupported, exposed and vulnerable to accusations of blame. When Sarah was struggling with depression, instead of supporting her, the minister excluded her and shared confidential information about her with others when she had expressly asked her not to. Joanna has sought help many times, and although she has received some helpful prayer ministry, she has been told on more than one occasion when she was really struggling, that no one could help her:

> When people realize just how deep the stuff is, they say it's too big, I can't cope with that, it's too big. So I think, how do they expect me to cope with it?[21]

Similarly Priscilla felt hurt by the local church's desertion of her when her first husband died of cancer, reporting that 'nobody bothered' with her. This left her feeling angry and as a result she stayed away for several years. Although Priscilla has returned to church and is now Churchwarden, she puts her commitment down to *God's* faithfulness to her, not that of the church community. She becomes frustrated with things she sees as unimportant:

> I struggle a bit sometimes – I think it's because I've been so dependent on [God] for everything and things have sometimes been so raw, that there are times when some of the protocol, I get cross with.

This echoes Sarah's argument that *Transformation* is the Church's true purpose and this involves getting dirty hands, but her experience has been of ministers who use red tape to keep people at arm's length and questioners at bay. In contrast, Jesus' encounter with the Samaritan woman was, according to Miriam, intimate and he did not judge her unconventional appearance; indeed despite appearances 'he went with it – saw what she really had and went with it'. Could it be that because Sarah and Miriam are theologically challenging, suggesting that church should be about dependency on God and transformative service of others that excludes no-one, they are still left out in the cold as regards formal ministry?

---

[21] Joanna commented that mental health professionals were also unhelpful, lamenting their lack of listening skills and their need to 'label' her:

'They'd sometimes say maybe it wasn't quite like that, maybe over the years you think it's something else, but that doesn't matter I don't think. The whole thing is, how you're feeling and what it's made you feel like. That's what the important thing is, not what it's like for other people or what the text book tells you what it should be like.'

The importance of listening attentively resurfaces in Chapter 5.

To summarize, *Knowing ministry* replaces the original code *serving God and others* because knowledge through experience of the meaning of dependence on God and knowledge of God's healing, transforming presence, become the dynamic for service. A Church which reflects this transforming action of God through its members, and leaders, is a sign of God's presence.

Core Category: *Knowing God's Timeless Presence Transforms*

Eventually the core category, *knowing God's timeless presence transforms*, emerged from the data, encapsulating the dynamic process by which the survivors collectively and individually live their spiritual lives. The grammatical ambiguity of this phrase allows for two meanings:

1. The survivors know God's timeless presence in their lives and this has transformed them and healed the effects of abuse, and continues to transform them and heal the effects of abuse.
2. Because they know and have experienced transformation by God's presence in their lives, this awareness equips and enables them to become God's agents for the transformation of others.

Thus the core category not only presents us with a theory about how and why survivors' spirituality might be authentic, it has also raised unexpected and important questions about who is suitable for ministry. In the literature review of Chapter 2 I argued that theological material from the survivor's perspective is sparse and deeply challenging. I am now able to include the observation that pastoral theology has been concerned almost exclusively with ministering *to* survivors, not what ministry should be accomplished *by* survivors.

In order to deepen the core category, I began 'selective coding' in relationship *only* to *knowing God's timeless presence transforms*. During this stage of coding, the concept of *boundaries* emerged as significant, as intuited by the theoretical memo at Table 4.7.

Selective Coding: Boundaries

Although some interviewees had talked about damage to personal boundaries caused by abuse, the spiritual significance of boundaries took time to emerge in which a reciprocal relationship between the survivors' *boundaries* with God and their *boundaries* with others began to develop. It also emerged that the balance of *boundaries* shifted at 'liminal' moments, that is to say at major life transitions such as death, a house move or divorce.

An incident in Tamar's interview illustrated the implicit nature of this concept. At the time of her mother's death from cancer, Tamar had been angry with her uncle for saying that he was praying for her. In response to her anger, he explained that he had been praying for peace, not for physical healing, and this was for Tamar 'a turning point'. She suddenly realized that bad things that happen are 'not necessarily God's fault'. I had first coded this passage as an incident under *spiritual awakening*. However, Tamar had explained later in her interview that God had, from that particular moment on, become personal for her and that she had 'let him onto [her] radar'. Thus God's crossing of Tamar's self-protective boundary (her radar) was commensurate with her growth as a Christian, but this happened at the time of a liminal experience: her mother's death. This proved an important connection as three other interviews show.

Two events in Esther's story are relevant. First, her earliest *spiritual awakening* came when, as a young nurse, she sat with a patient at the threshold of death. She began to realize there was a spiritual dimension to life and, after a childhood and youth of nominal religious adherence, God became 'real' for her. Second, after the divorce from her violent husband, she took out an injunction against him when he was threatening to return, even though she was faced with bullying opposition from a male member of her family. The establishment of this clear, self-protective boundary was at a time when 'all [she] had was God' and she was completely open to the divine.

For Miriam, who spoke explicitly about *boundaries* in her interview, I noticed that it was at the liminal moment of a parishioner's death (actually in the Chapel of Rest at the hospital) that her minister made the first sexual move on her. She explained how from that moment on her *boundaries* were being 'eroded to a point of extreme danger'; she felt confused, and psychologically dismantled by the 'coded messages' which the minister sent her through his sermons and by his distorted exegesis of scripture. One example of this distortion was when he interpreted Bathsheba's seduction by David as being God's will, intimating that adultery was not always wrong because it was to be through Bathsheba and David's line that Jesus would come. Ironically it was an *effect of scripture*, the story of Dives and Lazarus with its spiritual chasm,[22] which helped Miriam see that setting down a strong boundary-marker was the right thing to do in this situation: her boundary-marker was to refuse to be alone with the minister. It was after this attempt at re-establishing appropriate boundaries with the minister that she received a 'barrage' of angry texts and e-mails from him. Eventually having to leave her church community in order to protect herself, in her traumatic sense of loss she had a *special experience* which was a *Transformation* of *boundaries* between God and the world, between God and the Church, and between the Church and the world:

> It broadened everything out where I thought Christians are not better than other people, leaders are not better than people who aren't leaders, God is in everybody, God is in everything, God is in nature. I'm just as likely to find

22 Luke 16.9–31.

> God down in Sainsbury's as I am in St Peter and Paul. And that was quite a revelation, because although it sounds quite obvious, I don't think I ever really took it on board personally in the same way – it was like a massive impact on me – it was almost like, I don't believe in church anymore, which is an extreme. So it's almost like you're going from, there's all these holy places to there's no holy places; and there's all these places that are the streets and the cities, and all these other things that are just as much God as these. But I suppose what you're trying to do is get the whole thing to come together in the middle, or somewhere where you're just saying, God is in all of it, and even if you don't live more in this one or in that one or whatever, you're acknowledging that. I am acknowledging it in a way that I didn't before. I think I was thinking much more God is here in the holy places than over here in the world stuff.

Miriam's sense of the immanent God, who does not privilege the Church or its leaders, coincided with her re-establishing appropriate *human* boundaries: while simultaneously struggling with the church authorities for just treatment, she and her husband were committing themselves to healing their marriage with the help of Relate. She was excluded from the Church's disciplinary process, given no information about the outcome and no support, so that in a community where her *boundaries* had been inappropriately breached, it appears the ecclesiastical structures were working in self-protection against the victim, unable to initiate any process of reconciliation.[23] Meanwhile, Miriam is working at her own healing, is putting her important relationships on a sound footing, and she worships with the Quakers where she finds safety in her spiritual relationships:

> I've been going to Quakers because there I find silence, equality, no leaders, no preaching, no led prayers, no hymns, no coded messages, just a worship space, but in community because there are other people there. I've always believed you've got to have these three things: you've got to have your prayer, you've got to have your scriptures and you've got to have your community, your church. So I didn't feel that I could just think 'I don't need a church', because to me that is an essential part of being a Christian, just to keep you grounded. So I had to find somewhere, so that's the only place I felt safe.

Speaking more implicitly about relational boundaries, Deborah contrasted the development of her positive relationship with God with human relationships that have 'blown up in [her] face'. She reported that deep emotional and psychological scarring from her family relationships as a child has been transformed by God, who has shown a constant closeness, patiently waiting for her. Her description of her new connection with God uses very clear liminal imagery:

---

[23] According to MACSAS (2010) this is common. Sarah is battling with similar intransigence and protocol.

> God has always been in the background despite everything. He's never been that far away. I've pushed him away, but he hasn't been pushed. Perhaps I've shut the door on him, but he's the other side of that door. I've only got to open it and let him back in and that's what I'm trying to do now.

Removing the boundary with God – allowing God across the threshold – is in turn enabling her simultaneously to 're-build bridges' with her sons, opening the way for healed relationships.

I found that these stories prompted the development of my perception that:

- to the extent that proper *boundaries* were re-established with the abuser and/or significant others, the more open were the survivor's *boundaries* with God;
- conversely, the more open the *boundaries* with God that were experienced, the more appropriate the *boundaries* with others.

This was still only a theoretical idea, and I needed to check the 'fit' in the next stage of constructing the grounded theory. In the next two chapters I will offer my version of 'theoretical sampling' by comparing the core category and its three higher concepts with two challenging texts: the Book of Job and Marguerite Porete's *Mirror of Simple Souls*. In this I risked not being able to achieve 'theoretical saturation', but my perceptions were deepened and the major issues raised throughout this study will be discussed in the final chapters, giving a fuller picture of how survivors of abuse relate God, and relate to God.

Chapter 5
Crossing the Threshold: Job the Survivor?

A Foot in Both Camps: Introduction

In the spring I was walking to our allotment to prepare some of the beds for planting vegetables, when en route I passed by a family who were working together on the plot they had just taken over. I could not help overhearing the argument going on between the mother and her son, who was around ten years old. The boy had been given a pair of protective gardening gloves by his grandmother, but he refused point blank to wear them – not because he was unwilling to help clear the brambles and stones which would damage his hands, but because the gloves were the wrong colour. They were pink! Aversion to a certain colour purely because of the gender identity it represents may be a case of cultural irrationality, but for this youngster, crossing the 'pink' boundary was tantamount to social suicide.

All of the participants in my empirical study were women, so it may seem strange that I chose to add scriptural resonance to the developing grounded theory by exploring the experience of Job, a patriarchal man, rather than investigating the stories of the four women Trible portrays in *Texts of Terror*,[1] or other women characters who suffer abuse and exclusion in Scripture. Crossing the blue boundary might raise a feminist eyebrow, but there are two reasons why I chose Job as dialogue partner. First, Job is *the* archetypal innocent sufferer, as revealed by the profusion of theological reflection and commentary generated by the biblical account of his spiritual journey. Second, we have to be realistic and accept that there are no theological ruminations of such length and depth in Scripture from the viewpoint of an individual female speaker, which underscores Trible's point that female victims are mainly silent. Besides, at the outset there was no intended gender bias to my research design, since 'abuse' might be visited upon any citizen of a patriarchal society who does not meet the required person specification of the 'alpha male'.[2] In Chapter 6 we will indeed consider the voice of one female who crossed the blue boundary and braved the censure of male theologians who required that women remain silent about spiritual matters, unless censored by a man. In the present chapter, however, we find surprising parallels between my

---

1 Trible (2002).

2 The Oxford Dictionary definition of an 'alpha male' is 'the dominant male animal in a particular group', or a man who 'assumes a dominant or domineering role in social or professional situations'.

analysis of the interviews and Job's voice, when we begin to dig deeper down to what lies beneath the surface of the text. I will argue that Job crosses over important thresholds, but only when he has been excluded from the society of which he was once a leader. Then we see what happens when the 'alpha male' falls from grace. In comparison with the concepts emerging from the interviews, I ask whether Job in his predicament has anything to say about *God's timeless presence*. Does he undergo any *Transformation* throughout the 42 chapters of the book? Is there evidence of *Knowing ministry*? Here I present Job as someone who knows that God's timeless presence transforms, and in this knowing, becomes an effective agent of spiritual transformation in his community. Aspects of this community transformation will be shown to have implications for the concept of *boundaries*, which began to emerge as significant in the later stage of 'selective coding'.

Approaching the Text

A full biblical scholarly evaluation of Job is beyond the scope of this book, but it is necessary at the outset to consider the structure of the canonical text in order to establish grounds for viewing it as an integrated whole, the story of one person's transformative journey of faith. Further, Job's credentials as a survivor of abuse must be demonstrated, so that his story can be read from this particular perspective, following the method of Gustavo Gutiérrez who claims it is legitimate 'to read the Bible from the standpoint of our deepest and most pressing concerns'.[3] Gutiérrez maintains that this has always been the historical practice of the Christian community, and he proceeds to read Job from the context of the poor of Latin America. In similar fashion the following considerations provide the basis from which I engage with Job and discern its contribution to the concepts raised by the empirical research.

Integrity of the Text

The countless commentators on Job agree that the book presents copious textual and exegetical difficulties. Some of the text appears to have been 'piously' tampered with[4] or is just plainly incoherent;[5] there is a mixture of prose, soliloquy and poetic dialogue; and there are several possible interpolations, Elihu's six-chapter speech being the most universally accepted as a later addition.[6] Consequently there is

3 Gutiérrez (1987), p. xvii.

4 Pope (1965), p. XXV.

5 For example, Job 19.26 is notoriously difficult to translate yet it is an important verse theologically, concerning Job's hope of seeing God; see Habel (1985), p. 293.

6 Elihu appears suddenly in chapter 32 and his long speech seems unrelated to the rest of the text, adding nothing to the issues discussed in the Dialogue; see Pope (1965), p. XXVI.

divergence of opinion regarding the integrity of the text and whether the evidence for one single author and purpose stacks up. Textually the main discrepancy is found in the conspicuous mood change between the prose framework of the Prologue/ Epilogue, and the poetic Dialogue of the intervening 39 chapters. It is generally agreed that an old folk-tale about a righteous sufferer in ancient times was adapted to create this framework. Although hard to date, Job was probably written after the Babylonian exile,[7] and some commentators argue that the archaic setting was used deliberately by the redactor for literary effect. For example David Wolfers, who unusually suggests an earlier date of authorship, highlights discrepancies between references to the nomadic context of the Patriarchs on the one hand (Job mentions tent-dwelling and his wealth is measured in livestock), and references to city-dwelling and advanced legal process on the other.[8] Anachronistic time-settings are of course a convention found elsewhere in scripture, but some commentators discern an attempt by the author at camouflaging what is a heretical challenge made by the Dialogue to the traditional doctrine of retribution, with the purpose of rendering the poem acceptable to the canon of scripture. Namely, the 'lay' theology of the Dialogue[9] appears to demolish some Hebrew modes of reflection, calling the Deuteronomic Covenant and Yahweh's reliability into question,[10] and so the poet's radicalism must be tempered by the restoration of blessings to Job in the Epilogue. It is argued that this resolution would satisfy orthodoxy, accompanied as it is by Job's *alleged* repentance of his theological error in 42.6:

> Therefore I despise myself and repent in dust and ashes.

I stress alleged, as this is a contestable point to which I will return. The incongruence between poem and prose provokes René Girard's judgment that both Prologue and Epilogue are false, that they merely 'provide a semblance of unity to the chaos', a unity indispensible to both moralist and metaphysician, even as it is to the aesthete.[11] Likewise, Robert Gordis suggests in his literary appraisal of the text that the prose and poem are disjointed. He argues that there is no plot development in the Dialogue, only a growing intensity in the positions of the protagonists that has nothing to do with the heavenly 'wager' of the Prologue.[12]

In contrast other commentators discern integrity in the text as it stands, arguing that a skilful blending of parts indicates one clever artist's responsibility for the whole work, even if diverse sources and genres have been utilized.[13] This

---

7 That is, after 538 BCE.

8 Wolfers (1995), pp. 73–4.

9 Wisdom literature is placed in the sphere of the laity by Dermot Cox (1990), p. 13.

10 Brueggemann (1997).

11 Girard (1987), p. 46.

12 Gordis (1965), p. 4.

13 Pope (1965); Cox (1990); Wolfers (1995).

approach is favoured in literary and psychological interpretations of the text[14] and the following examples provide some precedence for my reading. Norman Habel discerns a plot development through three movements, shown particularly in plot anticipations.[15] A clear example is Eliphaz's prediction about Job in chapter 22:

> You will pray to [God] and he will hear you ...
> He will deliver even those who are guilty,
> They will escape because of the cleanness of your hands.[16]

This is exactly what happens in the Epilogue when Job intercedes and gains pardon for his Friends who were found to be incompetent.[17] Similarly, Dermot Cox sees the book as a three-part drama of Prologue/Dialogue/Theophany, and designates its genre as 'bi-polar' mashal.[18] The mashal gives two viewpoints, the divine and the human, thereby setting up a dialectic that enables the reader to think through these two perspectives and make up her own mind. Cox adds that this innovative method of theologizing proceeded by arguing from human experience, rather than by starting from the accepted tenets of tradition.[19] He suggests that Job's angry questioning of God's nature in the Dialogue is the central integrating problem of the book, and not suffering. With the tradition (represented by the Friends) rendered bankrupt, the Theophany becomes the only counterpoint to the lived experience of Job, and consequently the conflict has made possible a creative, dynamic relationship between Job and God, without mediation. This fresh idea, presenting God as creative artist rather than as judge, is reflected in the strong focus on creation in God's speeches.[20] Likewise Van Wolde suggests that the connection between the human and divine perspectives is key,[21] for it is only when Job begins to fight with God that he becomes an *active* believer. Thus the rebellion (Cox) or the 'ranting' (Van Wolde) which Job initiates in chapter 3, is vital to his spiritual progress. According to Van Wolde, the book hinges around Job's two monologues (chapter 3 and chapters 28–31) as the twin foci of God's response in two corresponding stages of the Theophany. While the development of the human/divine relationship in the poem is fundamental, the framework of the Prologue and Epilogue integrate this connection, in that God's concern at the outset with unconditional 'chinam' faith in 1.9 is mirrored by Job's growth into a believer who asks 'for nothing':

---

14 For example, Jack Kahn and Ellen Van Wolde offer psychological readings of Job, while Cox, Habel and the essays in *Semeia* 7 offer literary readings.

15 Habel (1985), pp. 25–34.

16 Job 22.27a, 30.

17 Job 42.8.

18 Cox (1990), p. 15.

19 Cox (1990), p. 79.

20 Cox (1990), p. 116.

21 Van Wolde (1997), p. 18.

> Chinam faith means not only a faith in God without a direct cause or reason and without a purpose or goal, but also a faith which is not necessary but possible. Job now sees that faith is not a divine demand but a human choice.[22]

This dynamic of spiritual transformation is identified by Susannah Ticciati as the development of Job's earlier uncritical piety of the Prologue into a mature piety in the Epilogue, having become rooted in something much deeper than 'perfection' as defined according to the Deuteronomic Covenant.[23] Her psycho-philosophical and biblical scholarly readings of the text present the poem as Job's journey of self-examination, involving the disruption of his theological preconceptions. This disruption takes him to the extremities of his identity, into an abyss, which eventually becomes the space in which he can encounter the truly 'Other/other'. God's direct communication with Job in the Whirlwind speeches of the Theophany, that is Job's experience of the embodiment, or presence, of the 'Other', affirms that 'Creation trumps the law'[24] because the latter is secondary to the former. The effect of this human/divine encounter is the flowering of the reconstructed community portrayed in the Epilogue. Job has changed, therefore he changes his society:

> Job's wrestling with God not only restores right relations between himself and God, but enables him to act as intercessor between God and the friends, bringing them also into right relations with one another.[25]

This is God's calling to Job and to all of humanity because:

> God is not simply an omnipotent and impassible deity [implying] that humanity is not simply that which is acted upon, all responsibility being removed from it. Rather God's involvement in creation and history invests humanity with a responsibility for the transformation of the world.[26]

Transformation, the nature of God's involvement and of human vocation will consequently be focuses of the dialogue between Job and the emerging grounded theory. However, having established that the text can be approached as an integrated story of a faith journey I turn first to the context of Job's predicament.

---

22 Van Wolde (1997), p. 139. 'Chinam' is from the Hebrew (הַחִנָּם / *haḥinnām*) meaning 'for nothing'.

23 Ticciati (2005b), p. 52.

24 Ticciati (2005b), p. 112.

25 Ticciati (2005b), p. 157.

26 Ticciati (2005b), p. 181.

An Ambiguous Identity: Job the Survivor?

There are many ambiguities in this text, not least those raised by Cox about ambiguity in the traditional understanding of God[27] and by Van Wolde about Job's piety.[28] In order to establish the context of Job's struggle I propose a further ambiguity in that Job could be viewed either as a survivor of abuse, or alternatively as 'rehabilitated' perpetrator of abuse. This dichotomy suggests that Job represents a significant case study for the struggle of working out reconciliation between perpetrator and victim within one single re-created and re-integrated identity. It may be going too far and be too optimistic to suggest that Job might even be a spiritual resource for perpetrators, given their intransigence,[29] but the possibility of seeing Job as perpetrator of abuse rests on the position he enjoys in the Prologue, as we will see.

I have argued earlier that many forms of abuse within patriarchal society reflect its ideology, theology and institutions, based as they are on male entitlement, hierarchy and abasement of the weak. Job is presented at the outset as a political and religious leader, a stereotypical 'Patriarch' in that his livestock and offspring are enumerated as his possessions, which tells us immediately there is none greater nor wealthier than Job (1.3). His righteousness and religious adherence are also stressed (1.1, 5). Thus we are assured in the Prologue that he is inevitably one who wields 'power-over'[30] others. His Dialogue speeches also show irrefutably that Job had had the status that accompanies patriarchal power, along with exemplary moral uprightness;[31] but having lost the one, he must necessarily lose the other in the eyes of the 'system'. Therefore Job's 'Friends', fully convinced of this equation, cannot accompany him to where his 'rant' leads him.[32] Job's dilemma is that he is likewise still enmeshed in this system: that is, his concept of his own innocence is determined by the doctrine of retribution, therefore his critique of this doctrine undermines his own ideology, an ideology which informs his own received notion of integrity. Because Job judges his own blamelessness by the values of the power structure in which he is embedded, it is difficult for him to relinquish his belief in it, and indeed this is his struggle throughout.[33] In other words, if the doctrine of retribution disappears, so does his integrity as judged by it; if the doctrine of retribution is relinquished, so must the patriarchal system be relinquished (and

27 Cox (1990), pp. 25–31.

28 Van Wolde (1997), pp. 12–18.

29 Poling (1991), ch. 4.

30 This would be in contrast to more democratic, mutual and consensual 'power-with' as described by Cooper-White (1995), pp. 31ff.

31 See for example 29.5–11, 14, 24–5.

32 On the cowardice and inability of the Friends to risk the same fate as Job, see Habel (1977), p. 232.

33 Ticciati (2005b), p. 61.

the status he should have within it). Hence, letting go of 'power' as defined by the system is his most torturing affliction. He is trapped by the circular equation:

his power = his integrity = his innocence = his power

Before the onset of disaster, when all seemed well with the world and responsibility for Job's downfall was therefore imputed only to God, there were inklings nonetheless that the Patriarch was on shaky ground. His over-scrupulous sacrificial observances described in 1.5 have been defined as obsessive and motivated by irrational fear,[34] but verse 1.10 is even more telling. In verse 10a the Satan has already complained that God has 'put a hedge around' (שַׂכְתָּ/śaǩtā) Job; and verse 10b recounts that his possessions have 'broken limits' (פָּרַץ/*pāraṣ*) in the land. Thus Job is well defended from harm, but he ventures over the boundaries of others. This is the classic scenario of an abuser, who takes advantage of the weakly defended and who is supported by a system of entitlement for the wealthy and strong.[35] Job's friend Eliphaz underlines this understanding of power when he describes loss of entitlement for the wealthy, who:

> will no longer be rich and his wealth will not endure,
> nor will his possessions *spread over the land*.[36]

The verb נָטָה (*nāṭāh*) meaning 'spread/stretch out, extend, incline'[37] is translated 'spread over/out' in NIV, ESV, and by Habel. Similarly, Pope has 'reach', but Gordis has 'remain' and Wolfers has 'established', both suggesting a temporal rather than a spatial meaning. For verse 29b, NRSV has 'nor will they strike root in the earth', which blends both nuances but JB offers 'no longer will he cast his shadow over the land', which conveys beautifully the idea of abusive power eclipsing territory.

Furthermore, Job describes people who now have the upper hand as follows:

> But now they mock me,
> men younger than I,
> whose fathers I would have disdained
> to put with my sheep dogs.
> Of what use was the strength of their hands to me,
> since their vigour had gone from them?[38]

---

[34] Kahn (1975), p. 44; Van Wolde (1997), p. 14.

[35] Poling (2005), p. 62 connects all forms of power abuse with exploitation of the vulnerable/outsider.

[36] Job 15.29 (NIV).

[37] Brown et al. (1996), pp. 639f.

[38] Job 30.1–2 (NIV).

These people seemingly belong to a starving underclass, having no land and being dispossessed. Undeniable in this passage is Job's contempt for these weak, 'useless' people with 'no name' (30.8) and the verses quoted above imply that Job gave them no aid in their destitution and redundancy. In the previous chapter, he told how others used to be silent in his presence, but we might ask: was this a mark of their respect, or of fear? Might the silence denote even a lack of voice? Could people not get a word in edgeways? And could Job's own silence in 40.4–5 signify dumbfoundedness at the recognition that he had abused his social power in the past,[39] when he now sees that the God he encounters is not a supporter of retributive justice, nor by extension patriarchy? For, unless Job lets go of his conditioned view of his own integrity as measured by the 'system', he cannot go beyond such a view to God's view. Does Job's experience of weakness and vulnerability cause him to know what being at the bottom of the pile entails? Are his true 'sins' laid bare: namely, the invasion of other people's boundaries (1.10); unilateral decision-making which fails to treat others as equals (29.22, 25); expecting and receiving service from others (29.5–6); and using charity as a sign of power to bestow, rather than as fair distribution of resources (29.12–14)? It is after all effortless for a wealthy man to give to widows and orphans, but what about giving to the despised of 30.1–8? The devastation and struggle with which Job's story presents us certainly might represent the recovery of a perpetrator, so rare in reality because of the horror of having to face one's own painful fragmentation and dreadful accountability.[40]

I reflect further on the changes in Job's perspective later in this chapter and turn now to the alternative possibility for which I have found strong evidence in the text, namely that Job can be recognized as victim of abuse, rather than, or perhaps even as well as, recovering perpetrator. There are two important indications of this characterization.

First, the anguish expressed by Job and his disclosure of persecution can be seen as the most powerful evidences of his victimhood. While Job might be advancing his case as 'victim' to deflect attention from his own role as perpetrator,[41] or to deny his sins as the Friends suggest he is doing,[42] it is crucial for any person disclosing abuse to be believed.[43] His grievance that the Friends are poor comforters because they refuse to listen to him and hold their own peace, let alone side with him against received wisdom, reflects statements made by interviewee Joanna as

---

39 Eliphaz suggests Job has abused his power in 22.6–9, though we cannot be sure whether the Friends' accusations are extrapolations from the evidence of Job's suffering as a *sign* of retributive justice, or are made about actual 'sins' committed.

40 Poling (1991), p. 72.

41 See Poling (1991), p. 66 for his description of perpetrators who see themselves as the ones now being persecuted, or as the vulnerable ones who were 'tempted' by the child, thereby blaming victims for what is their own violent and 'uncontrollable' behaviour.

42 Job 22.4–11.

43 Kennedy, M. (1999), p. 60.

shown below in Table 5.1. Nevertheless Job longs for the ministrations of a good listener because he needs to express his pain. The repetitiveness and circularity of the Dialogue speeches and their persistent anguish have been criticized as boring, but I demonstrated earlier that such oscillation is one of the hallmarks of survivor recovery.[44] In the last chapter I noted that interviewees reported varying degrees of success in finding quality ministry, and that finding a place to cry and feel bad over a prolonged period was invaluable.[45] Even with support, it is still a gruelling journey to healing because the pain lingers, returning in times of stress, and Job's further rant in 16.1–6 about the Friends' inability to listen reveals that his pain remains whether he speaks or not:

> If I speak, my pain is not assuaged,
> if I forbear, how much of it leaves me?[46]

His anguish may be exacerbated by the loss of his community, which is illustrated in 2.8 by Job's isolated location on the pile of ashes that identifies him as an outcast,[47] and this is reminiscent of Miriam's loss of her church community and of Esther's loss of family support when they decided to speak out. Job's excruciating mental, emotional and spiritual pain and his suicidal thoughts, expressed in his

Table 5.1 Comparison of Joanna and Job about being heard

Joanna	**Job 13.4–7**
I've been under psychiatrists and people like that but that was useless really, because I ended up saying to the psychiatrist, 'you're going exactly how your text book is telling you, you're telling me I'm this or that because the text book tells you it'. (*On Christian ministers:*) It's very, very frustrating trying to talk to people. Very frustrating, because they just keep saying too much of their own stuff instead of listening.	As for you, you whitewash with lies; all of you are worthless physicians. If you would only keep silent, that would be your wisdom! Hear now my reasoning; and listen to the pleading of my lips. Will you speak falsely for God, and speak deceitfully for him?

44 See p. 14.
45 See p. 70.
46 Job 16.6.
47 Gordis (1965), p. 234.

negation of the day of his birth in 3.1–26, are comparable to the experiences shared by survivors.[48] Job's lamentation from 7.13–15 shows a close parallel with Joanna's experience, as shown in Table 5.2.

Table 5.2 Comparison of Joanna and Job about suicidal thoughts

Joanna	**Job 7.13–16**
The worst time was the middle of the night and early hours of the morning and things would feel horrendous. When you feel like committing suicide it's about that time in the morning. I just used to think, if this is life I don't want it and I said that to Jesus. I said if this is what my life's supposed to be about, well then I don't want it. I don't want a life like this.	When I think my bed will comfort me and my couch will ease my complaint, even then you frighten me with dreams and terrify me with visions, so that I prefer strangling and death, rather than this body of mine. I despise my life; I would not live forever. Let me alone; my days have no meaning. (NIV)

Second, the overstepping of boundaries that is so characteristic of abuse is seen in the violation of Job's physical boundaries, for the Satan's second challenge of 2.4–5 demands that Job's flesh be penetrated 'to his bone' (אֶל־עַצְמוֹ/'el-*ʿaṣmô*), and the Dialogue assures us that the human protection of his skin has indeed been invaded:

> My body is clothed with worms and scabs,
> *my skin is broken* and festering.[49]

Jack Kahn, who reads the whole text of Job as if these were the words of a living person recording his thoughts and feelings during a series of therapy sessions, describes the skin as 'the borderland between the individual and the outside world, where all his interactions are represented'.[50] He suggests the skin disease of boils visited upon the erstwhile Patriarch demonstrates that his body was already showing symptoms of breakdown, as yet unexpressed, in the silence before Job's lament began, for 'throughout all this Job did not utter one sinful word',[51] but the boils speak volumes. The interviewees reported a variety of illnesses of differing severity, depression being the most often stated; Joanna suffers from several physical

48 Naomi and Joanna in particular (see p. 60).
49 Job 7.5 (NIV, emphasis added).
50 Kahn (1975), p. 35.
51 Job 2.10 (NIV).

disorders which she understands to be psychosomatic. Furthermore, Job's whole being revolts against the food he needs for nourishment, which he expresses thus:

> I refuse to touch it; such food makes me ill.[52]

Kahn identifies this revulsion towards food as a symptom of mental disorder,[53] a reaction that is supported in the literature on abuse.[54] Several interviewees reported eating disorders, such as incest victim Priscilla who describes the effect of becoming aware of what was being done to her:

> I suddenly realized what was happening, and that had quite a dramatic effect on me. At that time I became quite poorly. I stopped eating and became very, very depressed. I went down from about ten stone to about six stone in the space of about eight or nine months.

However, Job's illness is more than physical as illustrated by the attacks on him, which are described as arrows, penetrating deeply into his innermost self:

> For the arrows of the Almighty are in me,
> my spirit drinks their poison;
> the terrors of God are arrayed against me.[55]

When viewed as signifying Deuteronomic curse, Job's boils represent a *spiritual* defect,[56] which exacerbates his anguish. It is possible to connect this 'curse' with the stigma of mental illness today. Sarah, Naomi and Joanna have met prejudice regarding their depression, and there may even be a stigma attached to having been abused, a point which will be relevant to the discussion of survivors' ministry. I suggested earlier that there might be a reciprocal relationship between spirituality and healing from abuse, and it is clear that Job's healing is synchronized with his spiritual enlightenment. Accordingly, there are two positive outcomes of Job's experience similar to that of the interviewees: on the one hand Job finds that he is allowed by God to express extreme anger and yet remain acceptable, and on the other he absorbs a new, deepened and 're-framed' comprehension of God. Job's transformation, new knowledge of God and understanding of his own vocation are the subject of the next section, but here we note that Job's externalized belligerence

52 Job 6.7 (NIV).

53 Kahn (1975), p. 40.

54 Sgroi (1989); Ainscough and Toon (1993), pp. 125ff.

55 Job 6.4.

56 Ticciati (2005b), p. 61; Wolfers (1995), p. 115.

and rage are not only crucial to the plot as Van Wolde[57] and Cox argue,[58] but are key to his healing from abuse.[59]

Before turning to Job's contribution to the grounded theory, I must give attention to an author who provides the strongest description of Job as victim.[60] René Girard suggests that Job's fall from grace can be explained by the process of 'mimetic idolatry'. Having been once an object of veneration, the crowd has now turned on Job in an organized and ritualistic fashion; this ritual is presided over by the 'Friends' who were his former cronies, but who now vindictively denounce him. Girard's argument, that Job exemplifies the ritual victim, the scapegoat needed to unite a society in crisis, is based on his judgement that Job describes *real* persecution in the Dialogue, and that the Friends are *truly* violent in their speeches; moreover the concord that violence is *actually* taking place provides the Dialogue's only coherence. This idea of Job as 'victim of his people' helps fuse the two possibilities I have outlined above: on the one hand we can see him as abuser (the now discredited former leader of the dominating elite), and on the other we see that he is victim of this same oppressive regime (created by the envy and hatred characteristic of such elite social systems). More importantly I suggest that it is Job's identification with the vulnerable, moreover his *experience* of their condition that effects change in him and his community, whereas Girard maintains that the impact of Job's rebellion is qualified by the restoration scene in the Epilogue, that the 'Hollywood' ending conceals the raw subversion of the Dialogue. He compares Job unfavourably with Christ, who as the true representative of victims is a successful scapegoat because he shares their lot to the end. The key issue for me is whether Job has embraced his victimhood, become a survivor and therefore goes on to subvert the 'system' in the Epilogue. If Girard is right, then Job's original status, and with it a violent retributive God, is merely reinstated.[61] Girard's only concession that the Epilogue might hold any positive outcome is that in 42.8 God prefers Job's words over the words of the Friends, and we will return to further scrutinize the Epilogue Job shortly.

In sum, I have argued for reading the text as an integrated whole in which Job can be understood as being on a transformative journey; I have also suggested that Job could be viewed as survivor of abuse, as rehabilitated perpetrator, or possibly an integration of the two. I will now compare Job's spiritual journey with the core category and the three main concepts that were developed in my analysis.

57 Van Wolde (1997), pp. 26–7.

58 Cox (1990), p. 36.

59 Anger as an important aspect of healing is acknowledged by Flaherty (1992), ch. 5.

60 This paragraph draws on Girard (1987).

61 Girard (1987), pp. 144–5.

Saturating the Theory: How Job Relates (to) God

In what follows I argue that the climax of the book of Job, the Theophany of chapters 38–42.8, is the pivotal point for identifying the three higher concepts that emerged from the interviews, and that it deepens and modifies the concept of *boundaries* that began to emerge as significant in the later stage of 'selective coding'. Job's distinctiveness as survivor will consequently be further established as comparable to that of the interviewees, enriching the grounded theory. I will first demonstrate that *God's timeless presence* as revealed throughout the book, but concentrated in the *special experience* of the Theophany, is God's direct answer to Job's desire for encounter; second, that the *Transformation* of Job's faith from the naïve, pre-critical belief of the Prologue, through the anguished struggle of the Dialogue, comes to a deep, contemplative maturity in his silence before God in the Theophany; third, that in the Epilogue, Job the servant of God goes on to embody a *Knowing ministry*, having experienced vulnerability and extreme trauma, having been recipient of the inadequate ministry of others, and knowing the direct healing care of God's presence; and finally, that Job's revolutionized ministry reveals a new respect for *boundaries of justice and equality*, deepening this dimension of the grounded theory.

God's Timeless Presence

Although we hear directly from Yahweh only in the Prologue (1.6–12; 2.1–6) and in the dénouement of the Theophany and Epilogue (38–41; 42.7–8), God's presence is felt throughout the story. Presented in the Prologue as ruler of the heavenly court, completely separate and remote from events on earth, Yahweh is viewed as arbiter of retributive justice, which is mediated by ritualistic sacrifice and perfect behaviour. His presence is experienced therefore through the structure of the Deuteronomic Covenant's blessing/curse dichotomy.[62] The Satan is seemingly God's agent of 'curse', and much is made of their 'wager'. However, I read the Prologue as evidence of Job's undeveloped faith, typified by his 'black and white' understanding of reality. After the Prologue, the Satan is not referred to again anywhere in the book,[63] and as Job's spiritual understanding develops, an agent of God's 'smiting' on earth becomes redundant anyway because the blessing/curse polarization collapses. This polarization was already made ambiguous in the

---

62 Wolfers (1995), pp. 111–18 argues that the whole text depends on Deuteronomy 28, where God is described as establishing his covenant with the nation of Israel. Ticciati (2005b), pp. 53–4 also gives attention to the nature of Job's Deuteronomic Covenant faithfulness.

63 Wolfers (1995), p. 61 and Pope (1965), pp. XXXIV–XXXV argue that the poet was setting up the Aunt Sally of the dualist Persian Satan to be demolished as unfounded, speculative theology; alternatively Wolfers (1995), p. 61 and Cox (1990), p. 26 suggest that the Satan is merely a literary device.

Prologue since the Hebrew word בָּרַךְ (*bārak̆*) can mean both 'bless' and 'curse',[64] and since Job is ignorant of the wager, full responsibility is in any case placed on God. Besides, as none of the interviewees mentioned the Satan, we spend no more time on him here.

The name Yahweh disappears in the Dialogue, denoting perhaps Job's felt loss of the special relationship that the Hebrews normally had with their God,[65] illustrated by these reminiscences:

> O that I were as in the months of old,
> as in the days when God watched over me;
> when his lamp shone over my head
> and by his light I walked through darkness;
> when I was in my prime,
> when friendship of God was upon my tent.[66]

It is questionable whether this friendship truly embodied intimacy, considering Job's anxiety- and doubt-ridden state in the Prologue exhibited by his over-scrupulous sacrificing (1.5) and perfect behaviour;[67] both these practices of 'faith' were apparently approved of and therefore demanded by the remote, censorious Yahweh (1.8; 2.3). This level of understanding of the divine echoes Deborah and Esther's early attitudes to God and was well articulated by Miriam who found that true intimacy, knowing God's real presence and immanence in creation, came much later after a spiritual struggle and within a new revelation of God's nature:[68]

> I had an image of a parent figure who is controlling, distant and angry because I think I must have had that parent image of God underlying without being aware of it. I had to be a little bit scared of God, I had to keep God happy, seek God's approval, be always trying to impress God. The experience of abuse has forced

64 Van Wolde (1997), pp. 23–4.

65 Brueggemann (1997), p. 389. Habel (1985), p. 39 argues that Job is not a Hebrew, his home of 'Uz' being outside Israel, although Wolfers (1995), p. 83 challenges this. Such debate seems irrelevant, since Job's relationship with God is being dissected in a Hebrew canonical text. Anyhow, using pre-Mosaic terms for God in the Dialogue could strengthen Job's characterization as Patriarch.

66 Job 29.2–4.

67 Job is described as יָשָׁר/ *yāšār* (complete) and תָּם/*tām* (upright) and he retains this self-image throughout the Dialogue. Ticciati (2005b), p. 146 makes a distinction between these two terms showing how Job's clinging to his standing as תָּם/*tām* (of integrity/complete) diverges from being צַדִּיק/*ṣaddîq* (synonym for יָשָׁר/*yāšār*/upright) in the eyes of the Law. This inner *integrity* of Job's enables him to go beyond any notion of retributive justice and its demand to be *upright*, as will be shown in the section on *Transformation*.

68 See p. 55 for how the survivors' experience of *God's timeless presence* is intrinsically bound up with their understanding of *God's nature*.

> me to look to those sorts of attitudes that I had towards God and where they came from. When all of that happened, I felt let down by God, I felt abandoned, I felt unprotected and uncared for. I felt that all the efforts that I'd made in ministry and everything else had come to nothing and meant nothing and were not noticed. I felt I'd wasted my time and energy; I couldn't understand what God wanted and I realized I was trying to gain God's approval, scared of God's anger, saw God as ultimately violent when it really came to it, and random or chaotic in the way that things just happened to this one or that one. I got this kind of 'why me?' about it and can't see any justification for it and now I'm feeling that I have projected my stuff onto God, that that's where all of that stuff comes from. That isn't actually what God is – my experience of parenting that I've projected onto my father part of God.

This transition will also happen for Job, but meanwhile he must endure God's apparent absence, yet longs for God's presence. In 8.13 Bildad denounces Job as one who has forgotten God, but this seems incongruous considering that Job's discourse concerns nothing but God. In fact Job sets his desire for their encounter in the context of a trial, the only vision of divine engagement that his received theology allows him. Throughout Job's speeches there is a to-ing and fro-ing of God's absence and presence, first in 'never let[ting Job] alone for an instant',[69] and then two chapters later Job complains:

> When he passes me, I cannot see him;
> when he goes by, I cannot perceive him.[70]

This verse reveals that, although God's loving presence was not felt at the time of crisis, it did not mean that God was absent (indeed he is *passing* and *going* by), a reality some interviewees conceded. The dialectic of intermittent absence and presence recalls the painful faith process described by Joanna and Priscilla, although when God was felt as present they experienced this presence as comfort.[71] It is certainly not comfortable for Job when he feels God's presence again:

> [God] has torn me in his wrath, and hated me;
> he has gnashed his teeth at me;
> my adversary sharpens his eyes against me.[72]

Starting from the excruciating monologue of chapter 3, Job has, according to Ticciati, been 'thrown into a relation to the face of God, which at once obscures

69 Job 7.17–19.

70 Job 9.11 (NIV).

71 See pp. 56, 58.

72 Job 16.9.

and exposes, involving him in a dialectic of hiddenness/unhiddenness',[73] but this relation *will* become his 'comfort', and this painful process *will* become the foundation of his Epilogue ministry, as we shall see. The pain and violence expressed in Job 3 expose anger and the negative side of power, which are later addressed within the Theophany, what we might call Job's surprising *special experience* of God. This experience of direct contact with God reveals three dialectical aspects of *God's timeless presence* in creation: transcendence and immanence, hospitality and visitation, permissiveness and limit-setting.

The first dialectical aspect of God's presence as revealed by the Theophany, transcendence and immanence, is shown through God's redirecting of the context for encounter from a narrow courtroom as envisaged by Job, to the whole of creation which is the true venue of divine presence, and one which is unbounded by human constraints. This enables Job to move beyond a narrow definition of God as demanding judge, violent and cruel, to a much vaster understanding. This venue of the vast universe echoes what Esther said about her appreciation of God's 'hugeness' and Joanna's beautiful description of God's power revealed in the sunset:

> I feel God is all around us everywhere. He is the awesome things we see, the beautiful sun[set], the beautiful breathtaking beauty and although it's a job to give a description really, I just feel he's this power.[74]

As Job has pushed the boundaries of theology with his questioning, so God pushes Job's boundaries of perception towards contemplation of the natural world which God indwells, yet directs. Significantly, the Theophany takes place within a natural phenomenon, a tempest, and all four chapters relate *God's* continuing experience of the creation. Earlier Job had anticipated that a tempest would accompany God's longed for appearance:

> If I summoned him and he answered me,
> I would not believe that he was listening to my voice.
> For he crushes me with a tempest
> and multiplies my wounds without a hearing.[75]

Job had meant with these words that it would be an unfair show of divine power which would injure him even further 'for nothing' but the real encounter reveals the transcendent Creator as intimately and caringly connected to creatures, and God's candid poetry soothes. Starting from laying the world's foundations (38.4–6), we are shown how God was there at the very beginning of all things with a

---

[73] Ticciati (2005b), p. 143.

[74] See also Miriam's recognition of God's unboundedness as described in Chapter 4, p. 78.

[75] Job 9.16–17 (NIV).

beautiful image of morning stars singing together in choir (38.7); God has been ever-present, revealed by continued divine generativity in fathering the rain and mothering the ice (38.28–9). God's patient nurturing and devoted knowledge of every creature is demonstrated by the attention this divine speaker pays to counting the months of gestation of hinds (39.1–2), being in attendance at every birth. This whole speech turns round Job's negative, dark attitude towards his own beginning in chapter 3,[76] asserting that God has been there all along and has walked around (38.16b), seen (38.17), entered (38.16a, 22) and knows the paths to natural phenomena (38.19–20), even the dark places of the abyss and death (38.16–17). Like the interviewees, Job can now see that God *was* present but did not perceive it until this vital moment of insight. God's patience and eternal calmness within the storm now conveyed by poetic imagery[77] absorb the anger and rebellion of Job's words, and the arena of courtroom battle is replaced by the balance and splendour of the natural world. A meditation on creation which does not ignore violence and struggle, but incorporates all of reality into beautiful imagery, can help to heal the deepest of wounds. The sense of Job's silence in 40.4–5 which follows God's first speech is for me reminiscent of Psalm 131.2:

> I have calmed and quieted my soul; like a weaned child with its mother,
> my soul within me is like a weaned child.

A second dialectic found within the Theophany is one of hospitality and visitation, which is revealed when we observe that God has been listening attentively to the Dialogue all along. As a starting point, God appropriates the legal jargon which Job has used, ironically picking up many of his phrases and words and mirroring his demanding questions.[78] God also takes up images that the Friends have used to defend God, but redirects their focus. For example, Eliphaz speaks of overwhelming waters coming from God as punishment in 22.11, and God uses the same image in 38.34 but appears far more interested in the wonder of all watery and weather phenomena. Furthermore, the watering of uninhabited lands, the 'desolate wasteland' (38.26–7), is just as important as watering any other lands, which eliminates any idea of punishment by flood, and perhaps suggests God's provision and care for the dispossessed who dwell in the desolate ground (30.1–8). The close but silent attention which God has paid to Job reveals God's hospitality toward him, 'being there' for him, rather than marking this out as a

---

76 In her analysis of these 'Whirlwind speeches' Ticciati (2005b), p. 104 proposes that they turn around both of Job's painful monologues because 'the forces at play in God's speech … are the same forces that were involved in Job's pain and turmoil, emerging here in a new resilient and expansive form, [which] is suggested by Job's description of his affliction in 9.17 in terms of a "whirlwind" from God'.

77 Commentators note how the poet saved his best lyricism for God's speeches.

78 See Habel (1985), pp. 530–32 for an outline of parallels between God's first speech and Job's claims in the Dialogue.

censorious visitation. This surprise appearance, however, also discloses God's wish to be received. Indeed when Job becomes silent before God in 40.4–5, it is not in cowering submission, but in realization that God was there all along and Job therefore repays God the compliment of being listened to with care and attention. Job's anger has subsided in this true meeting of two persons *without judgment*: man of integrity meets God of attentive power. God has been to the depths of Job's abyss and found this treasured servant there, so that Creation's host is become visitor, and the human visitor on earth is become host to God. Ticciati regards Job's election as the commitment of God 'for naught' to creation[79] and Habel understands this to be the committed friendship, based in loyal love, which Job has been seeking all along.[80] Awareness of such divine immanence, even in the abyss, underlies the complete dependence on God related by the interviewees. Biblical commentators, who argue that God fails to answer Job's questions, bamboozling him with a show of power,[81] miss the point: the answer God gives *is* response, reciprocation, responsiveness. For despite Job's protestations of his own 'slightness' in 40.4,[82] he knows now that he is undeniably of value, because the great God has responded and entered into conversation with him. Interestingly the NIV translates the Hebrew verb קָלַל (*qālal*) as to be 'unworthy', AV has 'vile' and Wolfers 'contemptible', none of which agree with Brown, Driver and Briggs. Habel and Pope, on the other hand, have 'small' and Gordis has 'of small account', which convey much better the sense of Job's growing ability to relax and let go of the big questions, having been chosen as God's listener.

The third dialectical notion of the Theophany lies on the one hand in the permissiveness of God's toleration of Job's anger and creation's violence, and on the other in the Creator's limit-setting. In the last chapter we noted that God's 'permissiveness' was a conundrum for interviewees. In that God allowed them the freedom to be angry and express their pain and yet still loved them, there was a correlation with God allowing others to behave in the way they choose; for God's freedom is given to all. The Theophany in Job shows the wildness of some creatures such as the ass (39.5–8) and the ox (39.9–12), set free by their very Creator, and goes on to display the permissiveness in God's attitude towards the ostrich, the horse and the eagle (39.13–30). The stupidity, aggression and brutality of these three respectively are sanctioned by God, who does not judge, punish or mete out 'wrong'. Furthermore God's magnificent creations Behemoth and Leviathan are beyond comparison with any other creatures for pride and strength. These two beasts can be viewed symbolically as the extreme of human will to power: Behemoth, conceivably symbol of aggressive sexuality (40.16), cannot be 'overwhelmed' by the river (40.23), bringing to mind Eliphaz's reference to the punishing flood (22.11); and Leviathan is the epitome of raw power (41.9) whose

79 Ticciati (2005b), pp. 110ff.

80 Habel (1977).

81 For example Girard (1987), p. 142.

82 From קָלַל (*qālal*) meaning 'to be slight', Brown et al. (1996), p. 886.

hide it is not possible to penetrate (41.13). Such a reading is suggested by God's challenge to Job regarding the regulation of human evil and pride in the passage preceding the long description of these beasts:

> Have you an arm like God,
> and can you thunder with a voice like his?
> Pour out the overflowings of your anger ...
> Look on all who are proud and bring them low;
> tread down the wicked where they stand.
> Hide them all in the dust together;
> Bind their faces in the world below.
> Then I will also acknowledge to you
> that your own right hand can give you victory.[83]

In other words, it is only God who can approach Behemoth (40.19) and survive the experience of attempting intimate contact with Leviathan (41.3, 8, 33). It is only God who can stand the sight of such potential for evil. That God appears fond, even proud of these beasts (41.12) might signify God's absolute love of all creatures, but this is difficult to bear if one becomes victim of such terrible power. Cox suggests that only God really knows the extreme dark side of existence and that:

> Yahweh is conceding that he cannot just dispose of the wicked and unrighteous, for even they are part of the cosmic whole. They represent perhaps the liberty that God has inserted into creation – freedom implies the capacity to do wrong.[84]

The value of this freedom and the risk of pain that necessarily accompanies it are well summed up by Priscilla, when she reflects on the preciousness of her relationship with God in light of her hard experience, and on God's perpetual attempts to get close to her:

> I've got to this place in my life and I know it to be true, that I could, if I had to, go through it all again rather than give him up, and there's nothing that would make me give him up. Not a single thing. Because he has never given me up, and I'm a real prickly package – an awful lot of trouble sometimes.

This echoes well the shared desire of Job and God who will not give each other up, despite the struggle and the pain; as Brueggemann puts it, 'Yahweh is no easy, gentle partner, but then neither is Job'.[85] Perhaps one reassurance we can take from God's speeches is Cox's assertion that, 'given the liberty he has woven into the

83 Job 40.9, 11–14.
84 Cox (1990), p. 107.
85 Brueggemann (1997), p. 393.

fabric of his creation all [God] can do is restrain it within acceptable bounds'.[86] Because God is limit-less, governor of the vast universe (38.18), God can absorb the will to power of the limited, no matter how unyielding, and is not overwhelmed by creaturely extreme. God *knows* the abyss intimately.

God's limit-setting on the other hand, is designed to prevent potential overwhelming in the natural world:

> Who shut in the sea with doors
> when it burst out from the womb?
> when I made the clouds its garment
> and thick darkness its swaddling band,
> and prescribed bounds for it
> and set bars and doors,
> and said, 'Thus far shall you come, and no farther;
> and here shall your proud waves be stopped'?[87]

We can be sure God really is there and that there will be limits to the waves of grief. Furthermore, the magnificent limitlessness of the Theophany must be counterbalanced by return to finite (limited) existence, hence the Epilogue which appears to reflect the 'normality' of the Prologue. Brueggemann suggests that the great intensity which the Theophany has afforded Job has to give way to the mundane, although

> neither Yahweh nor Job will ever be the same after this intense encounter, any more than one is the same after stunning artistry or breathtaking therapy or sexual intensity. Both parties have seen beyond what had ever been seen before.[88]

Significantly, God's limit-setting encapsulated quintessentially in the Decalogue (notwithstanding their original patriarchal context) proved crucial, and ultimately protective, for interviewee Miriam. In the chaos caused by her minister's abuse of power and sexual predation on her, she found that 'when the inward sense was being lost' she clung onto the 'outward commandment'. When she felt confused by the situation, she thought, 'how can you get away from "thou shalt not commit adultery"?' Miriam believes that her following of God's limit-setting on human licence protected her and ultimately saved her marriage.

Consideration of the Epilogue will further address limit-setting but we note here that the experience of *God's timeless presence*, which helps us understand more of God's nature as location of hospitality and acceptance, provides an ongoing broadening of our spiritual capacity. So we turn now to the broadening of Job's horizons.

---

86 Cox (1990), p. 125.

87 Job 38.8–11.

88 Brueggemann (1997), p. 392.

Transformation

> If you came into my house you could have really eaten your dinner off the kitchen floor. It was immaculate. I was obsessively immaculate. I wore myself out by keeping it clean and during ministry, the Holy Spirit revealed that I only had peace if I felt clean, and of course I'd felt very dirty – but I had my whiteness, virginity, cleanness restored to me, and now [if] anybody who knew me then, and hasn't seen me for many years, came into my house they wouldn't believe it. We've got four dogs and it doesn't bother me. I don't have to clean anything now.

Describing the change that her difficult journey of faith has made to her life, Lydia demonstrates in this excerpt some of the *Transformation* we see in Job. In this section I will compare Job's transition through the stages of his story, noting some striking resemblances to Lydia's faith journey, and will pause to reflect on Elihu's attitude to experiences of suffering that 'these things are sent to try us'.

Lydia gave an account of herself as being raised traditionally in the Church, but related that by adulthood her faith was characterized by heavy church involvement which revealed the obsessive behaviour she described above. She explained:

> Looking back I know now that there were a lot of things that needed healing. But you think you're alright don't you? I was one of these – I would play in the worship group and it wouldn't matter if my kids were ill or anything, I'd have to be there. I was focused on – all of my energies serving God, all the time, because that's what gave me peace; at great cost, I'm sure, to my kids.

Correspondingly we noted Job's obsessive religiosity in the Prologue and his embeddedness in his faith tradition. We can add to this state the isolation that existed between himself and his family, for Job did not join in family meals (1.4), and he offered sacrifices not knowing whether this was a real need or not (1.5). At the first assault of the Satan, Job maintained his traditional view of God, continuing his habitual worship and attitude (1.21–2). Lydia explained that when addressing her experiences of Child Sexual Abuse for the first time in connection with her faith, that

> there was still no sense of pain from the abuse itself, only that it caused me [to] blame that for making me let God down. For years I just chugged along accepting that [celibacy] was my price to pay.

Lydia had believed that her largely celibate marriage was her punishment for being sexually active as a teenager, for having 'let God down'. The crunch came when her husband was charged with sexual offences against children:

> I began this new part of our life; then I began to experience a lot of pain. How did the children interpret it? How did I interpret abuse? I then began to experience the pain that I'd had when I was a child.

This painful questioning lasted a long time for Lydia, throughout her husband's trial and his prison sentence, and it has a striking correlation with Job's doubt following the Satan's second attack when his 'armour' was truly penetrated: Job may no longer sin 'with his lips'[89] but the torment has begun.[90] The ambiguity of his status – survivor on the one hand, possible abuser on the other – might be the hammer and anvil between which the question of his integrity before God, and the possibility of God's answer to him, is tortuously worked out in the Dialogue. Lydia was also caught between the two extremes of surviving abuse and intimate involvement with a perpetrator, exposed at once to the ignominy of both positions, for although she was no perpetrator herself, she was exposed to the pain of accusation as the supportive wife of one. Viewed from the angle of Job's final monologue and from Lydia's present perspective, there is in both an acknowledgement that it is in deep places where treasures from God are found. In Chapter 4 I described how Lydia was given the verse from Isaiah 45.3 by a random person at a retreat: 'I will give you the treasures of darkness and riches hidden in secret places.' She did not grasp the significance of this text at the time, but now understands that the 'treasures' are the love, support and good communication which her family now has and she is adamant that these were only discovered in the heart of their dark struggle together. Two passages from Job mirror this development: one is the poem to Wisdom in chapter 28, and the other is the centrality of family unity and care in the Epilogue.

Habel sees the central metaphor of Job 28 as 'the search for what is rare and precious',[91] and the image of mining for treasure in 'the extremity[92] of darkness' encapsulates this concept in verse 3. Isaiah's allusion to 'treasures of darkness' in 45.3 is made in the context of Cyrus' vocation,[93] and this verse is surrounded by references to God's creation of the universe, deeply reminiscent of the Theophany.[94] More significantly, although little evidence exists of a link between these two passages,[95] the important issue is the search made by humankind for God (exemplified by Job's quest), and that made by God for humans (portrayed in

---

89 Job 2.10b.

90 Van Wolde (1997), p. 25; Kahn (1975), p. 35.

91 Habel (1985), p. 393. On the poem's design see Habel (1985), pp. 391–5.

92 Ticciati's translation (2005b), p. 188 following Habel.

93 Cyrus the Great, who conquered Babylon in 540 BCE, allowed the Israelites who had been exiled there to return to Palestine.

94 The same Hebrew word (אֹצְרוֹת/*'oṣerôṯ*) is used in the Theophany in Job 38 for 'treasuries' of snow and 'storehouses' of hail.

95 Only Wolfers (1995) attempts to identify the author of Job with the prophet Isaiah and cross-references two verses from Isaiah 45 (verses 5 and 8).

Isaiah 45). Returning to Lydia, it was her hard questioning that brought her into 'deep'[96] contact with the God who was already searching her out. The probing of the Holy Spirit within prayer ministry afforded her an experience as effective as the Theophany was for Job, and both these survivors opened themselves totally to the possibility of God's active presence.

Ticciati notes that Job's deeper piety in the Epilogue lies under the surface of his Prologue faith, and she compares the two. Drawing on her reading of Job's 'Prologue piety' through the lens of the Epilogue,[97] the differences she elucidates will demonstrate how Job has been transformed. First, direct communication now exists between Job and Yahweh, for Yahweh had been remote in the Prologue, but now communicates with Job about religious service in 42.7–9. Second, a real community of family and associates gathers together with Job: Job is portrayed in 42.11 as eating with his brothers and former acquaintances and he is now hospitable, opening up his home and table (just as Lydia's home is now more relaxed) and there is a supportive family atmosphere (42.11b). Third, generosity from others is offered and received (42.11c), perhaps symbolic of the 'treasures' that have been discovered in Lydia's family, but also echoing the help that she was able to accept from her church community, which she had at first refused in the difficult times:

> [On] the first day of [the] trial, I thought I'm not going to make anyone at church vulnerable to – I'm not going to let them be associated with us, because it was pretty horrid, and there were lots of parents, lots of nastiness, and I couldn't see God anywhere. There wasn't one kind person, there wasn't anybody. I couldn't feel God in anything – complete panic. So I then took everybody's offer; I took everyone's offer after that of coming, because I knew then that God was in them.

Fourth, Job's service of God has moved on from being merely repetitious to a 'natural continuity … through the generations'[98] and his blessings are not just restricted to the 'work of his [own] hands' only (1.10), but received gratuitously without self-conscious effort. Lydia related how she is now able to let go of 'compulsion' to become an authorized minister and accept the gifts the Holy Spirit gives her, as and when necessary, and from her account it is obvious that she has a significant prayer ministry. Similarly the final *Transformation* of Job is his election by God as intercessor for the Friends, in conjunction with his own election of this God 'for naught',[99] and we will return to consider this vocation as his *Knowing ministry*.

---

96 Lydia used the adjective 'deep' five times in relation to her faith development.

97 See Ticciati (2005b), pp. 53–78.

98 Ticciati (2005b), p. 69.

99 Ticciati (2005b), pp. 110–13.

Beforehand, however, we consider the suggestion found in much of the early commentary such as Gregory's *Moralia in Iob*,[100] that Job's transformative struggle is somehow pedagogical. In this respect, Elihu seeks to teach Job and the incompetent Friends a thing or two. Just as the bulk of his speech emphasizes what the Friends have already tried to impress upon Job, Elihu takes up his idea of disciplinary suffering from Eliphaz's first speech (5.17) but he elaborates,[101] suggesting that God uses pain to communicate when dreams and visions fail. He speculates:

> … [people are] chastened with pain upon their beds
> And with continual strife in their bones.[102]

Although some commentators understand Elihu's speech as prefiguring God's viewpoint, pointing out that 'Elihu' is synonymous with God's fore-runner 'Elijah', God does not actually mention Elihu's contribution at all in the Theophany. Moreover, Elihu's main conclusion, that God is completely transcendent or 'does not dirty himself in dialogue with humans',[103] is comically dismantled by the appearance immediately after his speech of the immanent divinity in the tempest. Furthermore, the Prologue did not suggest that Job had anything to learn. Rather, Yahweh drew *the Satan's* attention to Job so that he might consider this man's uprightness (1.8), and the disaster visited upon Job is regarded by Yahweh in 2.3 as 'for no reason' (הַֽחִנָּם *haḥinnām*), that is, we can assume not even for Job's edification. Even though the Theophany takes the form of God's didactic questioning of Job's knowledge, this can be viewed as a continuation of the key legal framework of the Dialogue search for justice, with God using Job's terms of engagement. Thus, with the disappearance of the Satan from the story after 2.7 (as the one who should look on Job's integrity and learn) and the absence of any discipline of Job by God in the dénouement, we might draw the conclusion that the author abhorred the idea that there is any pedagogical purpose to suffering. Likewise the interviewees were adamant that their awful experience was not a test sent by God to teach them something,[104] and accordingly Pope suggests that Job and its theology could only be written by someone who had personal knowledge of immense suffering.[105] If they had learnt anything from the pain of healing from abuse, and if God had brought anything good out of their abuse at all, that outcome was, according to these survivors, not its guiding purpose, as this passage from Priscilla's interview shows, and bears repeating:

100 Schreiner (1994).

101 Pope (1965), p. XXVI.

102 Job 33.19.

103 Habel (1985), p. 53.

104 See Miriam and Priscilla's comments, p. 63.

105 Pope (1965), p. XXXVII.

> I don't think he let it happen, but when it did happen I think he was then able to change that, transform that into something that was good, so that out of that pain and out of that evil, good actually came, inasmuch as I was then able to talk to other people and get close to other people.

For Job there was some good to come out of the 'evil that the Lord had brought upon him': there was the later consolation of family and community in 42.11; there was his knowledge, not just that he was innocent but that what he spoke of God was right (42.7); and most significantly, because of his words he is affirmed as God's servant, a designation repeated four times in only two verses, which doubles the endorsement given by Yahweh to Job as 'my servant' in the Prologue (1.8; 2.3). This doubled endorsement harmonizes with the doubling of blessings to come in 42.10 and underscores the broadening of Job's spiritual understanding:

> After the Lord had spoken these words to Job, the Lord said to Eliphaz the Temanite: 'My wrath is kindled against you and against your two friends, for you have not spoken of me what is right, as *my servant Job* has. Now therefore take seven bulls and seven rams and go to *my servant Job* and offer up for yourselves a burnt-offering; and *my servant Job* shall pray for you, for I will accept his prayer not to deal with you according to your folly. For you have not spoken of me what is right, as *my servant Job* has done.[106]

This affirmation of Job's role as communicating, community servant echoes Priscilla's words above, and recalls the prayer ministry that some of the interviewees have. So we turn now to the *Knowing ministry* of Job. How does this compare with that of the survivors?

Knowing Ministry

By the Epilogue, Job has become intercessor for the Friends and is at the centre of a community of blessing, rather than isolated sacrifice-maker for his family. His new status comes about by virtue of his experience, since he now 'knows' something by having 'seen'. He does not just know *about* it in theory, learnt from a textbook. Beforehand he spoke of things he did not understand, things too wonderful for him to know (42.3b), but now he exclaims:

> My ears had heard of you
> *but now* my eyes have *seen* you.[107]

What he has seen is God's real presence in the tempest, and in all of creation, a presence which is not mediated by the Deuteronomic Covenant. Two further

[106] Job 42.7–8.

[107] Job 42.5 (NIV), emphasis added.

'visionary' experiences that have informed his new ministry can be added to this: he has seen how badly his friends behaved towards him, exposing the violence lying beneath their ideology (a place he too had occupied before); and he has seen the extremes and limitations of his own identity. These three experiences, seeing how God, his Friends and he himself are in reality, have prepared him for the Epilogue ministry, having brought about his 'repentance' of 42.6b. Habel translates this verse as Job 'repents *of* dust and ashes' because the verb נִחַמְתִּי/ *niḥamtî* ('repent') used with the preposition עַל/ *'al* usually means 'to change one's mind about something planned'. Joining this translation together with the verb מָאַס/*mā'as* (42.6a) which can mean 'despise' or 'retract' and has no direct object in this instance,[108] the basis for reading this verse as 'I retract and repent *of* dust and ashes' is strong.[109] The nuance is that Job's grieving can come to an end. He is changing his mind about the grief of his situation. Furthermore, as Job is already in the ash-pile[110] it makes no sense to see this 'repentance' as a newly adopted sign of repentance. This repentance is therefore not self-reproach, but resembles self-forgiveness: he no longer has to feel the weight imposed by retributive justice. Metanoia means throwing off the shackles of an unjust system. He now has the freedom of believing 'for nothing', a freedom that I will argue is within boundaries that are just and egalitarian. But first I address how Job's experience of God's presence, his Friends' behaviour and his own self-knowledge inform his Epilogue ministry.

I suggested above that Job experienced God's presence, as distilled in the Theophany, in three dialectical aspects of transcendence/immanence, hospitality/ visitation and permissiveness/limit-setting. Each of these aspects is now mirrored in Job's Epilogue ministry, since it is Job's direct encounter with *this* particular God that has summoned his vocation as intercessor. First, Job had previously offered sacrifices on his own initiative, but now it is God's initiative;[111] thus God affirms Job as his agent in 42.8 and continues to speak directly both to Job and to the Friends, so God remains immanently present. Kenneth Numfor Ngwa argues that 'the transcendent God becomes accessible in the context of prayer', with a combination of retributive and non-retributive action pervading the Epilogue in God's rebuke of the Friends and his favour to Job.[112] Thus God still makes judgment and gives blessings as transcendent Yahweh, but carries out the divine will through Job's prayer (as emphasized):[113]

---

108 Translators have to add 'myself' to make the verse mean 'I despise myself and repent'.

109 Habel (1985), p. 576; Gutiérrez (1987), p. 87.

110 See Job 2.8.

111 Ticciati (2005b), p. 67.

112 Ngwa (2005), pp. 127–31. One could argue that this combination of retributive and non-retributive action in the Epilogue adds a fourth dialectical aspect.

113 Van Wolde (1997), p. 149 suggests that rather than replacing the notion of retribution with non-retribution and thereby creating an alternative paradigm, the author

> 'My servant *Job shall pray for you*, for *I will accept his prayer* not to deal with you according to your folly. For you have not spoken of me what is right, as my servant Job has.' So Eliphaz the Temanite and Bildad the Shuhite and Zophar the Naamathite went and did what the LORD had told them, *and the LORD accepted Job's prayer*. And the LORD restored the fortunes of Job, *when he had prayed for his friends*. And the LORD gave Job twice as much as he had before.[114]

Secondly, we noted that Job became silent in God's presence, suggesting a mirroring of God's attentive hospitality, allowing God to be the visitor and literally to give vent in the whirlwind. Job becomes silent again in the Epilogue, God having the last word, but Job's actions speak louder than words. He plays the dual role of host and recipient: as host he has his house full of people, family and former acquaintances eating with him; yet even though we know from the previous verse that God has already doubled his possessions (42.10b), Job also receives gifts from the others:

> All his brothers and sisters and everyone who had known him before came and ate with him in his house. They comforted and consoled him over all the trouble the LORD had brought upon him, and each one gave him a piece of silver and a gold ring.[115]

While he has no need of money, Job is able to receive what others have to give 'chinam', gratuitously. Trading has disappeared from love relationships, just as Job has stopped bargaining with God.[116] Is Job's new way of relating the source of his community's change of heart? For they now console Job and concur with him about the unwarranted 'trouble' that came his way, whereas before they had deserted him (19.13ff.). Job's lived example as the sort of arbiter that he himself has been seeking throughout the Dialogue has perhaps impressed and transformed them. Habel suggests that Job's painful quest for a 'friend' (רֵעַ/*rēa'*) to console and represent him begins in chapter 6, proceeding through the much-discussed figures of the 'arbiter' (מוֹכִיחַ/*môkîaḥ*) in 9.33, his 'witness in heaven'(בַשָּׁמַיִם עֵדִי/*baššāmayim 'ēḏî*) in 16.19 and the 'defender' (גֹּאֵל/*gō'ēl*) in 19.25,[117] all of whom Habel sees as describing one and the same person. Job fails to find such a friend in his company, a person who is motivated purely by 'loyal love' (חֶסֶד-/*ḥeseḏ*).[118]

---

shows that in 'chinam' faith 'both a bad and a good situation can be possibilities, not as a reward for Job's behaviour but as God's free action'.

114 Job 42.8b–10. This fourfold affirmation of Job as prayer confirms the fourfold affirmation of his servanthood in verses 7–8.

115 Job 42.11 (NIV).

116 God's 'bargain' with the Satan has also disappeared.

117 See Gutiérrez (1987), pp. 56–64 and Ticciati (2005b), pp. 119–37 on these three figures.

118 Job 6.14.

Habel argues that it is Job himself who turned out to be the loyal friend, who knows that 'it is better to suffer with a friend than to defend his God.'[119] I would add that it is the sort of loyalty that he found in God's attentive hospitality, and this encounter with God's companionship in the backdrop of creation was foreshadowed by that with the jackal and the owl, both of whom know the desert and who were Job's only compassionate friends.[120] Perhaps this affirms the sense of the 'witness' of 16.19 that *real* friends who stay through wilderness experiences are in some way connected with heaven.[121] The ambiguity of whether Job sees this 'witness' as God, or someone else in heaven, resonates with the idea that if Job is the arbiter of 9.33, he is also *God's* agent, thus synthesizing within himself the divine and earthly, the transcendent and the immanent.[122] That he accepts this role in the Epilogue, becoming source of transformation for the community, recalls the redeemer passage in chapter 19 where he enigmatically states 'The root of the thing is in me'.[123]

Finally, Job's friendship is further demonstrated in the irony that it is now he who prays for the so-called 'Friends': they should have interceded and 'been there' for him, but they rebuked and victimized him instead. Thus Job, having seen their faults, and like God who permissively accepts even the stupid (ostrich), the aggressive (horse) and the brutal (eagle),[124] accepts them in this act; yet the requirement that they must now make sacrifice curbs their freedom and reminds them that God will have the final say. This sense of unlimited acceptance and love being tempered by the need for limits set on the chaos and evil of the world, particularly human will to power, is demonstrated in the Epilogue in terms of Job's recognition of *boundaries of justice and equality*, which we now address.

Boundaries of Justice and Equality

In comparison with the concept of *boundaries* as introduced at the end of the last chapter, it is clear that Job's intense experience is 'liminal'. First, he suffers both the death of his children and the breaching of the boundary of his skin, and then in the Dialogue he occupies the opposite bank of an experiential chasm from the

---

119 Habel (1977), p. 236.

120 Habel (1977), p. 236.

121 It is worth noting that the full phrase is הִנֵּה־בַשָּׁמַיִם עֵדִי/*hin·neh baššāmayim 'ēḏî*, which implies that the 'witness in heaven' should rather be understood as a 'witness who happens to be in heaven, as opposed to anywhere else he may have been instead'. I owe this insight to Revd. Adam Carlill.

122 Interestingly Elihu identifies this figure as an 'angel' in 33.23.

123 Job 19.28.

124 A comparison of the three comforters, Eliphaz, Bildad and Zophar with the ostrich, the horse and the eagle is an amusing thought. There is a certain amount of burying the head in the sand, aggression and picking over Job's carcass by the Friends.

'Friends'[125] who attack him from the safety of their side of a religious barricade with a 'barrage' of reproach. In his vulnerability and inability to traverse the barrier between them, Job comes into direct contact with the un-bounded, immanent God who 'walks around' the liminal places such as the abyss of 38.16, and who deals with evil where it dwells at the 'edges of the earth' (38.13). Job then arrives at a place where he shows attentive hospitality and ministry to others, and renews appropriate community relationships. My earlier perception about the reciprocal relationship between openness with God and appropriate *boundaries* with others is, however, developed even further in that we see radical change in Job's practice of social justice: the conventional, powerful Patriarch of the Prologue not only becomes silent, passive recipient of his community's solicitations, but he also pushes out the *boundaries* in terms of gender equality. He crosses the pink boundary, so to speak, and does so in two striking ways.

First, by naming his three daughters he literally en-*titles* them, which on the one hand bestows on them legal inheritance equally with his sons, and on the other hand identifies them with creation and beauty. Regarding their legal inheritance, there was an ancient Middle Eastern custom where daughters inherited under exceptional circumstances.[126] Accordingly the Old Testament records one instance where property was shared between five daughters; but their father had died without sons, so the purpose of their inheritance in that case was solely to keep the property in the Father's tribe.[127] Job's action is therefore without precedence, since we know that these three girls have seven brothers and their father still living. The purpose of the entitlement can only serve to equalize their status, as property owners in their own right. Regarding creation and beauty, the meaning of the daughters' names is significant: Jemimah means dove, Cassia means cinnamon tree and Keren-Heppuch means horn of antimony or mascara. Noting merely the peculiarity of these names, or suggesting they signify Job's relaxation into enjoyment of beauty, commentators pass over them. However, I suggest there is a motive of equality here, albeit embryonic. In God's universe as revealed by the Theophany there is a clear balance between fathering and mothering, between male animals (horse, ox, ass) and female animals (raven, ostrich, lioness, mountain goat, eagle and hinds).[128] Thus his daughters' names (zoological, botanical and adorning) may signify Job's newly discovered respect for *all* of creation, even that which might *appear* frivolous and 'weak'. Has Job's traumatic experience of dispossession bestowed on him an empathy with un-propertied females, restoring

---

125 Reminiscent of the Dives and Lazarus story to which Miriam referred.

126 Ngwa (2005), pp. 113–17.

127 Numbers 27.1–11; 36.1–12.

128 Elizabeth Johnson (1984) argues that in scripture, where the 'freedom and transcendence of God [are] beyond the adequacy of any human expression', female/mother metaphors are used in equal measure with male/father imagery, the Theophany in Job being the most emphatic example.

to them their rightful, equal place in creation, as God has shown him in the Theophany?

Second, the sense of gender equality in the Epilogue is underscored by the balancing out of women's presence and experience in the last chapter with men's presence and experience earlier in the book. For example, when translated literally and placed alongside each other, two verses illustrate this re-balancing:

Prologue Job 1.3	the *man*	Job was *greater*	than all the *sons*	of the East
Epilogue Job 42.15	*women*	were not found *more beautiful*	than Job's *daughters*	in that land

Furthermore, in 42.11 Job's sisters are mentioned alongside his brothers, whereas in 19.13 only his brothers were mentioned as those who had deserted him. Could it be that Job's experience of being excluded from society has identified him with, and made him notice, those who are subjected to painful exclusion by virtue of their social and biological roles? Certainly Job's identification with women's lived experience is found in the poem's use of language. For example, in 16.13 Job describes his agony as arrows 'splitting/cleaving' (from פָּלַח/*pālaḥ*) his innards in two. This is the same verb used in God's description of birth in 39.3a. Wolfers, who avoids the usual bland translation of 'bring forth/give birth', retains the painful sense of the Hebrew root in his translation:

> [the hinds] crouch down and *split* forth their young.[129]

Furthermore, in 39.1 God asks Job whether he is able to watch the birthing hinds 'writhing' (from the verb חוּל/*ḥûl*) and in 15.20 this same verb is used to describe *Job's* suffering ('writhes in pain all his days').[130] Does Job's experiential understanding of women's suffering, as if in labour, have a deep effect on his outlook?

The gender equality perceived in the Epilogue is a start at establishing just boundaries which are not based on gender lines. Although God needs no boundaries between Godself and creation – Yahweh is even undaunted by Behemoth and Leviathan – we creatures do need them, because persecution and power abuse are part of the human condition, as the Theophany attests. In this light, Job has seen the false lines drawn by theological rigidities and social structures which exclude and abuse, and which protect the entitled. Gone is his image of a remote punishing God, an idol which significantly had first been highlighted by his wife. Mrs Job does not appear in the Epilogue, but she was the one who told Job to 'curse God and die' in 2.9, that is, curse the *tyrant* God, since worshipping a despot who appears to

129 Wolfers (1995), p. 368, emphasis added.

130 ESV.

punish the innocent can have no integrity.[131] The further Job travelled into territory alienated from the powerful in society, unprotected by the 'hedge' of blessing (1.10), or rather un-blinkered by it (3.23), the more his radical new perspective would grow, a perspective which undermines the concept of retributive justice and the limits it places on 'righteousness'.

Checking the 'fit' of the developing concept of *boundaries of justice and equality* with the data, I found Miriam's interview helpful. We saw earlier in this chapter her movement away from a remote, patriarchal God-figure and how God's limit-setting became her protection. I suggested in the last chapter, that her experience of God's immanent unboundedness was also illustrative of a shift in boundaries at a liminal moment.[132] In addition, Miriam was led, as a result of her experience, into a new understanding of power and its abuse which she based on the concept of equality and on the importance of wielding authority responsibly on behalf of the vulnerable:

> I hate discrimination, racial discrimination, sexual discrimination; ageism, treating children badly, anything like that where I thought that people were being treated disrespectfully, I don't like, and I don't think God likes it – that's part of my theology. God doesn't like that, God didn't mean it to be that way, God is not hierarchical, God is not patriarchal. So those things are not part of my theology and I believe that in spite of God creating it that way, we do have power structures, and we do have people who have more or less power; like children have less power, and sometimes it needs to be set up that way, and it is set up that way because the adult is then protective and guiding and taking responsibility for everything. It doesn't mean that child is unequal in the sense that it's not just as valuable or as valid as a person, but it means that you take on certain responsibilities because you're able to do something they're not able to do at the moment. It's the same with someone who is a teacher or in a position of power because they've been given more education, because they've been given more money, because they've been given more status – these people have been given that power – it doesn't mean that they're a better or more valuable person. But they have got that power and they have to use it in a responsible way, for the people that they're in power over. So it's a big challenge because it does corrupt you and you're likely to misuse it and that happens all the time. We're all vulnerable to that but it's wrong, it's still wrong if you do it. And we have to accept that and admit it and face it.

Miriam's insights reflect at once Job's Theophany experience of permissiveness and the need for limit-setting. While unbounded exposure to God might be a safe and healing place, with creatures the risk of damage is ever-present, and limit-

131 Van Wolde (1997), p. 26 identifies Mrs Job as the catalyst for the 'rant' that gets Job through the trauma.

132 See p. 77.

setting must be fair and equalizing for all. We might take note that God's limit-setting was already present in the Prologue, in that God twice limited what the Satan was 'allowed' to do to Job.[133]

Conclusion

In this chapter I have argued that the Book of Job should be read as a whole, as the account of one person's journey of spiritual transformation; I have suggested that Job could be viewed as a survivor of abuse, although there is also the possibility of seeing him as reformed perpetrator. His characterization as survivor enabled me to compare Job's situation with the main concepts from the empirical study in that I demonstrated that Job's *Transformation* included a *special experience* of God, by which he came to know *God's timeless presence* in creation; this resulted in his *Knowing ministry* as intercessor and friend. Finally, this ministry included the reformation of the unjust *boundaries* of the elitist and excluding system in which he had been immured and from which he then suffered, and this reformative action reflects the equality and true justice he experienced in God's universe. Moving across the threshold of the patriarchal city walls and onto the ash pile of isolation opened up a whole new world to him.

133 See Job 1.12: The LORD said to Satan, 'Very well, then, everything he has is in your power, *but on the man himself do not lay a finger*'; and Job 2.6: The LORD said to Satan, 'Very well, then, he is in your hands; *but you must spare his life*.'

Chapter 6
At Home with God: Marguerite Porete's *Mirror*

It was all right with the king, with the church anyway.
The mob cajoled and laughed, some cried as she was burnt on the stake.
She however remained silent.[1]

Home Territory: Introduction

As a student I lived for a year near Stuttgart. I found that no matter how much German I picked up, I could not express myself emotionally in what was still a foreign language. If I became angry, excited or upset, I invariably reverted to English, my mother tongue. There is something visceral about the language we imbibe with our mother's milk, whereas learning a language in school or college has a different quality. This contrast is discussed by Walter Ong when he plots the development from 'orality' to literacy in the history of Europe. He shows how it was a 'learned' language that eventually became the foundation of theological discourse and education for the second millennium CE, namely Latin. This discourse was learned in what was a 'tribal', or male puberty rite setting, 'complete with physical punishment and other kinds of deliberately imposed hardships'.[2] Being based outside the home in male academia, Ong explains that Learned Latin was not only sex-linked, written and spoken only by males, it also had 'no direct connection with anyone's unconscious of the sort that mother tongues, learned in infancy always have'.[3] Thus the connection between sound and sight was lost because 'orality' embeds meaning in lived context for both speaker and hearer, whereas writing would concentrate meaning in language itself. The consequence was that 'Learned Latin' reduced any interference in academia, and therefore in theology, from the 'human life world'. That is to say, knowledge was established 'in a medium insulated from the emotion-charged depths of one's mother-tongue'.[4] As a result of the scholastic hold on the Church in the Middle Ages, any theology

[1] From 'She However Remained Silent: In Memory of the French Beguine and Mystic Marguerite Porete' by Carola Moosbach, *Traces of Heaven* (London: SPCK, 2002), by permission of SPCK.

[2] Ong (2002), p. 111.

[3] Ong (2002), p. 111.

[4] Ong (2002), p. 112.

in a language other than Latin was seen as anathema, a fact that proved devastating for a talented woman theologian of the thirteenth century.

In order to develop the grounded theory further, in this chapter I compare the core category established by the interview analysis with a vernacular spirituality from the Christian tradition, namely the work of medieval mystic Marguerite Porete. There is of course a gap of centuries, which might be expected to present difficulties when comparing her work with material from the contemporary world. This gap is somewhat reduced for me not only by the 'gut feeling' I had of a sort of 'home-coming' on first encountering her spiritual text, but also by the knowledge that Porete's voice was excluded by mainstream Christian theology. Moreover, I will use the method of comparison I used in the previous chapter with Job, applying the same conceptual framework from the empirical study to the words of a woman who was writing about God from her experience. To bridge the gap a little further, I will first set Porete's book *The Mirror of Simple Annihilated Souls and Those Who Remain in Will and Desire of Love*[5] within the context of the late Middle Ages, when an increasingly totalitarian church state abused and destroyed her, though failed completely to destroy her text. Subsequently, an evaluation of the *Mirror* outlining the Soul's seven-stage journey through the spiritual process of 'annihilation' will provide a basis for comparison with the higher concept *Transformation* from the interview analysis. Next, after assessing Porete's understanding of God, who is portrayed primarily as Lady Love, and her concept of divine/human union, I will relate this understanding to the concept *God's timeless presence*. Since the 'will' plays a crucial role in the direct, unmediated relationship with God that she describes, I also address the significant concept of *free will*. Consequently, I go on to consider the effects which divine union has upon the 'annihilated Soul' and the outpouring of God's love in creation, setting these observations in comparison with the interviewees' accounts of *Knowing ministry*. In summary, I suggest that Porete's prophetic treatise, which integrates intimate union with her divine lover and rigorous intellectual probing of religious ideas, can be viewed as a theological mirror which reflects in a positive frame the journey the survivors have made on the way home to God.

A Window on the Late Middle Ages: The Life and Death of Marguerite Porete

Porete's book, which was written in Old French, actually enjoyed wide translation and distribution for a thirteenth-century mystical text[6] in Latin, Middle French, Italian and Middle English. Kurt Ruh suggests that no other mystical work in

---

5 I will use the abbreviation *Mirror*, quoting from Ellen Babinsky's translation (1993) which is based on Guarnieri and Verdeyen's full critical edition of the Middle French text and the Latin translation, in *Corpus Christianorum: Continuatio Mediaevalis 69* (Turnhout: Brepols, 1986).

6 Lerner (1972), pp. 72–3.

the early fourteenth century surmounted European language-barriers more easily than the *Mirror*,[7] and this popularity is corroborated by the existence of no less than 13 extant manuscripts in an assortment of these four languages, all of which managed to survive severe papal censorship.[8] In a similar crossing of language boundaries, Porete scholarship has suddenly proliferated in the last two decades and appeared in no less than five languages, with English, French, German, Italian and Hungarian studies reflecting linguistically the geographical resting places of the 13 manuscripts.[9] Scholarly interest in this relatively obscure mystic now stretches across cultural/historical, theological, literary, sociological and feminist disciplines, as demonstrated by the conference held in Paris in May 2010 to commemorate the seven hundredth anniversary of Porete's condemnation and execution.[10] For Porete was burnt alive, with her book, on the Place de Grève on 1 June 1310 as 'relapsed heretic' because she had continued to propagate her teaching, having been banned from doing so by Guy of Colmieu, at some point in his tenure as Bishop of Cambrai between 1296 and 1306.[11]

Following Porete's demise, her book remained anonymous for centuries. The true identity of its author came to light only half a century ago and this discovery provides testimony to the vibrant theological discourse produced down the years by lay women. Much of this discourse has remained largely hidden, but whispers to us from the dark shadows of church history. Although Porete has not yet been pardoned by the Catholic Church, it is intriguing to note that her subtle text was known in monastic circles throughout the centuries,[12] but the assumption was made that the *Mirror* was written by a man.[13] Indeed Francesca Bussey suggests that the assumption of male authorship possibly conferred an orthodoxy on the

---

7 Colledge et al. (1999), p. lxxxii.

8 For information on history, locations and state of manuscripts see Falvay (2002b), pp. 148–50.

9 Falvay (2002b), p. 148.

10 See Groupe d'anthropologie scolastique (2010). Speakers included Robert Lerner, Dávid Falvay and Marleen Cré.

11 Field (2012), pp. 5–6.

12 See Cré (2000).

13 The author was called 'he' by the translator of the Middle English manuscript, MN, and by Richard Methley, the Carthusian who translated this text into Latin. Even Charles Crawford who published his English translation, *A Mirror for Simple Souls by an Anonymous Thirteenth-century French Mystic* (New York: Crossroad, 1981) after the discovery of Porete's authorship, thought the author was male. One historical anomaly discerned by Kocher (1998), p. 17 is that Porete's authorship was almost certainly known by the sixteenth-century Marguerite of Navarre, as revealed by her poem *Prisons*. The manuscript this reformist Queen read was the Condée text in Middle French, which was in the possession of the convent of La Madeleine in Orléans, with which she had connections. The codex has marginal notations made by three different female readers.

Mirror which saved it from further indictment.[14] It also shows that despite recent feminist appropriation of Porete's theology as distinctively female, it was by no means clearly discernible as such in past centuries, and this point has relevance regarding her condemnation as a heretic, as we will see. Astonishingly the *Mirror* was given the Benedictine imprimatur in its first modern English translation in 1927,[15] but it was in 1946 that Romana Guarnieri published her discovery that *Le Mirouer des simples ames anienties* was in truth authored by 'heretic' Marguerite Porete.[16] Although little is known about Porete's life, partly because the practice of burning heretics to ash was purposely to eradicate any trace of 'disease', it was from the few extant details of her death that Guarnieri pieced together the mystery. She noticed that three out of the 15 indictments used in Porete's trial and condemnation as found in historical accounts, can be found word-for-word in the *Mirror*. These excerpts, clearly taken out of context, would inevitably be denounced as antinomian heresy by the 21 theologians amassed by the Inquisitor, William Humbert, to assess the book.[17]

The three historical chronicles, the *Grandes Chroniques de France*, the *Continuation of the Chronicle of Nangis* and *La chronique de Jean d'Outremeuse*, which hold short accounts of her inquisitorial trial and death,[18] together with what is discernible as the *Mirror*'s autobiographical content, have provoked much speculation over whether Porete was a beguine. Semi-enclosed lay communities called 'beguinages'[19] had sprung up in the Low Countries in the late Middle Ages, appealing particularly to women. For this was an era of growing urban prosperity in Northern Europe, and in reaction to this newly acquired wealth, many lay 'poverty' movements were generated within the bourgeoisie. The greater economic, social and educational opportunities now available to women as well as to men allowed for beguinages to become centres of theological learning for evangelically-minded lay women.[20] Porete probably came from Hainaut and was itinerant around northern France and certainly the *Grandes Chroniques* calls Porete 'beguine clergeresse';[21]

---

[14] Bussey (2007), p. 87.

[15] Clare Kirchberger's translation, attributed to a male author, was published under the auspices of the Downside Benedictines.

[16] Published in 'Lo specchio delle anime semplici e Margherita Porette,' in *l'Osservatore Romano* on 16 June 1946.

[17] Babinsky (1993), pp. 22–3.

[18] Verdeyen (1986), pp. 88–92.

[19] For descriptions of beguines and beguinages, see Babinsky (1993), pp. 6–20; also Wogan-Browne and Henneau (1999). See Brenda Bolton (1976) on the demographic trends behind the rise of this lay evangelical movement.

[20] See Bernard McGinn (1998), p. 323 on growing literacy amongst the laity and changes in education in the thirteenth century. See Robin O'Sullivan (2006), pp. 148–55 on beguine education.

[21] Verdeyen (1986), p. 91.

although this might explain the source of her remarkable learning and theological training,[22] two factors call this identification into question.

First, the writing of the *Grandes Chroniques* post-dated the Council of Vienne which took place from 1311 to 1312. This date is significant in relation to Porete because the Council's main agenda, along with the suppression of the Templar order,[23] was to hereticize unregulated religious groups like beguines, and to delineate the supposed 'Free Spirit' heresy. The latter was achieved by using propositions, once again taken out of context, from Porete's *Mirror* as a frame of reference. Historically this resulted in the unfounded assumption that Porete was one of the 'prime movers' of the Free Spirit heresy.[24] By the time the aforementioned historical documents were written, in the wake of the panic at Vienne about women who evaded the authority of the Church, the term 'beguine' was generally being used derogatively for any unregulated, and by extension lax, woman and eventually became synonymous with 'heretic'. The attachment of the term 'beguine' to Porete as an unenclosed woman, who was a known heretic, was therefore a simple step. Porete's erroneous designation as a beguine thus became embedded in historical discourse.[25] The tragedy is that the hostility of the historical documents has been repeated in recent scholarship. Edmund Colledge called Porete the 'High Priestess of Free Spirit heresy',[26] and Ernest McDonnell described her, and 'beguines like her', as 'petty heresiarchs who pursu[ed] a life of moral laxity'.[27] It is striking that rigorous academics allowed themselves to be governed by hostile gendered discourses,[28] especially in view of Porete's trial records which never accuse her of lewd behaviour, a common characteristic of 'Free Spirit' trials.[29] It is therefore unimaginable that she committed actual antinomian crimes, otherwise the Inquisition would certainly have recorded them.[30]

Questioning Porete's identification as beguine would certainly never have occurred to hostile chroniclers and authors, yet neither has it occurred to the majority of feminist writers. Nevertheless, the second cause for doubt lies clearly within the *Mirror* itself, where Porete refers to beguines as her critics:

> O my Lover, what will beguines say
> and religious types

22 Bussey (2007), pp. 210ff.; Leicht (1998), pp. 59ff.; McGinn (1998), p. 244.

23 There are certain connections between Porete's trial and that of the Templars, 54 of whom were burnt in Paris only three weeks before her execution. See Field (2012).

24 Lerner (1972), pp. 47–9, 78–84.

25 Bussey (2007).

26 Robinson (2001), pp. 28–9.

27 Robinson (2001), p. 29.

28 See Michael Sells (1994) who outlines early scholarship which unquestioningly accepted the conclusions of Inquisitorial sources.

29 Bryant (1984), p. 207.

30 Lerner (1972).

When they hear the excellence
of your divine song?
Beguines say I err ...[31]

Obvious parallels exist between Porete and beguine writers such as Hadewijch of Antwerp and Mechtehild of Magdeburg in their common use of courtly love lyric to express their concept of divine love,[32] but in contrast she also draws on the rational (male) intellectual tradition, displaying a deep understanding of Trinitarian theology[33] and clear influences from neo-platonic thought.[34] Furthermore Porete asserts the possibility of *permanent* union with God, a concept which goes beyond any proposed by other women mystics.[35] Sympathetic scholarship has sought to defend the *Mirror* and establish its orthodoxy but even so, when compared with other female medieval writers Porete has been labelled an 'anomaly'.[36] The grounds for this categorization lie in the *Mirror*'s eschewing of bodily mortification and in its lack of emphasis on charitable works; Porete is therefore seen as unrepresentative of her contemporaries who in contrast focused on affective religious experience, the Eucharist, and somatic spirituality with its concomitant view of suffering as virtuous.[37] However, while her uniqueness is unambiguous, I believe we are not necessarily compelled to view Porete as a 'blip' in the history of spirituality. I see her rather as a significant voice that challenged the dominant two-fold medieval discourse of scholastic male orthodoxy and somatic female spirituality. Accordingly, Bussey argues that a continuation in Porete scholarship of her false representation as a beguine veils her true status as the voice of a community who had a theological discourse that was alternative both to dominant ecclesiastical theology and also to beguine spirituality.[38] This two-fold radicalism is illustrated by Geneviève Souillac and by Robin O'Sullivan, for on the one hand Souillac argues that the *Mirror*'s significance in the history of ideas lies 'in its intellectual relationship with an institutional and discursive locus: scholastic theology';[39] and on the other, O'Sullivan perceives Porete's intention was to contribute to, and correct, contemporary teachings on mystical epistemology within beguine communities.[40]

Paradoxically therefore, Porete was both typical and atypical of her generation of Christian thinkers. She was typical as a mystical theologian in that she engaged

31 *Mirror* ch. 122, p. 200.

32 Hollywood (1995); Robinson (2001); Newman (2002).

33 Lerner (1972), p. 201; McGinn (1998), p. 244.

34 Robinson (2001), p. 57.

35 Newman (1995), p. 152; Sargent (1997), p. 275; Robinson (2001), pp. 24–5.

36 Robinson (2001), p. xiv.

37 Bynum (1991), p. 124; Hollywood (1995), pp. 8ff., 96ff.

38 Bussey (2007), pp. 10, 81.

39 Souillac (1998), p. 263.

40 O'Sullivan (2006), p. 146.

deeply with scholastic theology, as had been standard for mystics up until the early fourteenth century, a point in history when mysticism and theology were about to diversify into a dichotomy of emotional spiritual devotion at one end of the spectrum, and at the other, cerebral theology as an academic subject.[41] However, Porete was atypical in that she was a female writing in this way; she did not write like her female literary contemporaries. It is this discrepancy that brought her the most intense inquisitorial censure because in her condemnation as 'relapsed heretic', she was specifically branded with the term 'pseudo-mulier' or 'phony woman'. Writing theology in the vernacular, as a woman was necessarily constrained to do, and moreover remaining unenclosed and free from the authority of a male confessor, meant that 'her construction as a heretic [was] linked to her deconstruction as a woman, an extremely vitriolic assault'.[42] Ultimately Marguerite Porete was silenced before politico-ecclesiastical powers who executed her for her boldness, or to continue the metaphor from the last chapter, for crossing the 'blue boundary'. Theology in the vernacular was very significant, as explained in the introduction, but gender was even more so. It is well documented that the sermons of Dominican Master, Eckhart, given in his native German also brought him accusations for heresy from the Inquisition in 1326, despite his reputation as a scholar. However, in Eckhart's case, his personhood as a man was never at issue, he was able to argue his case in Latin and he was never actually named personally as a heretic.[43]

It could, then, be argued that Porete's significance within the history of ideas quite accurately intersects the time when mysticism and theology were about to diverge as suggested by Turner's analysis. However, because scholastic theology, culminating with Aquinas, had already succeeded not only in delimiting the boundaries of thought, but also *how* one could think, and even *how far*,[44] Porete is again typical in that she was one of many alternative, excluded voices with radical theological views. For in the Middle Ages, those who challenged dominant

---

41 According to Denys Turner (1998), p. 214 in the Middle Ages one could talk about the theological and mystical tradition 'within a single, unified discourse and so could talk intelligibly about a mystical theology'. He offers lists of systematic theologians and mystics which until the mid fourteenth century would have contained the same names; since then 'hardly anyone who would be agreed to be of significance in the history of western Christian theology figures at all in the list of "mystics" and hardly any mystics make a significant contribution to the development of mainstream theology'.

42 Bussey (2007), p. 11.

43 Eckhart died before the verdict of his trial was received, when 28 articles attributable to him were deemed as heretical; he was posthumously excommunicated by Pope John XXII. Intriguingly, there are connections to be found between Porete's work and the sermons of Eckhart, who may have had access to a copy of her confiscated book. This seems very likely because in 1311, the year after her execution, Eckhart lived in Paris at the Dominican convent of St Jacques, contemporaneously with her Inquisitor, William Humbert. For an examination of the evidence for a connection between Porete's and Eckhart's theology, see Trombley (2010).

44 Souillac (1998), pp. 265–6.

ecclesiastical discourse were systematically exterminated like 'infectious diseases'.[45] As Miri Rubin writes, those who died for their faith in the later medieval centuries,

> were not Christians tested for their faith, but those exactly who criticized, questioned, or indeed rejected that faith: mystics, Jews, heretics. The fires of religious indignation as opposed to those of mere judicial disapproval, burnt for Marguerite Porete.[46]

What is extraordinary, however, is the preservation of Porete's words almost intact. As a rule history provides us with the Inquisition's trial records which reveal only inquisitorial concerns; the opportunity for 'heretics' to elucidate their thinking was severely limited, for they were required only to answer what were necessarily one-dimensional questions designed to root out particular errors.[47] We might view hostile records as a reflection in the inquisitorial mirror. Paradoxically in Porete's *Mirror* we have instead a window through which we can look in both directions and understand the real importance of how lay Christian groups of the time were seriously developing their faith. Accordingly, Bussey's thesis is that Porete belonged to:

> a community with a vigorous tradition of religious reform. *The Mirror* … both reflects and produces that reform tradition, a tradition founded in the didactic and transformative possibilities of religiosity on an individual basis sought eagerly within the public sphere.[48]

Thus Bussey sees Porete as representing 'an excluded lay discourse that saw individual transformation, critique and bold engagement with religious notions, as an essential aspect of transformative Christianity'.[49] This critique and bold engagement was offered, however, in a context that was becoming extremely dangerous.

As we know the winners always write our history, and the losers lose out. However, the *Mirror* presents us with an opportunity to subvert history on several counts. First, because against all odds the book survived the Inquisition's attempt to obliterate its challenging message; second, because Porete's astonishing self-imposed silence throughout her trial[50] prevented distortion of her speech by the

---

45 Ormerod and Roach (2004).

46 Rubin (1993), pp. 182–3.

47 McLaughlin (1973).

48 Bussey (2007), p. 200.

49 Bussey (2007), p. 19.

50 Porete's refusal to take the Inquisitorial oath is usually interpreted as undermining and stymieing the questioning process; however, it could be viewed as active, silent protection of her community.

hostile pen in court records; and third, because her text had not been censored by a clerical amanuensis which was the norm for 'acceptable' female mystics of the era,[51] we have a unique gift of words that describe one Soul's first-hand experience of unmediated relationship with God. An assessment of this gift will allow me to compare relatively uncensored medieval data on spirituality with live twenty-first-century data, and show how Marguerite Porete is rightly becoming more than a footnote in the history of Christian tradition.

Structural Survey: Design of the *Mirror*

The *Mirror* is a kaleidoscopic integration of genres including courtly love epic, parable, mystical treatise and poetry, with more than a hint of Boethian-style philosophical dialogue. However, whereas Boethius' *Consolation of Philosophy* personifies Philosophy as his female guide while he actually was awaiting execution, Porete's *Mirror* imaginatively personifies God as 'Lady Love' who guides the Soul to face spiritual 'martyrdom'. Its structure is a similarly complex interweaving of schemata and a cursory three-part outline suggests:

- a short Prologue containing an Exemplum from romantic legend based on the story of Candace and Alexander the Great,[52] in which the concepts of God's nobility, his identity as the 'Far-nearness' and the Soul's seven-stage journey to divine union are introduced;
- the core Dialogue explaining the journey of the Soul through annihilation, with Reason as questioner and Lady Love as divine guru;
- a substantial Epilogue, mainly in the first person, giving an in-depth commentary on the Dialogue with examples from scripture of annihilated souls, for example John the Baptist, Mary Magdalene and the Virgin Mary.

While the seven-stage transformative journey is the basic spiritual scheme, this is fleshed out further by a process of three 'deaths' occurring before 'annihilation' at the fifth stage, which is the stage the author stresses is the main focus of the book.[53] Because the complex exposition with diverse schemes makes the book seem repetitive, its structure has been described by hostile academics as incompetently or deliberately disordered.[54] However, building on Huot de Longchamp's treatment of their interlocking nature, Amy Hollywood has shown how the three

---

51 Thus Bussey (2007), pp. 9–10 argues, 'somatic discourse … accepted as a given in much scholarship, may not always have been as central to women's experiences as we have thought'. She acknowledges, however (p. 75), that Porete's text has been edited in translations.

52 Babinsky (1993), p. 223.

53 *Mirror* ch. 58, p. 135.

54 Colledge et al. (1999), p. lxxiii.

'deaths' and the seven-stage journey can be integrated.[55] Furthermore, Irene Leicht incorporates into Hollywood's analysis of the *Mirror* Porete's secondary three-tiered descriptions, some of which will be elucidated shortly, and Table 6.1 shows how these various schemes fit together. Leicht argues that the *Mirror*'s repetitiveness, rather than showing lack of structure, spirals around the central pivotal chapters 54–9 like a helix, delineating a process of 'ruminatory' spiritual formation.[56] We observed earlier how a similar dialectical, repetitive process of transformative spiritual experience was key for survivors (and for Job). In what follows, the *Mirror*'s depths will be plumbed with relation to that process which emerged from the interview analysis.[57]

Table 6.1 How the Mirror's various schemes and stages fit together

Death (1) of sin	**Death (2) of nature**	**Death (3) of spirit**	**Death of body**
Life of grace	Life of the Spirit	Godly life	
Soul	Spirit	Pure, heavenly bride of peace	
Slaves	Slaves and merchants	Free ones	
The ruined	The lost/the sad	The annihilated	
The actives	The contemplatives	*The unencumbered*	
Seraphim wings pair 1: The goodness of the Incarnation	Seraphim wings pair 2: Salvation through the Passion	Seraphim wings pair 3: The free Soul led by the Spirit	
Raison	Raison	Amour	
Stages 1 and 2: Life according to the virtues and commandments	**Stages 3 and 4:** Dependence on love and readiness for martyrdom	**Stages 5 and 6:** Rest of the free and clarified souls in nothingness and in the clarity of God	***Stage 7:*** *With God in paradise*

Based on Leicht (1998), p. 200 with my additions in italics.

55 Hollywood (1995), pp. 97–103; n. 35, p. 257.

56 Leicht (1998), pp. 157–61 refers to Jean Leclercq's account of monastic exegesis, *lectio* and *meditatio* combining within the term *ruminatio*, describing a constant chewing over of scripture until digested.

57 For systematic readings of Porete's theology see Amy Hollywood (1995) and Bernard McGinn (1998); see also Irene Leicht (1998) for the most comprehensive theological analysis.

Journey to the Homeland: The Seven Stages of 'Noble Being'

Joanna Maguire Robinson[58] treats the annihilated Soul's 'nobility' as the *Mirror*'s central hermeneutical theme and argues that to see oneself as elected daughter in the lineage of the 'King' makes Porete's spirituality esoteric, designed for an elite group of pre-elected souls. I disagree with this assessment. While election of the Soul is certainly important, it is Fine Love (God) that has made her *find* nobility,[59] the Soul's knowledge of her election being activated only following her recognition of her own wretchedness. The path to this discovery is potentially open to anyone because we are all created beings, and I read Porete's so-called 'elitism' as her realistic acknowledgment that not every created being will choose this difficult journey. It is unsurprising therefore that the *Mirror* admonishes us that it is a 'very long road from the first stage of grace to the last stage of grace',[60] and informs us at the outset that all the stages must be experienced without exception.[61] That said, the *Mirror*'s main focus is 'annihilation', the crucial experience which involves the 'spiritual death' that enables the Soul to move from Stage Four to Stage Five, and remain there. Details of earlier stages and the first two deaths are sketchy, and consequently I will give a short summary of Stages One to Four, followed by a more detailed assessment of the all-important Stage Five and how the Soul is transformed into God through union. Parallels can then be drawn with the interviews.

Stage One signifies the foundational experience of becoming Christian, which involves baptism and the Soul's assent to keeping God's Commandments. The Soul is saved by God's grace and has died to 'mortal sin',[62] which was presumably a stage attained by all in medieval Christendom. Stage Two occurs when the Soul realizes there is more to loving God than selfish gain and is prepared to make sacrifices by living the evangelical life, after the example of Christ.[63] Souls who are in either of these first two stages are called 'actives' and although they have been saved by grace for all eternity, they are deemed 'ruined souls' because they still remain enslaved to Nature, Reason and the Virtues; that is to say, they are slaves to the 'works' of body, mind and spirit. A second death, to Nature, is required before the Soul can move into the next state of being, which comprises Stages Three and Four. In Stage Three, the Soul recognizes that she has multiplied her good works from her desire to give to her beloved (God) the things which she knows he[64] loves. She now appreciates that this 'work', even though it might be

---

58 Robinson (2001).

59 *Mirror* ch. 122, pp. 198–9.

60 *Mirror* ch. 60, p. 137.

61 *Mirror* ch. 1, p. 81.

62 *Mirror* ch. 62, pp. 139–40.

63 *Mirror* ch. 118, p. 189.

64 God's gender appears interchangeable in the *Mirror*, so personal pronouns for God will reflect Porete's usage in this chapter.

virtuous, is in truth motivated by love of herself because it is motivated by pride in her own accomplishments. In order to rid herself of this self-centeredness, she must relinquish the works of charity which she loves and which make her feel virtuous as a giver:

> In order to accomplish this martyrdom, she obliges herself to obey another will, in abstaining from work and from will, in fulfilling another will, in order to destroy her own will.[65]

From this point on, focus on the will becomes central to the journey. However, the reference here to obeying 'another will' indicates the Soul's *conscious* submission to external authority, because the Soul is still reasoning out by her own intellect what is beneficial for disciplining her will.[66] Because she is still in control of her will this is not yet annihilation for she is conforming her will to another's, which is not *God's*. Stage Four of the Soul's journey leads her into further relinquishment of the good deeds she had formerly relished and into a life of contemplation, which brings with it the delights of God's love. Herein lies danger; for these delights are ecstatic, and lead the Soul into the pride of thinking that she has now reached the heights of spiritual perfection.

Souls in these twin Stages Three and Four are called 'contemplatives', a term which incorporates a further distinction between 'lost souls' and 'sad souls'. Lost souls are 'lost in their works',[67] that is to say they are lost in spiritual pursuits, for they experience a dialectical cycle of anxiety and desire; on the one hand they need to prove their worthiness of the gifts they already have from God, even to the point of martyrdom, while on the other they also desire the sweet consolations of God, which are experienced through hard-won meditative 'works'. This is still a life 'over which [one's soul] has lordship', since she thinks, mistakenly, that she has everything.[68] In this, Porete both critiques and departs from the somatic practices of contemporary women religious by maintaining that a life of contemplation, which seeks delights 'through pain or through the peddling of pain's remedies'[69] (that is, through bodily mortifications), is not the highest spiritual goal. She maintains that because of their perpetual striving to suppress sensuality in order to achieve purity, such souls can have no real peace,[70] which is an important concept in the *Mirror*. The following excerpt clearly suggests that the author has herself experienced this

---

65 *Mirror* ch. 118, p. 190.

66 This might, for example, denote submission to a superior in a beguinage according to Babinsky (1993), p. 231 n. 113; it could reflect Porete's early experience and supply a clue as to why she may have parted company with the beguine sorority.

67 *Mirror* ch. 55, p. 132.

68 *Mirror* ch. 118, p. 190.

69 *Mirror* ch. 86, p. 162.

70 *Mirror* ch. 90, p. 166.

'dead end' in the spiritual life, otherwise she would not have been aware of any deeper spiritual understanding and its deeper peace:

> … love has deceived many souls by the sweetness of the pleasure of her love, which overtakes the Soul as soon as she comes near to it. Against such power none can prevail. This is known by the Soul whom Love has carried higher beyond herself, through Fine Love.[71]

There is a subtle but very important difference here between 'love' and 'Love'. The former signifies yearning, desirous natural love, in which the Soul is still 'with herself … prideful and charmed',[72] and still ruled by the senses; the latter signifies Divine (Fine) Love, which has no master.[73] Nevertheless, 'sad' Souls who are at this stage still have the potential for experiencing Fine Love, because they have the ability to perceive that there is yet more to come. This perception helps them move into the fifth stage through the process of annihilation, because their sadness is the misery of knowing that in reality they do not yet have God's 'sufficiency'; they are not fooling themselves that they have made it spiritually. Because they continue to seek God's sufficiency, and call for help, 'Lady Understanding' will guide them.[74]

In the next phase, which is presented as 'annihilation by Love', the Soul dynamically straddles Stages Five and Six where she has been brought into lasting union with God. From here the Soul cannot slip back to an earlier state because the Soul has died a third 'death to spirit' and is thereby annihilated for good. The Soul is now justified by faith, and not by works:

> This Soul knows no longer how to work, and without fail she is thus excused and exonerated, without works, by believing that God is good and incomprehensible. This one is saved by faith without works, because faith surpasses all work, as Love herself witnesses.[75]

It is striking that the *Mirror* champions belief in justification by faith a full two centuries before the Reformation era[76] and Porete explains that this belief is generated only when the Soul has contemplated the ultimate Being of God and how all of creation comes from God; simultaneously she realizes that she would not exist in reality outside of God and his gift. The Soul has reached the understanding that the material universe came from nothing, and therefore as a material being she is nothing, *except for* the gift of God's own will which he gave

71 *Mirror* ch. 118, p. 191.
72 *Mirror* ch. 110, p. 182.
73 Babinsky (1993), p. 231, n. 114.
74 *Mirror* ch. 57, p. 134.
75 *Mirror* ch. 11, p. 89.
76 See Souillac (1998) for a discussion of Porete's identity as prophet.

her freely from his goodness at creation.[77] The key to transition into this state, where the purity of the divine transforms the Soul into itself, is the *will*: God wills that her will should be returned to him as freely as it was given to the Soul by God in the beginning 'without a why'.[78] This reveals that God's motive for creating the Soul within time was that she might 'attain' what is hers; that is to say, 'to be established in [her] nothingness',[79] which means being in eternity with God. In a movement of God's pure light (the initiative is always God's), which one might call a 'theophany', the Soul sees clearly that her will *can* be moved from the place of her present wretchedness where it ought not to be, to its rightful place with God 'where it ought to remain'.[80] Her wretchedness has been revealed by its stark contrast with God's total goodness, and she sees that she is now less than the nothingness which she had before God created her *ex nihilo*, because it is her will (not her nature or any of the senses) that has caused her to sin. She now realizes that 'it is impossible that [she] sin, if [her] will does not will it'.[81] Because her will has been removed from its pre-creation origin in God and used by the Soul for her own ends, even if those ends were intended virtuously, she is completely wretched. Moreover, because of the uttermost depths of this wretchedness, which is less than nothingness, or an 'abyss' into which she has fallen, it is only God's essential Love which he is perpetually giving (because that is God's nature to do so) that can possibly fill it; that is, the abyss becomes the place where she is filled with God's utter goodness to the extent of her utter wretchedness,[82] because God has to be God and give to her.

Rendering her will back to God means that God can then dissolve the Soul's will into the divine; therefore she is transformed *by* God's Love *into* God's Love, where she remains in a state of peace.[83] This peace is maintained in the Soul because it is now God who acts through her, without her human will or motives getting in the way:

> if she does any exterior thing, it is always without herself. If God does His work in her, it is by Him in her, without herself.[84]

---

77 This is described as the Trinity being imprinted into the Soul at creation, now activated and fuelled by Love; see *Mirror* ch. 50, p. 128.

78 *Mirror* ch. 89, p. 165. The gift of free will from God 'without a why' and its reciprocation from the creature is paralleled by gratuitous 'chinam' faith in Job.

79 *Mirror* ch. 69, p. 144.

80 *Mirror* ch. 118, p. 191.

81 *Mirror* ch. 89, p. 165.

82 *Mirror* ch. 117, p. 187.

83 *Mirror* ch. 118, p. 192.

84 *Mirror* ch. 81, p. 156.

Porete illustrates this phenomenon with the metaphor of fire transforming iron into itself because it is the stronger element.[85] The result is that the 'iron' of the annihilated Soul can act now only out of the 'fire' of God's essence – Divine Being, Will and Action are one. The affections of both human spirit and reason have lost their tenure, for now when the Soul acts virtuously, or charitably, this action is motivated by eternal Love, that is, by God's Love working in her. There is no human 'pay-off' for her wilful self-seeking desire, and the character 'Reason' dies in shock at the Soul's contemplation of eternity without lack, for God's 'sufficiency' has no lack;[86] this is just too much for human logic.

Thus far, Reason personified has been an important tool for bringing the Soul through the early stages of spiritual learning, acting as a necessary foil in the Dialogue.[87] A comparison could be drawn between Porete's use of Reason and the role of Job's so-called 'Friends', but in the *Mirror* Reason represents explicitly the institutional church and its unrefined understanding of scripture, which the author suggests has misled many souls.[88] Reason's intellect, as an element of created being, is limited, and he cannot grasp the teachings of Divine Love. The annihilated Soul, on the other hand, is 'in possession of free being' which she can never lose.[89]

The commentary in the Epilogue asserts that this stage of annihilation is not reached without a painful struggle on the Soul's part. The climax of this struggle, when she decides there is no turning back, is depicted as a courtly trial of love comprising three torturous challenges which require her to will situations which are contrary to her own will.[90] Unable to respond, she faces a paradox: on the one hand, she can accomplish God's will only if she *changes* her own will; but on the other hand, if she changes her will, she would still be doing her own will, because the essential nature of God's will is that it is *unchanging*; it is the characteristic of humans to have a shifting will. The only resolution for the Soul is that she relinquish her will to God, whence it came. The discrepancy in nature between human will and divine will (changing and unchanging respectively) underlines what Porete has earlier proposed about the 'identity' with God that annihilation brings: this identity is not one of nature, but one of being. Lady Love explains:

> I am God by divine nature and this Soul is God by righteousness of Love. Thus this precious beloved of mine is taught and guided by me, without herself, for she is transformed into me.[91]

85 *Mirror* ch. 52, p. 130.
86 *Mirror* ch. 87, pp. 162–3.
87 Babinsky (1993), pp. 33–4.
88 Robinson (2001), p. 35.
89 *Mirror* ch. 118, p. 193.
90 *Mirror* ch. 131, pp. 211–15.
91 *Mirror* ch. 21, p. 104. See also ch. 43, p. 123.

Because the Soul at this stage is 'hidden' within God, sin cannot come near her because it is not possible for God to be penetrated by sin.[92] Thus she is at peace, having left behind the 'warfare'[93] that was taking place with her own will, a conflict which was driven by her strivings against vice and which brought constant reproach from a guilty conscience. Love describes for us the difference between the two states:

> There is a great difference between the sweetness of peace, which surpasses all senses and which remains in the delights of full sufficiency the Lover gives through the juncture of love, and the war which creates reproach. One who remains in will is often in such a war, whatever good works his will might do. But that one has peace who remains in willing nothing where he was before he had will. The divine goodness has no reason to reproach him.[94]

The peace of Stage Five incorporates moments when Stage Six occurs. This is a complete overcoming of the Soul by the highest power in a 'ravishing', when God gives God-self to God-self within her, 'without appropriating anything' from her.[95] Like the description of divine union given by other mystics, Porete's is highly erotic, but her version denies that God takes any power from the Soul and incorporates the integration of transcendence and immanence. This integration is encapsulated by Porete's unique term for God, the 'Far-nearness', or the 'loingprès', the Trinity who is within her, and yet far from her. The Soul is so empty of herself in 'such an abyss of humility which she has within her',[96] that she actually cannot see God: rather, God sees Godself in her (as a 'mirroring' of the divine), and so the Soul is transparent or 'clarified'. This movement also happens only at God's initiative[97] and is able to happen because the Soul has become goodness (God) by means of goodness (God): God can now see the divine goodness in her, therefore *she* is not there:

> And so nothing is, except He who is, who sees Himself in such being by His Divine Majesty through the transformation of love and goodness poured out and placed in her.[98]

While this is a foretaste of heaven beyond material existence and concludes the Soul's earthly contemplation of God's Being, it is not the indescribable glorification that Stage Seven of the journey will bring:

---

92 *Mirror* ch. 44, p. 124.
93 *Mirror* ch. 44, p. 124.
94 *Mirror* ch. 111, p. 183.
95 *Mirror* ch. 118, p. 194.
96 *Mirror* ch. 118, p. 193.
97 *Mirror* ch. 61, p. 138.
98 *Mirror* ch. 118, p. 194.

> The seventh stage Love keeps within herself in order to give it to us in eternal glory, of which we will have no understanding until our soul has left our body.[99]

This unknowable dimension of Love is characteristic of the *Mirror*'s strong apophaticism and accounts to some extent for its complexity, and the author is in fact explicit within the text about the difficulty of speaking of these divine things:

> This book has been created by human knowledge and the human senses [which] know nothing about inner love, inner love from divine knowledge. My heart is drawn so high and fallen so low at the same time that I cannot complete this book. For everything one can say or write about God, or think about Him, God who is greater than what is ever said, everything is thus more like lying than speaking the truth.[100]

Because Stage Six is a short-lived glimpse of the indescribable eternal glory of Stage Seven, its intensity prevents the Soul from remaining there for long, and so she returns to Stage Five. This echoes the return to normality as described by Brueggemann after the breathtaking intensity of the Theophany in Job,[101] but the annihilated Soul is no longer able to revert to earlier stages 'for God has sanctified His name within her and there the Trinity is at home'.[102]

The lasting effects of annihilation, of being 'unencumbered' of the self and the Soul being at home with God, will be addressed later, but now in light of Porete's account of spiritual transformation, I will highlight points of resonance with the concept of *Transformation* from the survivors' interviews.

Building the Theory: Transformation

All nine interviewees described their faith journeys as long, painful struggles. Each began their journey at what Porete would name 'Stage One', being baptized into the Christian faith and having either a family church background, or influence from Christian friends or teachers early on. Later in life they each made a personal commitment which brought extra, and for some heavy, involvement in church work, correlating with Porete's Stage Two when evangelical dedication takes hold. That said, I will not attempt an exhaustive categorization of the interview data into all of Porete's stages, or make a judgement on how far each interviewee might have come along the path to 'annihilation'. This would undermine the basic tenet of my methodology in which I refuse to impose an external framework on what the interviewees said. Rather, I will point out some remarkable parallels between the survivors' stories and Porete's central themes of relinquishment of

99 *Mirror* ch. 118, p. 194.

100 *Mirror* ch. 119, pp. 194–5.

101 Brueggemann (1997), p. 392.

102 *Mirror* ch. 22, p. 104.

self-justification by 'works', the 'trial' of the will followed by peace and *special experiences* of God's love that transform. These parallels will strike not merely verbal similarities, but deeper resonances.

First, Lydia's interview shows clearly the theme of relinquishment of self-justifying works. She spoke candidly about multiplication of her works in order to feel pure and clean, and about her obsessive need to serve, even at the expense of her family, and we saw in the last chapter how this was comparable with Job's Prologue piety. The relinquishment of this hyperactivity was accentuated when, at a point of crisis, Lydia's vicar took away all her ministry. While this was a situation beyond her control, she nevertheless accepted, and furthermore endorsed this imposition of external authority. Her receipt of prayer ministry at that difficult stage brought her the consolation of healing,[103] but it was not until she reached the depths of 'humiliation' at the time of her husband's imprisonment that she experienced God's total presence: in Porete's terms, the opposites of Lydia's own wretchedness and God's goodness put her in a place where she experienced a 'profound, overwhelming sense that God said it [doesn't] matter because Jesus is holding your hand'. She exclaimed that for her this was 'one of those moments when you *know*'.[104] This was a point of no return for her, and brought a revelation that Lydia has held onto. She describes herself now as one who has been crucified with Christ, and she is 'facing only one direction', with 'no plans of [her] own', which corresponds to Porete's identification of the annihilated Soul as Christ-like 'exemplar'.[105] On relinquishing control to God, Lydia acknowledges that, 'God, Jesus and the Holy Spirit are not ones for answering your prayers how *you* want them, but are in the business of being in it'. The *Mirror*'s Trinitarianism will be addressed more fully in the next section, but this statement suggests that the presence of God, Jesus and the Holy Spirit gently challenges Lydia's will, but accompanies her in difficulty. Lydia went on to describe the annihilation of her plans and her subsequent total dependence on God as a 'privilege', which is not far from Porete's concept of 'nobility'.[106] Regarding this 'privileged' knowledge, Lydia reflects:

> I don't think you can impart [this] to someone without them finding it or God choosing to reveal it to them. You can only point them in the right direction.

This strikes a chord with Porete's assessment of the concept of annihilation:

---

[103] Even before annihilation occurs, Porete maintains that those living fully the life of Spirit (sad souls) receive healing and the ardour of their spirit has 'healing powers' (*Mirror* ch. 90, p. 166).

[104] Lydia's emphasis.

[105] *Mirror* ch. 109, p. 181; ch. 117, pp. 186–7.

[106] See p. 123 and n. 59.

> If you do not understand, I cannot help you. This is a miraculous work, of which one can tell you nothing, unless it is a lie.[107]

A difficult dimension of Lydia's journey was the sense she had of 'falling into the pit' and thinking that she could never fall any lower, yet she did. Even so, she found there, underneath everything, 'God's everlasting arms', which has echoes of the 'abyss' where annihilation and full encounter with God's love occurs.[108] A further resonance is how in retrospect Lydia has puzzled over her earlier obsessive strivings which bore fruit, despite them being initiated by her own will and not by God's will. She theorizes that because God's essence is Love, he blesses human strivings for the good anyway. This echoes Porete's idea about a work that 'when the intention is truly for the sake of the love of God, it is very difficult for it not to yield some fruit, unless the work be evil'.[109]

Second, Miriam's interview contains the theme of the 'trial' of her will. She related how at a time when she was very isolated and her marriage unstable, her faith and intense desire to serve God became bound up with her feelings towards an abusive minister who lavished attention on her and professed his love for her, claiming that this love was pure and was the will of God.[110] A key moment came when Miriam chose to relinquish this intense exploitative relationship, a choice that shows great inner resolve, because extricating oneself from this type of abuse is extremely difficult for two reasons: the minister has a 'godly' status, and the parishioner has invariably been forced into a position of isolation from the community.[111] I suggest in what follows that Miriam's experience at this point of relinquishment *resembled* the challenge that Porete's Soul faces in the courtly trial, which is a threefold test of the will, culminating in her 'love' being surrendered. The Soul had to imagine knowing that:

a. God would be pleased if she should love another better than God;
b. God could love another better than her;
c. God loves her less than someone else loves her.[112]

Porete describes the result of this trial as 'martyrdom', after which the Soul has 'departed from [her] infancy'.[113] I am setting aside here the fact that Miriam is of course relinquishing the minister and not God, first because I understand both tests to be a challenge to the distortion of *human* love, and second because the intensity

---

107 *Mirror* ch. 132, p. 216.

108 *Mirror* ch. 34, p. 123.

109 *Mirror* ch. 124, p. 204.

110 See MACSAS (2010) on predatory clergymen targeting vulnerable, (usually) female parishioners.

111 Kennedy, M. (2003).

112 *Mirror* ch. 131, pp. 211–15.

113 *Mirror* ch. 131, pp. 214–15.

of desire on the Soul's part and on Miriam's part[114] are comparable. Miriam explained how excruciating it was that she had to face the idea that:

a. she must choose her marriage over this minister;
b. perhaps the minister really might love/choose his wife/ministry over her;
c. her husband was really the one with whom she had to sort things out, even though she felt uncared for by him.

Although it was not *her* will, Miriam chose to relinquish the relationship anyway because she knew that it was right to do so; that is, she changed her will for the sake of 'real' love, and she was, in her words, 'devastated' by the loss.[115] Subsequently her healing began with a *special experience* of God's election:

> I had this picture of Jesus proposing to me, wanting me, choosing me, personally, that was really amazing, and I just felt, if Jesus chooses me, what do I care about anyone else whether they choose me or not?

This 'election' as spouse nudged Miriam into evaluating the difference between divine and human love, and she apprehended that real spiritual consolation is not about intensity of desire, and certainly not about emotional manipulation, but about peace.[116] Likewise, the *Mirror* refers to God as the Soul's spouse[117] and stresses that the 'land of freeness', the 'country of absolute peace',[118] unfurls when one relinquishes one's own will. Only then does the Soul stop making desperate attempts to win love by reasoned method or creating love by human desire, since both these actions are works of the human Virtues, not of Love. It is only divine Love residing in the Soul 'at repose' that accomplishes the work of true Charity, without human effort or desire.[119]

---

114 It is important not to make the same error as church hierarchies by judging Miriam in this and in what follows. She was the *victim* in an extremely abusive situation.

115 Kennedy, M. (2003) stresses the deep loss for a parishioner in this situation, because in losing an intense relationship that gave her self-esteem, as well as losing her church community, she feels as if she has lost God.

116 Making reference to Gerald O'Mahoney's *Finding the Still Point* (Guildford: Eagle, 2002) Miriam explained ecstatic consolation as being at the furthest point from peace; Porete likewise warns against seeking consolations because 'whoever would wish the comforts of God through the feeling of consolation, the consolations will impede the enterprise of Fine Love' (*Mirror* ch. 26, p. 108).

117 For example *Mirror* ch. 19, p. 102; ch. 36, p. 117.

118 *Mirror* ch. 52, p. 130.

119 *Mirror* ch. 6, p. 84. Interestingly, since Miriam's traumatic experience she has started worshipping with the Quakers, appreciating there what appears similar to the *Mirror*'s spirituality outlined in ch. 9, p. 87.

An important issue that I must signal here, but which will be addressed more fully in Chapter 7 is the following conundrum: what is the relationship between 'annihilation' as a positive form of spirituality and enforced (or manipulated) 'surrender' that is abusive? Furthermore, can the action of 'surrender' to a more powerful being, even though this is God, ever be positive for a survivor of abuse? That said, the description of divine work/movement in the annihilated Soul at rest, at its height in Stage Six, bears remarkable similarity to the *special experience* of God's initiative and 'overpowering' which Naomi and Joanna described. Both women found these events difficult to explain, resembling the apophatic statements found in the *Mirror*, which regularly assert the impossibility of conveying divine knowledge in words.[120] Naomi described her experience of being overwhelmed by God's love as follows:

> There was somebody here – I don't know whether I was asleep – there was somebody here who I knew was heavenly. Whether it was God himself or whether it was an angel, I don't know, but it was a real presence and it took me into this place, and I couldn't see – there [were] very bright lights – but I knew there were lots of people there and they were singing, and the singing was just lovely. I just felt that my heart would burst.

Along with the 'repose' which Naomi seemed to be in, not knowing whether she was asleep, the presence of bright light recalls Porete's Stage Six when 'a ravishing Spark and Light joins her and holds her very close'.[121] In addition, the 'unseeing' nature of Naomi's experience is similar to God's Love taking the annihilated Soul up into the Trinity,[122] where she cannot see herself because of the deep abyss of humility which she has within her: 'Nor does she see God on account of the highest goodness which He has.'[123] Moreover, God's initiative is described by Porete as:

> the Divine Goodness pour[ing] out from (His) bosom, one rapturous overflow of the movement of Divine Light [which] … dissolves this will into God … not being able to place itself there without such Light.[124]

The bliss of being bathed in light was described as follows by Joanna when she spoke of her *special experience*:

---

[120] See Slee (2004), pp. 76–9 on apophaticism as a characteristic of women's faithing strategies.

[121] *Mirror* ch. 68, p. 143.

[122] *Mirror* ch. 122, p. 201; ch. 138, p. 220.

[123] *Mirror* ch. 118, p. 193.

[124] *Mirror* ch. 118, p. 191.

> I was in this beautiful golden sea and Jesus was there … [we were] all of us standing in this golden sea, and just this beautiful, beautiful light; oh and it was just, I can't put it in words it was just so beautiful.

In her narrative about a time when she had been suicidal, Joanna described God's intervention as follows:

> I wasn't asleep because I was sitting bolt upright in the bath … there was just this like, total distance, such a distance just keeping me in this place until I'd got over that feeling that I wanted to do this.[125]

It could be argued that Divine Love as described in the *Mirror* 'dissolved' Joanna's will into God's own will, giving her life, and her sense of God being close by intervening, yet remaining at a distance, strikes a direct chord with Porete's unique term for God as the 'Far-nearness'.[126] Similarly, Lydia described God as 'so close and yet so far', conveying the apprehension of God's real but unknowable presence. Thus we now turn to the identity of this God.

In the Lady's Chamber: God and the Soul

> O very high-born one, says Love to this precious pearl (Marguerite),
> it is well that you have entered the only noble manor.[127]

I argued earlier that the *Mirror* can be viewed as offering the voice of an alternative theology, with a two-fold challenge to the conventional mind-set of the era. These challenging aspects of Porete's treatise are clearly demonstrated in her doctrine of God. It is true that her close engagement with dominant ecclesiastical discourses surfaces in a largely orthodox Trinitarianism with a profusion of dogmatic formulations,[128] and her main characterization of God as Love and the Soul's heavenly spouse closely resembles beguine spirituality. However, there are some unconventional, and one could argue even original aspects which underlie both discourses.

---

125 The water Joanna was sitting in was freezing cold when she 'came round' from this experience. Unable to find a more suitable term, she called her state a 'trance'.

126 The 'loingprès'.

127 *Mirror* ch. 52, p. 133.

128 For example, the Father's ungenerate origin is referred to in *Mirror* ch. 67, p. 143, and the dense Augustinian formula: 'He is who is, because He is what He is of Himself: Lover, Loved, Love' appears in ch. 113, p. 184. On the *Mirror*'s deep commitment to Trinitarianism see Orcibal (1969), Epiney-Burgard and Zum Brunn (1988), Randall (1995) and Babinsky (2003).

First, the *Mirror* asserts the *triple* nature of the Son in that the Son's identity as a human being has a body and a soul, the latter being the place where the will resides; this furnishes him with three natures, not two as per Chalcedon, these natures being one physical, one spiritual and one divine.[129] This theological idea is idiosyncratic to Porete, but it proves important for her soteriology because according to her the will is the crucial factor in sin, not the body. Being joined to the Son facilitates our salvation because God 'joins human nature to Divine Goodness in the person of the Son in order to pay the debt which we had committed by our unrighteous will'.[130]

The second unconventional aspect which sits alongside its orthodox Trinitarianism, is the *Mirror*'s espousal of the purely perichoretic nature of the Trinity, with the Holy Spirit portrayed as the main actor of the Godhead. While perichoresis is not *un*-orthodox, its non-hierarchical character has often not been achieved in patriarchal theologies. 'Subordinationism' within the Godhead, and in particular the downgrading of the Holy Spirit, has accompanied both Eastern and Western traditions in Trinitarian theology.[131] Indeed, Catherine Randall sees the *Mirror*'s portrayal of the Trinity in action as Porete's 'prolonged and thoughtful dialogue with church doctrine' in which she employs 'literary techniques to illustrate, empower, and expand traditional theological positions'.[132]

Third, Porete thoroughly dismantles the medieval Church's concept of a God who demands virtuous service and charitable works of human effort. She pushes the boundaries of God's love till they disappear and the Soul becomes identified with, but not erased by, the divine. The Soul then acts as co-worker/lover/redeemer with God, and furthermore, the nature of the Soul, by virtue of this intimate relationship with God, is endowed with eternity like her Creator in that she returns to her pre-existent state in the Trinity, an idea clearly influenced by neo-platonic philosophy.[133] This vital concept was particularly misunderstood – or misconstrued – by the theologians who condemned the articles from her book, as it evidently was by the beguine community, and the apparent abdication of the Christian Soul's need to act in charity has brought Porete wider criticism for advocating a sort of quietism. We will return to this issue when I address *Knowing ministry*, but first I consider the nature of God and of the annihilated Soul. Since 'Love' was the main attribute attached to God by the interviewees, I will proceed by outlining the *Mirror*'s understanding of God as Love and God's action through the Holy Spirit. Next, I show how the concept of God's united, unbounded presence within the annihilated Soul, who realizes her virtual existence in the Trinity, resonates with

129 *Mirror* ch. 14, p. 96.

130 *Mirror* ch. 111, p. 183.

131 On Eastern and Western subordinationism and the down-grading of the Holy Spirit, see Weinandy (1995), pp. 8–9, also D'Costa (2000), ch. 1.

132 Randall (1995), p. 230.

133 Robinson (2001), p. 57.

the major category *God's timeless presence*. The role of the will in the annihilated Soul's identity with God then sheds more light on the interview data.

The *Mirror*'s fundamental understanding of the nature of God is as self-giving Love, and this 'noble' Love seeks union with Her creatures. Much is made by feminists of Porete's characterization of God as predominantly female,[134] but this is not as relevant here as the dynamic nature of God as ever-present Love; in fact God's gender in the *Mirror* appears inter-changeable.[135] Although the genre of courtly love lyric is seen as the literary expression of the early development of the ego-subject in late medieval European culture,[136] and furthermore that Porete's use of 'nobility' as metaphor for true love in the court of heaven has been judged as signifying an elitist doctrine,[137] it is then surprising, and in my estimation more relevant, to find that the *Mirror*'s society is an inclusive community with a proliferation of diverse figures in dialogue. Apart from Lady Love, Reason and the Soul, the Father makes an appearance, as do the personifications of Divine Righteousness, Discretion, Faith, Hope, Charity, Truth, Courtesy and even 'Nobility of the Unity of the Soul'. Interestingly Reason, Unrighteous Will and Holy Church the Little,[138] who prove obstructive to the Soul's journey, dwell nevertheless within the court of heaven. While Lady Love (God) presides, these figures who are often acerbically criticized,[139] are included in Her paradise, even as murderers are, should they ask for mercy. The Soul wonders in fact at God's generosity in granting paradise even to fools and villains.[140] A further intriguing aspect is that the characters supplement each other and can even speak for one another with no loss of their own identity. For example in chapter 66, Love speaks on behalf of the Soul, and in chapter 88, Reason's speech is taken over by Lady Love. This dynamic interplay is compared by Randall to the nature of the Holy Trinity, and in support of her argument she quotes Colin Gunton, who proposed that in God 'there is no breach between the "one" and the "many", because of the part played by the person conceived relationally'.[141] Randall reminds us that 'persona' from the Greek 'προσοπον', originated in the vocabulary of drama and so Porete was, in her theatre of God's court, 'recuperating' the notion that conveys the meaning of underlying persons in one God rather than 'reforming' it.[142]

[134] For feminist interpretations see Hollywood (1995); Lichtmann (1995); Newman (1995, 2002).

[135] See quotation below at n. 163.

[136] Newman (2002).

[137] See Robinson (2001).

[138] Porete's term for the institutional Church.

[139] For example, those who live by Reason are called 'donkeys', *Mirror* ch. 68, p. 143.

[140] *Mirror* ch. 121, p. 197.

[141] Quoted from Colin Gunton, *The Promise of Trinitarian Theology* (Edinburgh: T&T Clark, 1988), p. 192.

[142] Randall (1995), p. 244.

God, who eternally desires relationship as Trinitarian deity and moreover who is limitless, unconditional Love,[143] is seen as synonymous with his limitless Goodness. Limitless Goodness and Love invariably gives where there is need, because it is not in God's essentially just nature to deny needy souls:

> He is total goodness, and one must give alms to the poorest lest one take from them what is theirs by right. Now God cannot do what is unjust, for then He would destroy Himself.[144]

This Goodness which connects with the human soul, is identified elsewhere in the *Mirror* as an attribute of the Holy Spirit,[145] and Goodness personified is seen both as agent of creation and as agent of annihilation.[146] Moreover, Goodness is synonymous with the *gift* God gives:

> [God] retains what he also gives, that is, the great gifts which he has to give are the same things which were never given ... Love has so much to give and so sets no limit to it; in one moment she makes of two things one.[147]

On this passage Babinsky notes that Porete's radical understanding of God being equal to God's gifts means that 'to receive the gift of grace is to receive God'.[148] Grasping this idea is crucial for understanding how union with Love, the 'most High', comes about; that is, union comes about through an act of the Holy Spirit which effects the Soul's transformation into God by the condition of God's Loving act, which then dissolves her into himself:

> Since I possess His total goodness, thus I am the same as He is through the transformation of love. For the stronger transforms the weaker into itself.[149]

The notion of the identification of the Soul with God who works within, leads to the next consideration: that the *Mirror* describes God's united, unbounded presence within the Soul which requires her to divest herself of material, rational and affective impediments. This divestiture is one of the *Mirror*'s leitmotifs: the annihilated Soul becomes naked, 'nue', before God,[150] which is an erotic, but safe and peaceful place to be. It is safe because God wants only her good and

---

143 Unconditional because the Soul believes that 'it is without return that He has given me His love', *Mirror* ch. 122, p. 201.

144 *Mirror* ch. 117, p. 187.

145 *Mirror* ch. 11, p. 89.

146 *Mirror* ch. 111, p. 184 and ch. 118, pp. 191–2 respectively.

147 *Mirror* ch. 77, p. 150.

148 Babinsky (1993), p. 227 n.62.

149 *Mirror* ch. 117, p. 188.

150 For example, *Mirror* ch. 54, p. 130; ch. 89, p. 165.

'she cannot fear anything if God dwells in her. For He is everywhere present, omni-potent, omniscient, and total goodness'.[151] The paradoxical state which then arises, the Soul's elision into God, is totally affirming and positive, and is helpfully addressed by William Corduan who uses the term 'sublation' for this phenomenon. He argues that because the term 'annihilation' carries negative connotations in English theological discourse of condemnation to non-existence, 'sublation' is preferable as it 'carries the double meaning of negation of self while being absorbed into something higher'.[152] Even so this concept will require further attention in the next chapter as there are questionable aspects to absorption, suggesting the idea of self-effacement, an issue I have already raised in the previous section. Here we merely observe that annihilation brings an overriding sense of God's presence because 'appropriately, one finds something in the place where it is, and because [God] is everywhere, this Soul finds Him everywhere'.[153]

Porete understands God/Love as the only *true* reality, on whom human existence and destiny are contingent, for 'God is Who is, from whom all things are, and [the Soul] is not if she is not of Him from whom all things are'.[154] Since God's 'Being' is integrated with his Love and Goodness, the Soul's union with Love gives her true 'Being' and this has enabled her to leave her nothingness: 'this conjunction places the Soul in being without being which is Being'.[155] The Soul has been moved there by God/Love, for she cannot lift herself,[156] and this action gives her God's 'sufficiency', or completeness, and she needs nothing else.[157] Simultaneously the 'stripping away' brings Porete's Soul into the security of 'repose', to the place where she was in the beginning. Her free will, God's great gift to humanity from God's Being and substance, and the only part of us that is not of material nothingness, is repositioned whence it came,[158] and therefore it is re-fused with God, whose Being is eternal. Thus one becomes 'unencumbered' of oneself for eternity[159] by willing God's will, which always was the return of his beloved 'nakedly and freely, without a why':[160]

> [The Soul] sees by Light that the will must will the Divine Will alone without any other will, and that for this purpose this will was given. And thus the Soul removes herself from this [*that is, her own*] will, and the will is separated from

[151] *Mirror* ch. 5, p. 84.

[152] Corduan (1992), p. 516.

[153] *Mirror* ch. 30, p. 110. Compare this with Miriam's experience quoted on p. 78.

[154] *Mirror* ch. 118, p. 191.

[155] *Mirror* ch. 115, p. 185.

[156] *Mirror* ch. 118, p. 193.

[157] Perhaps this completeness parallels the inner integrity/completeness that Job finds in God, in being 'תָּם/*tām*'; see Ticciati (2005b), p. 155.

[158] *Mirror* ch. 118, p. 191.

[159] *Mirror* ch. 127, p. 208.

[160] *Mirror* ch. 89, p. 165.

> the Soul and dissolves itself, and (the will) gives and renders itself to God, whence it was first taken, without retaining anything of its own, in order to fulfil the perfect Divine Will.[161]

This idea of God's eternal presence now resident in the Soul brings us to the third consideration: the concept of the 'will' which is so central to the process of annihilation. The generous gift of free will stems from God's desire for our freeness:

> Uncreated Goodness possesses properly of herself free will and she gives us free will also by her goodness, free will beyond her power, without any why except for our sakes that we might be of her goodness. Therefore we have will, departing from her goodness and outside her power, in order for us to be even more free.[162]

Moreover, God cannot and does not *demand* this gift of free will back from us:

> He has freely given me my will, and thus He cannot repossess it if it does not please my will. The supreme height of Love has given me such nobility by her goodness through Love that she can never take from me the freeness of my will if I do not will it.[163]

In other words, at Creation God has gratuitously put part of Herself into the human Soul's keeping, and with this comes the opportunity to be united with Her, if we choose to render this will back to Love; this union gives the Soul a true *eternal* freedom, equal with God's because we share 'willingly' in God. This lofty position brings peace, security and nourishment. Beforehand, by contrast, 'this Soul always had warfare as long as she retained the will within her outside of her being',[164] that is, in human strivings outside of her *true* being in God.

Paradoxically, a significant aspect of the process of annihilation appears to be the absolute depths of 'wretchedness' which the Soul sees in herself and which has been caused by her removal of her will from God. In other words, human action apart from God always leads to such wretchedness, for God's eternal will is not in it, and this will is therefore changeable. It is God's constant (non-forceful) Goodness and Love which simultaneously negate and fill this wretchedness, because of the incredible 'largesse' of the divine.[165] In annihilation the human will is synchronized with the divine will, which always only wants good, and so the Soul, whose separate human will and desire are now melted away into nothing, is also exemplar of always only wanting good, characteristically doing God's will.

---

161 *Mirror* ch. 118, pp. 191–2.

162 *Mirror* ch. 111, p. 182.

163 *Mirror* ch. 103, p. 176.

164 *Mirror* ch. 118, p. 192.

165 *Mirror* ch. 80, p. 155.

For me this begs further questions regarding survivors' spirituality which are related to the important issue already raised about the paradox of surrender and annihilation: Have those who have been abused already had an experience of 'divestiture' which similarly leads to annihilation, when the boundary of their will has been crossed or negated (in violence), in their case without a choice? Can divine will more easily cross damaged boundaries, than boundaries that are more intact in non-abused people? More crucially, can divine will repair the damage of violence because God's love is greater than – or at least as great as – the wretchedness of the perpetrator? We will return to these questions in the next chapter when considering the relationship of power and powerlessness in abuse. For now we note that for Porete, the 'melting' of human will into God's will results in a form of radical obedience, since God, eternally present in the Soul, performs works of perfect Charity through her, while she remains in perfect peace. Indeed the *Mirror* reminds us that a state of love from which true charity flows cannot be achieved by human effort; it can only be achieved by God because 'a work of charity was never accomplished by a human body. The ones who accomplish such a work could not accomplish it by themselves'.[166] God is now the Soul's house-mate, but before considering the 'accomplishing of Love's will'[167] and the outcome of annihilation in terms of action, we turn to the interviews for a comparison of Porete's view of God with that of the survivors.

Building the Theory: God's Timeless Presence

In her description of God, interviewee Sarah echoed some of what we have observed in the *Mirror*. She said that for her, 'God is love and everything good, and all goodness is from God'. Alluding to the Holy Spirit's role in her journey of faith she explained:

> this is where God comes from within and this is where the inner strength is. I didn't learn about God from the outside; I think he developed me from within.

Sarah related an incident which illustrates her belief about the Spirit within: she was once asked to preach in church without any notice, when the minister was taken ill at the last minute. She attributes the powerful sermon she gave to the Spirit who 'takes us over and does what it wants with us, when it wants to, when it's needed'. She drew the conclusion from this that 'when God needed somebody to preach his word, he found somebody' and for Sarah this was not a negative experience, but an empowering one. Furthermore, the direct presence of 'God within' is apparent for her particularly when she prays, for she mused, 'surely it can't be me that's praying?' In a similar vein, for Esther, being totally dependent on God, means letting go of all her problems and anxieties:

[166] *Mirror* ch. 71, p. 146.

[167] *Mirror* ch. 7, p. 85.

> You have to let go … letting go and letting God. [I think] I'm in charge … but no, you've got to let God be in charge and let him take over.

Esther repeated the phrase, 'let go and let God' several times, and also said that at the crisis point which transformed her life, 'all [she] had then was God'. Like Porete's Soul, complete dependency on God and exposure to him in their anguish is not seen by these survivors as negative or submissive; rather this dependency is experienced as bringing healing, peace and self-worth. Lydia expressed this type of dependency by saying that she now 'lives only for God'. The process of healing was explicitly linked by Lydia and Esther to God being their secure place, when all else has been lost, or taken away.

I mentioned earlier the immense loss in Lydia's story and how the healing of her loss had brought her insight into her earlier struggles to achieve. Porete's Soul laments similarly:

> Alas, I have not left this work for Him (to do)! For if I had allowed Him to do what was pleasing to Him, He would have freed me as soon as He gave me this thought about Himself. But I did not wish that He heal the fear of such a loss (of myself). My thoughts have made me follow many false steps: I think to find Him by my works, but I will not accomplish it, nor do I accomplish it, except through loss.[168]

Furthermore, reliance of the Soul on God's 'sufficiency' is echoed by Lydia when she explains her complete trust in the Holy Spirit, which now involves:

> every day wanting that potential space [within all life from conception] to be completely filled to saturation with his Spirit to empower and direct that day, and then relying on the gifts of the Spirit when we need them, when necessary – whatever [God] think[s] I'll need I will gratefully receive it.

Lydia made the following connection between her new awareness of God's presence with her through trauma and the text of Isaiah 43.2:

> 'When you pass through the waters I'll be with you, you will never be consumed by the flames. You are my child and I love you with a perfect love' … that just expresses the truth that you're not cremated and you're not drowned.

The annihilated Soul is described in the *Mirror* as the 'phoenix',[169] and passing through flames is also a metaphor used by Porete for the Soul's transformation into God's ardent love:

---

168 *Mirror* ch. 127, p. 208.

169 *Mirror* ch. 11, p. 89.

> Such a Soul, says Love, is so enflamed in the furnace of the fire of Love that she has become properly fire, which is why she feels no fire. For she is fire in herself through the power of Love who transforms her into the fire of Love.[170]

The ardent Love of God shared with the Soul was referred to by Miriam who related Jesus several times as 'lover' and as a 'friend' who is 'equal to me'. After being exploited sexually by her minister, she feels she has learnt so much more about God's real love:

> I think romantic love has its place. But the love that I think of as being God's love is the love of everything, everyone. Everything is included in it and it's love that includes justice, peace, truth, respect, equality – that is the love that God is. I can forget all the other stuff that had been twisted and tried to be turned into something else, and just believe in the love of God that I've learnt even more about through the experience. So God is love.

While Porete certainly uses romantic love to convey her message, Miriam's experience of distorted romantic love perhaps echoes the *Mirror*'s critique of normative female spiritual practices, warning us that the involvement of human will and desire can, and does, deceive.

A further striking resonance between the *Mirror* and the empirical material is found in Naomi's interview. Having struggled throughout her life with enormous trauma, she reported the following:

> As I've got older, I realize that really it all comes down to free will. *God gives us the choice of free will and people choose the outcome of their life and God is a gentleman. He's not going to step in and change things for me or for anybody else because we each have our own choices to make* and many people make the wrong choices but that's their fault. It's not God's fault. He's offered the way.

The emphasized portion echoes plainly how the *Mirror* portrays noble, chivalrous love. God does not change God's will, which is for us to dwell in peace in Her court; neither does God enforce a change of human will, for he is a 'gentleman' according to Naomi, therefore enforcement would overcome the very freedom he has bestowed upon us. However, we can become one with God's will by relinquishing self-will, although freely choosing God's will does not mean we are one with it by our own effort. What freely relinquishing human will does mean, is that God can transform us into himself, and this union brings his will into the world 'in us, by him in us, without ourselves' as Porete would say.[171] Do we choose to carry on our own wilful way, or do we 'let go and let God', to use Esther's words? Fascinatingly, these survivors who might find such a choice excruciating,

170 *Mirror* ch. 25, p. 107.

171 *Mirror* ch. 81, p. 156.

who have had their will overcome when they were at their most vulnerable, are actually willing to let God use them as agents. So we turn now to what the *Mirror* says about *Knowing ministry*; what agency does the annihilated Soul have in comparison with the interviewees?

Charity Begins at Home: The Difficult Works of the Virtues

Assessment of the process of annihilation and the nature of eternal Love has shown that at the heart of Porete's theology are the key concepts of the primacy of faith in God's Goodness, and the insufficiency of works which are motivated by human will. To evaluate how these themes are cashed out in terms of ministry is difficult, because practical details in the *Mirror* are sparse, since its crucial assertion is that the annihilated Soul is 'unencumbered' of works, and that what she does is motivated purely by Love/God. Therefore to assess the Soul's ministry would be in reality to assess explicitly God's work in the world. I will proceed therefore by considering first what the annihilated Soul does *not* do, and then by suggesting three specific aspects of 'annihilated' ministry which can be found implicitly in the *Mirror*.

According to Porete, 'works' must not be the result of a prayer bargain in which either God grants or blesses what the Soul asks for, or the Soul does what she *thinks* is God's will. This type of prayer bargaining is illustrated by Porete's satire of 'merchant' souls who are always seeking a return on their virtue, and the observation undergirds her downgrading of the Virtues from their usurped position as masters of the Soul.[172] She asserts that their rightful place is to be the servants of Love. In this, Porete starkly challenged the acts of penance and the pursuit of virtues which were central to 'orthodox' female spiritual discourse, and as such her 'heresy' is highlighted by the first indictment cited in the condemnation of 31 May 1310, one of the three which Romana Guarnieri connected with the *Mirror*:

> That the annihilated soul is freed from the Virtues and nor is she any longer in their service, because she does not have them as far as their practice is concerned, but the virtues obey according to her good pleasure.[173]

What Porete perceived was that true Virtues are not to be practised as a demonstrative, desirous way of obtaining divine love, but that they *result* from spiritually mature love, as Michael Sells explains:

> Apophasis of desire results in a radical conception of selfless love, deity as love, and authenticity as involving acts that are ends in themselves rather than means.[174]

---

[172] *Mirror* ch. 6, ch. 8 and ch. 21.

[173] Quoted in Verdeyen (1986), p. 52.

[174] Sells (1994), p. 118.

It is possible that Porete's thinking may have been influenced in this by the work of William of St Thierry, who considered the virtues 'as ordinary *consequence* of our deification in Christ'.[175] Porete underscores the uniqueness of God's creative initiative and ability by explaining that

> it is necessary that [God] do this without me, just as He created me without myself by His divine goodness ... for the purpose of working between Him and me and the difficult works of the Virtues ...[176]

She seems to say more about what practices the Soul *no longer* does than what she does do as a result of a return to her pre-creation 'nothingness', in that 'she does not pray, no more than she did before she was',[177] and

> such a Soul neither desires nor despises poverty nor tribulation, neither mass nor sermon, neither fast nor prayer, and gives to Nature all that is necessary, without remorse of conscience ...[178]

It is clear how this would appear antinomian, and was judged so by the Inquisition who were given this quotation as one of the indictments taken out of context from her book.[179] However, if the excerpt is reunited with what actually follows it in the *Mirror*, we see that it is because God is now identified with the Soul that she can only but act in a well-ordered and 'lawful' fashion, for God can do no other:

> ... such Nature is so well ordered through the transformation by unity of Love, to whom the will of this Soul is conjoined, that Nature demands nothing which is prohibited.

She does perform rituals out of 'good habit',[180] but Porete clearly anticipated negative ecclesiastical reaction to this attitude because she uses Reason to question the Soul's repudiation of the spiritual practices which Reason argues are the 'food of holy souls'. Love answers this criticism:

> This is true for those who beg; but this Soul begs for nothing, for she has no need to desire something which would be outside of her. Why would this Soul desire

---

175 Epiney-Burgard and Zum Brunn (1988), p. 19, emphasis added.
176 *Mirror* ch. 111, p. 183.
177 *Mirror* ch. 136, p. 218.
178 *Mirror* ch. 9, p. 87.
179 This indictment is found in the *Continuation of the Chronicle of Nangis*. See Verdeyen (1986), p. 90.
180 *Mirror* ch. 7, p. 85.

> these things … since God is surely everywhere …? This Soul has no thought nor word nor work except the practice of the grace of the divine Trinity.[181]

The 'practice of the grace of the divine Trinity' indicates the Soul's two-fold knowledge that accompanies annihilation: on the one hand she knows the grace of God's presence which negates past hurts, sins and wilfulness; and on the other she knows that she does *not know* God at all, and cannot know God at all. Such knowledge puts her at rest and this restfulness negates anxiety about the present:

> This Soul has no anxiety about sin which she might have ever committed, nor about suffering which God might have suffered for her, nor about the sins or anxiety in which her neighbours remain.[182]

In other words, annihilation annihilates both will and desire, and therefore by extension sin (which is engendered by free will) and anxiety (which is generated by desire).

Having established her 'knowing' apophatic spirituality in general, I suggest there are three specific ministries that the annihilated Soul naturally engages in which are evangelistic, educational and pastoral respectively. First, as evangelistic 'exemplar', other souls may come to see God's total goodness in her, and the realization of this goodness becomes the trigger for their annihilation. She humbly qualifies this by stressing that they see this goodness not because of her good works, but because of her absolute wretchedness:

> The salvation of every creature is nothing other than the understanding of the goodness of God … Nothing was ever understood if not my wretchedness. Since the divine goodness is understood by them through my wretchedness, and their salvation is nothing other than understanding the divine goodness, therefore I am the cause of the salvation of every creature, for the goodness of God is understood by them through me.[183]

Second, the author assures us that the book was written with an educational motive to help the 'little ones' expand their intellect and to understand the spiritual journey. It is difficult to avoid the idea that Porete speaks directly through the central character of the Soul when she acknowledges her own need for teaching:

> When Love saw me think about her, on account of the Virtues, she did not refuse me, but instead she freed me from their petty service and guided me to the divine school.[184]

181 *Mirror* ch. 16, p. 99.
182 *Mirror* ch. 16, p. 99.
183 *Mirror* ch. 117, pp. 187–8.
184 *Mirror* ch. 122, p. 198.

She also expresses the paradox that speaking of God didactically is more like lying than real divine knowledge, and in satisfying Reason's questions throughout the Dialogue the Soul realizes that she has probably been vindicating herself.[185] Through writing, however, she realized this book was indeed Love's action, unencumbering the author's Soul in the process, and teaching her that nothing of human will can compare with true divine knowledge,[186] which she nevertheless is trying to convey to her community. Third, a pastoral attitude of silence, non-judgment and equality are coincident with 'martyrdom of the Spirit', leading to the 'high' life of peace. The following lengthy excerpt from the Trinity's praise of the Soul, and her response, illustrates her new position which echoes some of the aspects of Job's Epilogue community:

> Now have you tasted my feast,
> And you have savored our wines,
> Says the Holy Trinity,
> No one but you knows how to speak of it
> And thus you will not be able to give your heart
> In any other practice for any price.
> I pray you, dear daughter,
> My sister and my love,
> Through Love, if you will,
> That you no longer will to tell the secrets
> Which you know:
> The others will condemn themselves because of it,
> Where you will be saved,
> Since Reason and Desire govern them,
> And Fear and Will.
> Know, however, my chosen daughter,
> That paradise has been given to them.
> *The Chosen Soul:* Paradise? says this chosen one, would you not accord them something else? Thus indeed murderers will have it, if they wish to cry for mercy! But in spite of this I will keep silence about it, since you wish it.[187]

Love's broad *boundaries of justice and equality* are shown in that few come to annihilation, but all are saved through God's grace, and those who fail now to see and accept God's unconditional love will receive the same gift of paradise. Inability to accept God's love brings no retributive or eternal judgment and Love wills that the Soul is quiet about what she knows because reasoning, logic and

[185] *Mirror* ch. 97, p. 171.

[186] *Mirror* ch. 119, p. 195. She calls the work of this book 'small', whereas it seemed such a great thing originally; echoing perhaps Job's recognition of his 'smallness' (see p. 78).

[187] *Mirror* ch. 121, pp. 197–8.

words keep souls in fear and control. As in the analogy of the farmer who has tilled the ground and must wait for the seasons to do their growing work, after the earlier preparatory stages of the journey she now needs to remain 'silent and at rest' so that God can do his work.[188] This life is called the 'peace of Charity', which includes obeying nobody but Love; abandoning one's own needs and attending to the need of others; having no shame, fear or anxiety; being unbowed by anything that might happen to the self; and giving to all what one has of worth.[189]

Building the Theory: Knowing Ministry

Porete's belief that a developed spirituality entails relinquishing unnecessary practices surfaced in the interviews. The *Mirror*'s three implicit ministries of evangelism, education and pastoring are equally relevant, especially what might be called spiritual 'attentiveness' to others. The following comparison between the interviews and the *Knowing ministry* of the annihilated Soul illustrates each in turn.

First, regarding religious practices, Miriam was originally energized for ministry through her experience of the Holy Spirit and now, feeling no compunction about ritual and church structure, she worships with the Quakers where silence and equality of views about God are respected.[190] Naomi still worships in a mainstream denomination and follows spiritual practices, but maintains that her faith is not dependent on the Church:

> I discovered [my faith] in the Church, but I don't think the Church is always helpful. It isn't dependent on going to church, it isn't dependent on the Bible. It's dependent on my little relationship with God.

Second, helping other survivors was the overarching reason for all nine women deciding to participate in this study. In this respect, Joanna conveyed an evangelistic motive of wishing to share with others her knowledge of the presence and love of God which she had experienced in the depths of her despair, offering an example to others of how her 'wretchedness' is still a place where God can be encountered. Educationally, Naomi feels called to the ministry of leading others into a deeper spiritual relationship with God, a ministry for which she has been censured. Porete's Soul knew she would face similar opposition[191] and accordingly, Sarah and Miriam have been robbed of their teaching/preaching ministries even though they have theological gifts which have been shaped by their hard experiences. Sarah criticized the rational and detached way in which church authorities responded to spiritual needs rather than instinctively and compassionately reaching out. Porete's view that the Soul is 'closest to the Far-nearness, when she no longer

188 *Mirror* ch. 124, p. 206.
189 *Mirror* ch. 4, p. 82.
190 See excerpt from Miriam's interview in Chapter 4, p. 78.
191 *Mirror* ch. 122, p. 200.

takes Holy Church as exemplar in her life' and that she is operating 'under the work of Humility',[192] because no longer governed by Reason, strikes a chord with Christians like Sarah who are dissatisfied with ecclesiastical bureaucracy and protocol which often get in the way of effective pastoral response.

Finally, attentive spirituality is a quality that has been discerned in the prayer ministry of interviewees Lydia, Priscilla and Esther, as well as in the Job of the Epilogue. Their attitude reflects an open, silent, listening, non-judging, non-evangelizing and giving love that eases the anxiety, fear and suffering of others. This type of ministry is demonstrated in the following excerpt from Esther's interview where she spoke about the phone call she had made that morning to the mother of two boys who had already had a double mastectomy:

> Now she's had secondaries in her spine and in her sternum and she was terrified. Well, spinal surgery is very frightening. So I phoned her up and I said do you want to talk about it? I told her how fantastic they'd been to me, and I would have been in a wheelchair now if they hadn't done that surgery. So I said, when you go in, when they give you an anaesthetic, and they say you must count to ten, don't count to ten. Just say to yourself, All will be well, all will be well. Oh, she said, I'll do that ... This girl, she's having her operation today, and I said can you remember that? She said, yes, I'll remember that, what a good idea, she said. And she's not a Christian. I didn't tell her that was Julian of Norwich. I just didn't want to. So hopefully she'll remember to say, All will be well, all will be well.

Esther epitomizes the life of 'the peace of Charity' in which the Soul 'cannot bow on account of anything that might happen to her'.[193]

Integrated Living: The Prophetic Legacy of Marguerite Porete

Geneviève Souillac argues that Marguerite Porete's 'prophétisme' is clear from the *Mirror*, because her book is testimony to the dual prophetic process of seeing and saying; that is, central to the text is the cognitive understanding of contact with the absolute, coupled with the drive and responsibility to transmit the message that has been understood.[194] As with all true prophecy, Porete's words show this 'dual demand, this feeling of being pulled in two directions, of participating in two dimensions'.[195] Belonging to a specific concrete historical milieu, Porete certainly lived in sharp tension between her God and the medieval world. This holy woman's life, writing, execution and the subsequent fate of her text, mirror in myriad ways

---

192 *Mirror* ch. 134, p. 217.

193 *Mirror* ch. 4, p. 82.

194 Souillac (1998), p. 267.

195 Souillac (1998), p. 271.

the turbulence of her environment, for she did not compromise her drive to integrate the paradoxical and 'to deliver the absolute in relative terms, to make the dialogue between eternity and time co-exist between the prophet and the world'.[196]

It could of course be said that prophets are known by their results, by the fruit of their spiritual gift, and so what can we deduce from Marguerite's grisly death and virtual oblivion? She did not survive the abuse meted out to her, and accordingly Rubin reminds us that Porete 'uncannily' alluded to, and embraced, the fate that was to be hers[197] only a few years after writing the following:

> This Soul is scorched through mortification and burned through the ardour of the fire of charity, and her ashes are thrown into the open sea through the nothingness of her will.[198]

Perhaps what we can deduce for the present, is that testimony given by Christian survivors of abuse about their relationship with God has provided direct and fresh evidence of the value of a theology of annihilation, and we can agree with Gert Groote who observes that when 'something holy is being said', there is an irreplaceable 'directness and freshness of the mother tongue'.[199] Indeed the contemporary interviews show that the spiritual experience of these nine survivors echoes that of a medieval woman who foresaw the abuse she was to receive at the hands of the Inquisition, and said it anyway in her native French.

Did the divine reside in this prophet? The encounter of the annihilated Soul and God as we have examined it in this chapter has raised important issues about free will and the surrender required in order to be at home with the God of love. Such integrated living, which enables a flowering of ministry, will be discussed further in the next chapter and so after all, despite her brutal end, Porete's prophetic ministry may not yet have ceased bearing fruit.

---

196 Souillac (1998), p. 271.

197 Rubin (1993), p. 176.

198 *Mirror* ch. 85, p. 160.

199 Cré (2000), p. 38.

Chapter 7
The Authentic Spirituality of the Annihilated Soul

Introduction: Boundless Love, or Love of Being Bound?

Lucia, a married woman, has a chance encounter with a concierge in a conventional Viennese hotel. She realizes immediately that she has met this man before and her intense, erotic love for him is rekindled. Maximilian visits Lucia and reveals his passion for her. The film *Night Porter*[1] proceeds with a series of flashbacks to over a decade before, and we learn that during the Second World War, Max had been a doctor in the Nazi concentration camp where Lucia had been a Jewish prisoner. In the camp he had singled out Lucia and abused her physically and sexually while other inmates looked on, silently and impotently. Both perpetrator and victim survived the war. What is shocking is the choice Lucia now makes of giving up her secure married life to live with the night porter in his flat as his willing partner. They become imprisoned in this space, locked into a devoted relationship in which he takes care of her, and feeds her. Finally, in a bid to escape the encroaching threat from the group of war criminals who wish to keep the past buried, Lucia and her lover walk out into the street, hand in hand. He is dressed in his Nazi uniform, she in the girlish dress she had worn on entering the camp. Rather than be separated, they court assassination and are indeed gunned down, annihilated together in their grotesque and scandalous love.

Night Porter was, and is, a controversial film, not merely for its depiction of a sado-masochistic relationship between a Nazi officer and a Jewish victim, but for deep ambiguities in its sexual characterization of Lucia. Director Liliana Cavani has been accused by Rebecca Scherr of misreading the lived experiences of survivors of the Holocaust, in that she abstracts these events into a work that 'center[s] on the erotic female body', and offers a narrative that 'grossly misrepresent[s] historical facts, by transforming the memory of the Holocaust into a "sexy memory"'.[2] With this in mind, it has been incumbent on me to proceed with care when describing the stories of survivors of abuse and their relationships. For in the last chapter I suggested that there is something of an 'erotic' and unbounded relationship between the annihilated Soul and God. The bizarre image created by the all-powerful, yet intimately loving Max and the childlike passion of Lucia, is one which strikes a disturbing chord. What is missing from their claustrophobic

1 *Night Porter*, directed by Liliana Cavani (Criterion Films, 1974).

2 Scherr (2000).

relationship, however, is any sense of freedom to grow, move out and share their 'love'. They are doomed to a symbiotic relationship that can lead to no other end but death; they are not called out to the vibrant, individuated life which we would see as healthy for survivors.

In the interviews, Joanna reflected on how her childhood in an abusive household and her sexual assault by a priest had rendered her open to further attacks as an adult. Esther spoke to me about coming to terms with how, during her early years in the concentration camp, she had been 'conditioned for humiliation'; in her opinion this had led to her submissive acceptance of long-term psychological and physical battering from a brutal husband. Lydia explained how her personal boundaries were changed by the sexual abuse she had suffered as a child, resulting in difficulties setting healthy boundaries as a teenager and adult. According to the emerging grounded theory in my study, such experiences of human boundaries left shattered by abuse appear somehow to have facilitated, or at least been accompanied by, open boundaries with God. Although for each of these women openness to God has been transformative, has healed to a greater or lesser extent the effects of abuse, and has enabled them to help other people and to deepen their relationships, some important questions remain unresolved. These questions concern the true nature of survivors' relationship with God and I must now attempt to address them. In what follows I will try to discern in this spirituality the fine line between abusive human bondage and the contours of a boundless relationship with a powerful 'Other'.

The first raft of issues concerns the possibility that the survivors might be repeating unhealthy patterns in their relationship with God, rather than manifesting an authentic, transformative spirituality. That is, does their dependence on God denote an erasure of human will comparable to, and a repetition of, the experience of abuse? Is their unbounded experience of God a further submission to a powerful 'Other' who overwhelms? In addition, when aligning the survivors' spirituality with the spiritual discipline of annihilation, is there a difference between crossing boundaries by *choosing* to render the will to God, and the boundary of will being violated *without a choice*?

Second, if the experience of abuse can produce an authentic spirituality resulting in positive transformation and transformative ministry for survivors, is suffering and/or abuse a prerequisite for this, or any, authentic spirituality? Taking this a little further, does God indeed 'will', or at least condone, abuse *in order that* human beings can have knowledge of God, and therefore do God's bidding in the world? To put this in terms of atonement theology, are self-sacrifice and abuse necessary in order for God to be present in the world and for authentic ministry to happen?

Finally, an issue relating to the community of believers, are those who hold the boundaries of ministerial practice themselves boundary-less in God's presence? How open are the leaders of Christian community to their own re-creation in God? For if the Church's ministry is founded on authentic spirituality, do we see evidence of 'annihilated souls' at work? And if so, where do we see them at work?

As a way of proceeding, I will bring these questions into dialogue with contemporary debate in feminist theology which centres on issues of autonomy and vulnerability. I will first address the paradoxical concept of 'surrendering agency' as captured by the survivors' living faith and dependence on God, and which is echoed in Porete's *Mirror*. Second, I will show how Sarah Coakley's review of the Pauline 'hymn' of Philippians 2.5–11 resonates with the spirituality of the survivors as a 'kenotic spirituality' which 'holds vulnerability and personal empowerment together, precisely by creating the "space" in which non-coercive divine power manifests itself'.[3] Subsequently, a differently nuanced reading of the Philippians passage will turn the conventional focus from pre-occupation with Christ's self-sacrifice to the key theme of resurrection in a way that develops Coakley's concept of 'kenosis'.[4] I present this kind of spirituality as 'listening with the Other', an attentive listening within God's timeless presence, which can form the foundation for authentic Christian praxis in community. This praxis resonates with the characteristics of a healing Church as suggested by the interviews, and by the Epilogue ministry of Job. Third, all these considerations culminate in a discussion which focuses on the paradox of God's presence which is immanent within, but transcends the limitations of creation. I suggest that God's 'holding company' for the violated can be discerned at the edges of human boundaries, a potentially transformative location where creation is free from bondage, and God is free from the connotations of a 'power' that crushes or symbiotically controls the other.

Subsequently in the final chapter I will offer some concluding comments about who might provide spiritual 'holding company' for others in our risk-conscious society. I will also address there the implications raised by my study about the difficulties met when the interviewees have offered themselves for ministry, which surely for survivors is a generous and God-motivated action, full of 'largesse'.[5]

Surrendering Agency

In contemporary Western culture where choice and autonomy are of paramount importance, how can dependence on God be consistent with the need for agency, particularly for those whom I have argued have been the victims of patriarchal values and entitlement? How can the openness of the vulnerable soul to a powerful 'Other' be different from an experience of violation? Yet the grounded theory seems to suggest that complete 'surrender' of the will, whether this surrender is by choice or by violation, results in a comparable spiritual effect. We saw particularly how in Porete's *Mirror* the process of annihilation, that is, *choosing* to relinquish one's will to God, has strong correlations with the spiritual experience of survivors whose will was at some point taken over *forcibly*; direct experience

[3] Coakley (2002), p. 5.

[4] Meaning 'self-emptying', as discussed shortly.

[5] *Mirror* ch. 4, p. 82 and ch. 37, p. 117.

of God's timeless, transformative presence, when the boundaries of the self are down, appears to have equivalent significance in both situations. This implies that the element of *choice* has little relevance regarding the receipt of direct spiritual experience of God; rather the diminishment of boundaries and the relinquishment of will are the factors which count. In relation to Job, it could be argued that in the Prologue he *did not* choose the abuse that came upon him, while at the end he *did* choose to surrender himself to silence, and he experienced God's presence in both circumstances. The point I am making is controversial, and clearly I am not suggesting that abuse is at all acceptable, just because it might have the same positive result as a life of spiritual discipline. Rather, what I am suggesting is that experiences of abuse and advanced spiritual discipline bring us by default into the identical 'spiritual space' where boundaries are relinquished and will 'surrendered'.

That surrender of the will seems a more relevant concept in authentic spirituality than choice might seem reactionary to a contemporary outlook that views the exercise of choice as central to our identity,[6] and personal power as sacrosanct.[7] It may even seem counter-intuitive to my feminist stance in this book, in which I have argued that women need to be released from the oppression of male entitlement and *lack* of agency. Accordingly, Daphne Hampson has argued that feminism requires unequivocal female autonomy, or self-rule, and that Christianity is necessarily heteronomous because it is centred on a transcendent God; thus a spirituality which involves vulnerability and dependence on an external God is inappropriate and inauthentic for women. Notwithstanding deconstruction of patriarchal imagery, Hampson maintains that relating to a God who is 'other' can only mean subordination, since the 'apartness' of a transcendent God presupposes hierarchy.[8] Her position begs the following questions, however: Are vulnerability and autonomy necessarily mutually exclusive? Are ideas of hierarchy, subordination and 'obedience' in relation to God, experienced as fully present but 'other', relevant anyway? For if it is possible to have autonomous selves relating mutually as different human beings can each with the other, as Hampson suggests happens in feminist meetings,[9] then why not with God who is 'other', unless the 'being' of God is something she does not wish to relate with mutually, or cannot relate with mutually? By eschewing otherness or transcendence in God, Hampson

---

[6] See Peter Ward's argument (2002), p. 73 that people now seek meaning through exercise of choice so that their lifestyle choices and consumer purchases shape their identity; he maintains therefore that the spiritual quest is driven no longer by need, but by desire.

[7] See William Schweiker (1995), p. 212 on late modern post-theism in which, he argues, meaning and value are created by human agents in a 'morally neutral' and materialistic world. The acquiring of human power as the source of agency required to create and project 'reality' on the world is therefore 'the first imperative of such an outlook'.

[8] Hampson (1996b).

[9] Hampson (1996b), pp. 14–15.

is led ultimately to locate her deity in a deep dimension of the self.[10] But might not this deity of Hampson's equate with the patriarchal God, the male narcissistic idol,[11] who is a symbiotic projection of the self, and not truly transcendent or 'other', no matter how deep that dimension is?

In what follows, I explore the possibility that personal agency and surrender of will to God are not mutually exclusive. I also argue that dependence on God is not subordinate dependence as if on a perpetrator of abuse, for that would entail continuing to accept the implications of patriarchal theologies that present God as an abuser,[12] or at least as an extension of human power. It was very clear from the research participants that the God on whom they depend and to whom they are open is not abusive, but a God of love who allows them to be who they are, patiently nurturing them. Gendered nomenclature was not a particular problem overall, but the patriarchal traits of overbearing domination and coercion in God's behaviour were denied by all the interviewees. Commensurate with feminist Christian theology the concept of God as conquering, powerful Lord had been relinquished, thus the survivors' dependence on God does not necessitate being beaten into a submissive 'surrender' to God in defeat, or being trapped in a symbiotic, inward-looking relationship; rather it involves relationship with positive, life-giving Presence that also empowers human relationship with others. The consensus was that God is to be trusted, and the parameters of their relationship with the divine are safe and healing. Similarly in Porete's *Mirror* we found a spirituality that does not demand self-harm, but advocates a surrender to a 'gentle' or 'noble' God, like that of melting into a lover.[13] Thus surrender to God appears to be different from surrender to an abuser, for it is not in God's nature to abuse.

However, what about the person's agency? Is the power of God merely *over*powering, bearing in mind that the adjective 'all-powerful' was almost universally attributed to God by the interviewees? And how can we be sure that God is not abusing the privilege of unbounded intimacy with creatures? The difficulty of holding dependence and agency together is discerned by Alastair McFadyen in his analysis of feminist theology. He acknowledges the importance of 'right relation' for the achievement of a differentiated self by means of deepest mutuality with others. That is, right relation from a feminist viewpoint is neither a flight into the female sin of 'sloth' as dissipating self-abnegation toward others, nor an aping of the patriarchal sin of 'pride' as unbridled self-assertion over others, but a 'proper economy of the self in relation'.[14] He also addresses the problem that feminists like Hampson have with the notion of grace given 'from outside'

---

10 Hampson (1996a).

11 See McFague (1987) and Burrus (2000).

12 In addition to the feminist critiques of atonement theologies as divine child abuse and Trible's *Texts of Terror* on the abusive nature of the biblical God which have already been noted, see Gerard Hughes (1985), p. 34 for a presentation of God as a terrifying uncle.

13 *Mirror* ch. 80, pp. 155–6.

14 McFadyen (2000), p. 155.

by a more powerful entity, a transcendent God, with whom it is impossible to have a mutual relationship on an equal footing. His radical resolution is based in his comparison of the relational dynamics of abuse with the action of the will in Augustine's theory of original sin. In the Augustinian theological system, will that is forcibly conscripted nevertheless involves a *contribution*, or participation of personal will, because Augustine understood personhood and will to be inseparable. This participation of the will holds true, even in a situation in which a person is not to blame morally, since apportioning blame comes within a *moral* framework of personal responsibility, to which a victim of abuse cannot be, and must not be, subjected. Thus, according to McFadyen, when the victim's will is conscripted into abusive acts, there necessarily occurs her personal participation in the abuse. Indeed in Chapter 2 we noted how the conscription of the victim's will in 'allowing' abuse to happen produces great difficulty at the third stage of recovery, when there is a need to accomplish self-forgiveness for being part of the abusive situation. In a similar vein, feminists have become aware of how women under patriarchy do collude with the powerful in their own oppression; they have had to do so in order to survive, and this involves unavoidable co-operation in what are pathological relationships. It is, then, possible to have a colluding relationship with someone more powerful in which the will of the less powerful person is in *co-operating* action.

The theological point I am trying to make is that these relationship dynamics may be paralleled in a relationship with God, but in this particular case, the 'person' with whom we are relating is not equivalent to an abuser. McFadyen argues that relationship with God reorients the will distorted by pathological human power relations because, in contrast, it is *empowered* by the Holy Spirit rather than disempowered; the consequence is that the person's will becomes good, in and of itself:

> This goodness which results from the Spirit's action really is the will's own goodness and the resultant action also belongs to the will as its own.[15]

This concept closely correlates with the transformation of the Soul through the Holy Spirit in Porete's *Mirror*, the Soul stating plainly that 'since I possess His total goodness, thus I am the same as He is through the transformation of love'.[16]

But how is this not a form of symbiosis, and by extension abusive? The key issues to address are the results of the transformation relationship and the nature of God. Pathological relational dynamics of *abuse* lead to a distorted self. This distorted self becomes isolated, is controlled, and unable to relate or speak to others about the abuse; the self inhabits a constricted place where transcendence and joy are 'blocked'.[17] Perpetrators of abuse do not seek a true relationship with,

[15] McFadyen (2000), p. 176.

[16] *Mirror* ch. 117, p. 188.

[17] McFadyen (2000), p. 237.

or nurture the *particularity* and *individuated* self of the victim,[18] and this begs the question therefore: Is the interviewees' unbounded relationship with God likewise symbiotic, leading to distorted and disoriented identities, in which case it would be abusive? Clearly the effects of the interviewees' relationship with God have to be the decisive factor. We have heard the interviewees speak universally of a God of love who builds their self-esteem, has broken the bounds of their earlier understanding of a remote, demanding, censorious God, and also of their own transformation into *agents* of speech about this love, of reaching out to others in need and most crucially, of being able to re-establish healthy boundaries with others. Their agency in work, family relationships, ministry and seeking justice is clear, and even when in some cases they have been rebutted, their struggle carries on. Although it could be dismissed as a subjective judgement about the women, I have to add that I regularly found in my encounters with the participants a vibrancy, hospitality and love of life that totally belied the dreadful experiences they had suffered.

Finally, McFadyen's thesis asserts that the human will is unreliable and alterable, since concrete pathologies of abuse strongly suggest that

> willing is entwined with relational, social and structural processes and dynamics that have the power to shape identity, interiority and life-intentionality and to confuse the internal mechanisms and criteria by which decisions are made.[19]

The unreliability of the will is also powerfully illustrated by Porete's three trials of the Soul,[20] as outlined in the previous chapter. Thus, both writers agree that action in conjunction with God's will, which is *unalterably* good, is true agency for this action can only ever be good, and motivated by love. Agency as separate from God is not true agency at all, for it is buffeted by any power games or relational structures that are influencing human will at the time. Hence when the will is with God 'where it ought to remain',[21] it is constantly, timelessly good. This does not denote a self-effacing absorption into God,[22] but a *sharing* of power and the capacity to love in a relationship that is non-competitive.[23] For both the annihilated Soul and the interviewees, this is the life of faith: co-operating with the God of love, as united agents of love, owning the act together.

---

18 See Poling (1991), p. 104 for his analysis of symbiotic merging of perpetrator and victim.

19 McFadyen (2000), p. 172.

20 *Mirror* ch. 131, pp. 211–15.

21 *Mirror* ch. 118, p. 191.

22 Recalling Corduan's definition of the term 'sublation', see p. 138.

23 McFadyen (2000), p. 164.

Listening with the Other

What is the hallmark of this life of faith? How is dependence on God lived out practically and with integrity? In order to explore these questions, I consider 'kenotic' spirituality as evaluated by Sarah Coakley who wishes to challenge, and offer a corrective to, liberal feminism by rescuing the important spiritual paradox of 'losing one's life to save it'.[24] By developing the passage Philippians 2.5–11 from which the term 'kenosis' is derived,[25] I then move the discussion on to the concept of 'kenosis' as spiritual praxis in community, and in communion with God.

In correlation with the argument in the previous section, Coakley believes that the main objection to 'kenotic spirituality' is associated with the horror in our Western culture of any form of vulnerability and submission, because the 'surrender' involved can only be viewed from the perspective of cost to personal freedom.[26] In feminist theology this has resulted in a doubly negative understanding of 'kenosis' which reflects McFadyen's analysis of 'the pathological dynamics of abuse'. For on the one hand Rosemary Radford Ruether compares 'kenosis' unfavourably with forms of bullying found in the 'masculinist' world, while on the other Hampson reduces it to 'self-destructive subordination' for women, for whom 'the theme of self-emptying and self-abnegation is far from helpful as a paradigm'.[27] Coakley believes that misunderstandings about 'kenosis' have led to flaws in both Radford Ruether's and Hampson's approaches. In order to clarify exactly what she is arguing for, she categorizes all the past understandings of Christ's 'kenosis' since Chalcedon into six broad interpretations,[28] explaining that misapprehensions have been common throughout the history of commentary on the Philippians passage. The six options are:

> Christ relinquished his divine powers;
> Christ pretended to relinquish divine powers;
> Christ, as human, chose never to have the wrong sort of worldly powers;
> Christ revealed divine power as humble;
> Christ took on human flesh without loss or restriction;
> Christ experienced a temporary withdrawing of certain divine characteristics.[29]

---

24 Coakley (1996), p. 83.

25 Since Philippians 2.7 contains the only New Testament appearance of the verb κενόω (*kenóō*), meaning 'I empty'.

26 Stogdon (2007).

27 Quoted in Coakley (1996), p. 82.

28 The complication of *divine* emptying only became significant after the Council of Chalcedon in 451CE, with its commitment to Christ's dual nature and to divine omnipotence and omniscience; in other words, the question had to be asked: which nature was being emptied, and of what? See Coakley (1996), pp. 90ff.

29 See Coakley (1996), pp. 89–96 for a summary of the readings.

Coakley selects an interpretation of 'kenosis' that is loosely compatible with the third option, suggesting that the 'emptying' is located in Christ's *human* choice never to grasp worldly power, and this becomes normative for humanity. With this explanation she hopes to bridge the gap between Ruether, who aligns the attitude of the self-emptying Jesus with feminist values because it challenges patriarchy, and Hampson who suggests that only for men 'kenotic' spirituality might be an appropriate antidote to the male problem of needing to dominate. Interestingly, Coakley's understanding of 'kenosis' is based not on a comparison with the narrative of scripture, despite post-war twentieth-century scholarship which largely connects this passage with gospel narrative,[30] but on her own personal experience of contemplative, wordless prayer. In silent prayer she believes space is made for the 'unique intersection of vulnerable "non-grasping" humanity and authentic divine power, itself made perfect in weakness'.[31] This spirituality she calls 'practising the presence of God',[32] which is precisely the term used by survivor Priscilla to describe her prayer life. For Priscilla, moreover, God's presence is a constant and can be accessed by her at any time.

To extend Coakley's interpretation of empowering wordless prayer, I now offer a differently nuanced reading of the Philippians passage. By setting this passage in the wider context of κοινωνία (*koinōnía*), meaning 'community/fellowship/communion/partnership', and by shifting our perspective from a focus on the *suffering* of Christ to that of the *resurrection*, I suggest that in this epistle the apostle Paul is alluding to his own encounter with God in the resurrected Christ, and to his own subsequent spiritual praxis. By urging this praxis on their communal life, Paul was encouraging the Philippians into the attentive post-resurrection spirituality that he was working out for himself in 'fear and trembling' (Phil 2.12) as the basis of Christian community action. This is what was exemplified by Christ's 'kenosis'.

Coakley concentrates on the seven verses of Phil 2 which, since Ernst Lohmeyer's analysis of its strophic structure in the 1920s, have been viewed universally as a liturgical hymn, interpolated into the letter.[33] Her sharp focus on these few verses is inevitable, since the Christological battles that she set out to analyse have been centred round that all-important term ἐκένωσεν (*ekenōsen*) in verse 7. Therefore the dimension of community spiritual practice is skimmed over, yet the keynote of the whole letter is κοινωνία (*koinōnía*).[34] Sharing in the 'fellowship of the gospel' (Phil 1.5) and contributing to this collective work are crucial (Phil 4.14–15), underlining Paul's view that 'love must be embodied in

[30] See for example the parallel drawn between the Philippians passage and John 13.3–17 in Hawthorne (1983), p. 78.

[31] Coakley (1996), p. 110.

[32] Coakley (1996), p. 108.

[33] Coakley (1996), p. 85.

[34] Martin (1974), pp. 46–50.

action'.[35] References to community relationships are plentiful throughout the epistle: Paul calls the Philippians his 'partners' and 'fellow-workers' in the gospel (1.7; 4.3) and appreciates the positive relationship he has with Epaphroditus, a true companion who was sent to him from the church in Philippi (2.25; 4.18); he exhorts the Philippians that they should be of 'one spirit and of one mind, struggling together in the gospel' (1.27), and significantly he asks Syntyche and Euodia, two members of the church, to 'think alike in the Lord' (4.2). The same Greek verb φρονεῖν (*phronein*), with the same meaning 'to think alike in the Lord', is used in the first few verses of chapter 2, which form an introduction to the so-called 'hymn'; translated literally this phrase would read, 'think this in you what also [is] in Christ Jesus'.

Equally significant is Paul's expression in this letter of his longing to know intimately, 'the power of [Christ's] resurrection' and the 'κοινωνία/*koinōnía* of his sufferings' (Phil 3.10). What is striking in this verse is that the experiencing of Christ's resurrection *precedes* communion with Christ's sufferings. In this there is clearly an allusion to Paul's *special experience* on the Damascus Road that burst the bonds of his patriarchal faith, an experience that was referred to several verses previously (Phil 3.2–7); this *special experience* was the all-important event which empowered Paul to act as apostle. Is, then, the practice of communion with God through *resurrection* experience a Pauline prerequisite for ministry? Such an idea appears to be encapsulated in Paul's insistence that the Philippians should 'have the mind of Christ', stressing that it is 'God [who] is the one at work within you both to will and act for good purpose' (Phil 2.13), resonating clearly with Porete's basic premise in the *Mirror* that the annihilated Soul acts not by herself, but by God's will.[36] Could we interpret the key message of Paul to the Philippians as '*knowing God's timeless presence transforms*', because knowing the transformation of resurrection, and the dissolution of rigid conceptual and theological boundaries which accompanies God's presence, precedes Christian ministry? Was Paul encouraging the Philippians to share, like Christ, in the praxis of 'kenotic' communion with God as the basis of authentic ministerial action?

The twin themes of community spirituality and of taking the resurrection of Christ as the starting point for ministry also combine in the praxis of 'kenosis' described by Rachel Muers as a 'surrender of communicative power' before God's silence. In her attempt at rescuing silence from the passive role it normally has, subordinated to speech and to the power of the word, she advocates an active *hearing* which emulates God's listening.[37] She argues that when God hears, particularly victims such as Hagar and the slaves in Egypt, God can determine the context for human freedom:

---

35 Martin (1974), p. 48.

36 *Mirror* ch. 81, p. 156.

37 Muers (2004), p. 166.

> God's listening is integral to understanding who God is both in relation to Godself and in relation to the world and … this listening in turn shapes who people are in relation to God and each other.[38]

Drawing on Dietrich Bonhoeffer's theology, which was shaped over against the silencing power of Nazi propaganda, she argues that the only true 'place to stand' as the basis for creative, transformative silence is the resurrection of Christ. The standpoint of resurrection destabilizes any attempt at using the crucifixion as an ethical starting point for the practice of faith because as a concrete historical event, the cross can be aestheticized or instrumentalized in order to achieve certain ends, perhaps as discussed in Chapter 2 in the encouragement of self-sacrifice of the vulnerable by those in power. In contrast, the resurrection is the given that *cannot* be distorted, since it is unknowable and therefore resists systematization.[39] In a sense the resurrection is non-rational, or rather it is beyond reason. In community therefore, keeping a 'kenotic' space for the 'other' in worship or pastoral care is a way of 'acknowledging and coming to know, entering and coming to inhabit, a common place to stand before God'.[40] This place is non-prescriptive and creative and resembles the 'attentive listening' of Job which he returns in compliment to God, the Other, who attentively listened to him, and which he models in the re-created Epilogue community. For Paul, this may also be how we share in glory: by making a listening space within our humanity for God to be God with us, where we discover our true being and vocation.

Notwithstanding any complexities created for interpretation of the Philippians passage since Chalcedon, Christ's humanity does not have to be disconnected from divinity; rather, in 'kenosis', humankind and divine-kind are acting in co-operative, creative communion and this requires openness to the Other/other. This co-operative communion is something to be emulated, but as something beyond reason it cannot easily be conceptualized. So it is possible that the 'hymn' of Philippians 2 was Paul's attempt at encapsulating in poetry, rather than in technical language, Christ's practice of the presence of God as 'attentive listening', the basis for joint action. The passage is crammed with a parallelism of doubled terms and ideas, the hallmark of Hebrew poetry:[41]

Let the same mind be in you that was in Christ Jesus,
6 who, though he *was in the form of God*,
did not regard *equality with God*
as something to be exploited,
7 but emptied himself,
taking the form of a slave,

[38] Muers (2004), p. 15.

[39] Muers (2004), pp. 82–4.

[40] Muers (2004), p. 180.

[41] See Ancient Hebrew Poetry (2005).

being born in human likeness.
And *being found in human form,*
8 he humbled himself
and became obedient to the point of death –
even death on a cross.

As shown by the emphasis, 'being like God' is doubled in verse 6, and 'being in human likeness/form' is doubled in verse 7. Additionally, there is a balance between humanity and divinity, both acting in tandem:

> in verse 7 *in relation to God*: Christ *emptied himself,*[42] taking *the form of a servant*;
> in verse 8 *in relation to humanity*: he *humbled himself*, becoming *obedient.*

This is a parallelism of both action (emptying/humbling) and attitude (becoming a servant/obedient).

The word ὑπήκοος (*hupēkoos*) used in 2.8b is interesting, because although this adjective is invariably translated 'obedient', it could have the meaning 'suffering' in the sense of suffering/allowing something to happen. This is therefore descriptive of someone's attitude to an action, rather than a moral judgement of character. Thus Ernst Käsemann argues that 'Philippians 2 tells us what Christ *did*, not what he *was*.'[43] Furthermore, the verb from which ὑπήκοος (*hupēkoos*) derives means 'to listen attentively' (ὑπακούω/*hupakoúō*). To listen attentively has the sense of subordination only if one believes that taking a listener's position is a matter of subservience, as discussed by Muers. This nuance of listening attentively connects with Paul's use in verse 7 of the term δοῦλος (*doúlos*), a slave or servant, whose job it is to listen. Could this 'kenosis', so hotly debated, denote silence before God and attentive listening in the same way that God is silent and listens? Making ourselves attentively present in communion with God, as Christ did, empowers the mystery of our transformation, for 'our citizenship is in heaven'.[44]

The significance of a listening community of Christians as advocated by Muers, exemplified by Job and perhaps envisaged by Paul, reflects the type of church some of the survivors found instrumental in their healing; it also is the sort of ministry they themselves offer to others as a result of their transformation. Survivor faith, furthermore, is resurrection faith because having come through victimization and trauma, it is the experience of their re-created self, and categorically *not* the emulation of suffering, that holds them with God.

---

42 Not *of* anything as there is no genitive following on.

43 Coakley (1996), p. 85.

44 Phil 3.20a. Interestingly, the Philippians are described here as 'being' citizens in heaven recalling the same verb of 2.6, υπάρχων (*hyparchōn*) Christ 'being' in the form of God.

God's Holding Company

That Paul advocates entering an open space of communion into God's presence as a purposeful spiritual discipline rather than seeking 'suffering' for spiritual highs is underscored by the apostle's view of genuine love in 1 Corinthians 13.3:

> If I give all I possess to the poor and give over my body to hardship that I may boast, but do not have love, I gain nothing.[45]

This verse echoes Porete's disapproval of bodily mortification in the human quest for true spirituality and needs to be kept in mind for what follows. The contention that a person's boundaries being transgressed through violation can engender a spiritual experience parallel with that of an 'annihilated' Soul, still begs the question whether abuse might therefore be *God's* intention: Does God will abuse so that we can experience and know his presence, and then go on to serve him? Certainly the interviewees understood their awareness of *God's timeless presence*, and God's gifting of them for ministry to others, as emerging from the awful suffering of abuse, evil being turned to good.

In the following exploration of God's re-creating presence in dire circumstances I aim to show that God's action cannot be pinned down to divine cause and effect, and that God holds the boundaries for creation when there is overwhelming chaos, with the result that spiritual illumination and transformation are inevitable accompanying graces in dark places. By describing God as our 'holding company' I do not intend to portray God as a controlling parent company, but I draw on the aspect of this term which implies that God holds – and most crucially – shares the risk of our operating as free agents, it also incorporates the concept of the 'holding' environment that is vital for allowing survivors to develop a healthy identity by being active agents in their own recovery.[46]

In Chapter 2 I touched on Rebecca Ann Parker's testimony to the 'Presence' who limited the damage being done to her when she suffered horrific sexual violation as a child. Acknowledging the tragedy that some victims are destroyed, she nevertheless reflects on the 'salvation' she received in that terrifying moment when she thought she was going to die:

> In that moment I knew that there was a Presence with me that was 'stronger' than the rapist and that could encompass my terror. This Presence had a quality of unbounded compassion for me and unbreakable connection to me, an encompassing embrace of me and … of the man raping me. I understood that if I died, I would somehow still be with this Presence, this Presence would 'take me up', this Presence was 'greater than' death, and 'greater than' the power of the man who was raping me. *This Presence could not stop the man from killing*

45 NIV.

46 Higgins (1994), pp. 68–72.

> *me, if he chose to. And, at the same time, it could stop him.* Because, I knew, if he noticed it he would be stopped. He would not be able to continue … You couldn't be aware of this Presence and do what the man was doing to me. He only could do it by not noticing, not knowing. So, *this Presence did have the power to save me from death and there is a way in which I believe it did. The man did stop short of killing me, and I think it was because some part of him could not ultimately deny the knowledge that he was raping God. Not that I was God, obviously, but that the Presence was there and in raping me he was going against the Presence. The man was stopped by the Presence, that's what I believe.* The Presence saved my life. But he might not have been stopped. He could have killed me. Molesters do kill.[47]

The highlighted portions illustrate that Parker's experience suggests that God's presence limits damage (perhaps as Yahweh did for Job in the Prologue)[48] and holds the person in life. Parker struggles with the ambiguity that such awful experiences do in reality bring spiritual revelation, such as gifting her with personal knowledge of, and deep faith in God at an early age; this also suggests that when boundaries have been violated, victims may be rendered open to Presence in a similar way to those who undergo advanced spiritual discipline. Such spiritual discipline is of course arduous, and therefore only taken up by a small few.[49] But could this exposure in some cases be the 'only way' to healing? Indeed Parker's therapist described her client's experience of 'Presence' as comparable with what the prophets begged not to have to undergo: exposure to the dreadful vision of God, and as such beyond what a child should have to endure.[50] However, she suggests it may have been the only way for God to offer her ultimate safety.

In order to understand why human boundary violation might open one up to boundary-less relation with God and the spiritual significance of this, the following argument draws on Rowan Williams' insights on the doctrine of creation *ex nihilo*, as well as on McFadyen. As finite beings our boundaries are crucial for containing our identity. Identity is always formed in the context of relationships, what Williams terms the 'conversation' we enter at birth.[51] To maintain his/her own identity structure a perpetrator's needy action overruns the victim's boundaries. The victim's alternative reference points are thereby destroyed, and his/her identity becomes bound into a stranglehold of total dependence on this most intense of relationships.[52] The only escape from this 'bondage' is to find another equally compelling symbiotic relationship, and thus addictions (which involve being bound to a powerful substance) are often a result of abuse; it is therefore

47 Brock and Parker (2001), pp. 211–12.

48 See p. 112.

49 Reflected in Porete's alleged 'elitism'.

50 Brock and Parker (2001), p. 210.

51 Williams (2000), p. 71.

52 McFadyen (2000), p. 61.

no surprise that Cohen and Densen-Gerber found in their research that 84 per cent of the addicts they studied had been victims of child abuse.[53] The literal corollary of giving up an abusive relationship (or an addiction) and its powerful boundedness is to have absolutely *nothing* to depend on. However, there is one alternative: that is to resort to the total fundamental dependence we have as *creatures*. This creaturely dependence is a reality we normally try to avoid at all costs, because otherwise we would have to face the fact that none of us are 'free agents' at all. For in order to maintain the illusion of our self-regulating individuality and our status as givers/agents, human beings create symbiotic relationships with external objects (these can be real or imaginary), which hide our need. We thereby avoid the truth that we are creatures dependent on relationship.[54] So, I am who I am because I am (symbiotically) my car, my child, my image, my drug and so on.

An experience of boundary-less-ness, perhaps at a 'liminal' moment when our boundaries shift,[55] can feel like annihilation, a loss of identity; but in this moment a possibility presents itself. That is to say, the experience of having nothing at all to depend on can become total dependence on what appears to be in-finite nothingness, a dependence on the true ground of our being, that is, God's loving presence. Now, God does not hold us in a stranglehold; God holds us in the infinite freedom of God's self-gifting love. Because God is different from humans, completely free of the world, God does not *need* God's own identity bolstering by relationship with others.[56] This, consequently, is not a repetition of symbiotic relationship. Rather, God can *hold* a victim while a new, and free, identity is re-created out of the 'nothingness' of victim identity – an identity which is nothing because it is lost in in-finiteness or boundary-less-ness. I believe this to be what Porete described as the Soul being 'established in [her] nothingness'[57] which she understood when she realized the creatureliness of the universe.[58] Only a God who is beyond nothingness, who does not need our bondage, can 'allow' or enable this to happen.

Abuse is unequivocally not the ideal route to deep spiritual knowledge and practice, but when violence does overpower, the presence of God provides a sort of emergency 'flood plain' of spiritual breadth and depth that holds the destruction and becomes the 'only place to stand'. Here begins resurrection. Parker argues categorically that there is no *need* for any horrific experiences purely so that people can become aware of Presence; Presence is there all the time. Furthermore, if only those who suffer terrible violation have access to knowledge of God, then those untouched by violence are 'let off the hook from the call to reverence the presence

53 Cohen and Densen-Gerber (1982); see also Anderson (2005).

54 Williams (2000), p. 70.

55 See p. 77.

56 Williams (2000), p. 73.

57 *Mirror* ch. 69, p. 144.

58 *Mirror* ch. 118, p. 191.

of God in all of life'.[59] Consequently, she repudiates any idea of our 'atonement' through Christ's torture and death, claiming that there was no reason for Jesus to die violently and rise for us to know that God's creative power is greater than death, for Judaism already affirmed this.[60] God's love does not *vindicate* the violated as some kind of recognition of, or reward for their difficult and painful 'work', a view also repudiated by Porete; rather, resurrection happens as an *inevitable result* of God's accompanying presence in dark places. Williams might add, that Christ's resurrection happened because Jesus was uniquely open to divine act.[61]

As a retort to those who would suggest that the 'blessing of divine revelation' was worth the horror she experienced as a child, in the vein of 'these things are sent to try us', Parker affirms that she would gladly turn over such blessings to anyone willing to live with the awful consequences of child rape. Interviewee Priscilla, who was a victim of incest by her grandfather over several years and who acknowledged the blessings of knowing God's constant presence, love and hope that she sees as a gift accompanying her abuse, said this about her terrible experience:

> If somebody said to me, you can go back and have that not happen, but not have that relationship with God, I would go through all of that again for that relationship. I wouldn't want to change that. If it was either or, there's nothing that would make me not want to have that relationship. Although it was awful and it was horrible, I'd rather that than not have God.

These words appear to contradict Parker's stance, but it seems to me that Priscilla was not expressing a masochistic desire for abuse, for indeed we noted earlier her insistence that God does not send abuse as a test, or have a plan in which we are to be damaged and thereby taught something.[62] She also stressed in her interview that she wishes the incest had never happened. But it did. That cannot be changed. What Priscilla is perhaps trying to express, is that the irreplaceable love and presence of God which she has come to know through that experience and which she cannot deny, are now part of her identity. Once experienced, there is no going back; as Lydia remarked, she now faces 'only one way'. Abuse and its healing expose survivors to an all-encompassing, unsurpassable love that holds. It is as if Priscilla is choosing now, in the present, what she wishes had not happened in the past: her past violated will can thus be healed, because she is (sur)rendering her will by choice to God – not to the abuser – to God who is Love and with whose presence she timelessly has union in freedom, right to the extremity of any darkness and human symbiotic violation she has experienced.

---

[59] Brock and Parker (2001), p. 212.

[60] Brock and Parker (2001), pp. 212–13.

[61] Williams (2000), p. 76.

[62] See pp. 62–4.

Perhaps it is inevitable that participants in resurrecting love become themselves agents of God's holding presence in the dark places that are painful to enter because

> our openness to God is our readiness for the action of a generosity creative of community to be 'enacted' in us – our readiness, therefore to challenge and resist the making or remaking of exclusions and inequalities in creation.[63]

It may be a place to which we normally do not want to go, which we approach in 'fear and trembling'. Yet experience of resurrecting love transforms even the broken into true agents, who then by nature act in love.

One challenging question remains for me: Can even a perpetrator be held and healed? Porete believed God's goodness and love are as deep as the abyss of human wretchedness;[64] Job survived the breakdown of the violent system of retributive justice which endorsed his entitled and privileged, but false and controlling life; Lydia believes that her husband could be healed if he would choose to have the healing ministry which he avoids because, according to her, he feels he is 'past being helped'. My answer has to be a hopeful but very tentative yes, for it would mean a difficult path of relinquishing bondage and choosing freedom, of entering boundary-less nothingness, the abyss bounded only by timeless Love that lies beneath us all.

---

63 Williams (2000), p. 76.

64 *Mirror*, ch. 117, p. 187.

Chapter 8
What Lies Ahead: Conclusions and Implications

Evagrius Ponticus: A theologian is one whose prayer is true.
Naomi: There's so much further we can go.

Throughout my research, the response of senior clergy who asked about the subject of my thesis, *How Survivors of Abuse Relate to God*, usually resembled: 'that's good, because we need to know how to minister to these people'. The innate and unexamined violence behind such an attitude is breathtaking, and hence my stress at the beginning on precluding any outcome on 'how to minister' to survivors. Despite the question posed at the end of the previous chapter, this also holds true for outcomes on 'how to minister' to perpetrators. My sole intention has been to engage with theological debate by listening directly to voices of Christian survivors speaking about their faith. In the last paragraph of her book *Keeping God's Silence*, Rachel Muers relates that several people with whom she had shared her proposed project suggested that she conclude with some blank pages. She comments that the end of any theological book can indeed be an invitation to share in keeping God's silence and accordingly the end of this book might best be left as an invitation to share in keeping God's silence on the matter of abuse. There certainly is no 'Hollywood ending', and I can only offer what rainbow of hope lies in the testimony of the nine women I interviewed.

While the grounded theory has provided important knowledge about their spirituality, that *knowing God's timeless presence transforms* them, it also raised a surprising issue about the ministry of survivors. It transpired on the one hand, that having this spiritual 'knowledge' is transformative for others, and yet on the other hand survivor ministry seems absent from formal authorized positions. In this concluding chapter therefore I make some comment on these implications, particularly about why survivor spirituality might have importance for Christian spirituality in the twenty-first century, when individual choice and personal power are at a premium. There are also questions to be asked about the place of survivors in the ministry of the Church, the importance of unbounded relationship with God and appropriate boundaries with others within ministerial preparation and praxis. Although one author notes the large proportion of survivors in the caring professions,[1] I found only one article on the ministerial vocation of survivors of Child Sexual Abuse. The article was written to assist mentors in supporting the

[1] Higgins (1994).

steadily growing number of self-disclosed survivors through selection, not as an encouragement for survivors themselves.[2] This may be a lacuna in my research, nevertheless I will first consider the need for an authentic spiritual voice in a consumerist society and the apparent absence of survivors' voices in ministerial practice, which could perhaps have a reciprocal connection.

In the previous chapter, I referred to Peter Ward's view that in contemporary Western culture people seek meaning for their lives by constructing a lifestyle through their individual choices.[3] By exercising consumer choice they are demonstrating that 'spiritual hunger, desire and pleasure are just below the surface'.[4] Consequently, building on Zygmunt Baumann's concept of 'liquid modernity' Ward's vision of a flexible 'liquid' church involves replacing outdated evangelism, which has been constructed around the task of convincing people of their *need* of Christ, with a range of spiritual experiences that stimulate and feed their *desire* for God. 'Solid church' is fixed in location, serving the *needs* of those who see church as a heritage site, a nostalgic community or a refuge.[5] Although I would argue that the Church still has an extremely important role as refuge for the vulnerable, it should also be a spiritually challenging place that encourages spiritual maturity. Accordingly, Ward suggests that 'liquid church' would realize that for those wanting a profound and real experience of God, it would need to provide 'a high level of authenticity in its spirituality, and integrity in its allegiance to Christ'.[6] Thus ordained leaders who were chosen as safe 'fort-holders' of 'solid church' in the past should give way to leaders and spiritual directors perceived as being enlightened, for

> [those who] have met with God, been in his presence, found themselves changed by his Spirit will be the guides, the teachers who lead by example of their holiness, discipline, and passion.[7]

In this Ward echoes the findings of Patricia Davis' research on girls' faith which I mentioned in Chapter 3. The girls were seeking meaning but reacted against the Church's inauthentic '*Forrest Gump*' spirituality; consequently they were forced to find meaning elsewhere.[8] Christ's metaphor describing religious leaders as 'the blind leading the blind'[9] springs to mind. However, to turn that metaphor around and apply it positively to a different scenario, if I were trapped in a dangerous building at night and all the lights went out, the person I would want as a guide

2 Loftus (1986).
3 See n. 6, p. 154.
4 Ward (2002), p. 73.
5 Ward (2002), pp. 25–9.
6 Ward (2002), p. 77.
7 Ward (2002), p. 90.
8 Davis (2000).
9 Matt 15.13–14.

would be a blind person who had knowledge of all the corridors and exit routes – someone who knows their way around in the dark because they are familiar with that perilous journey.

It appears from my research that formal authorized ministry for the nine survivors I interviewed has been hard to realize; even informal ministry has sometimes been rejected and criticized as 'going too deep'. It is beyond the scope of this book to evaluate all the implications of survivors as authentic spiritual guides and there must surely be some assessment of any minister's spiritual maturity. However, I raise here three points about quality of ministry, particularly apropos Sarah's understanding of the Church's purpose which is to 'heal a broken world'. First, the healing of the survivors seems to offer some common and hopeful ground to the addicted,[10] for they understand from the inside that the pain of surrender of self is not fatal, and that the presence of God within surrender is transformative, loving and equalizing. In comparison with Schermer's observations this would resonate with the AA's 12-step path that involves trust in a higher consciousness, or God.[11] Holding a space with integrity for others to experience loss, surrender and pain is perhaps a clearer task for those who have inhabited this space long-term, and have learnt not only to live within it but have seen the grace that has blessed them *as a result* (not as a reward).

Second, I wonder how many authorized ministers have entered this seemingly desolate space in preparation for their deeply spiritual calling, whether by choice of spiritual discipline or because they themselves are survivors? Interestingly, the word Horeb, where Moses and later all the Israelites encountered God in preparation for their vocation is related to the Hebrew word חָרְבָּה (*ḥorbāh*), which means desolation or waste.[12] Might such preparation, like the 40 days of Christ in the wilderness, be crucial for those who purportedly seek the healing of this violent age? Dietrich Bonhoeffer certainly thought such ministerial preparation was necessary, springing from his theological premise of 'cheap grace' and his conviction that the resurrection is 'the only place to stand'.[13]

Third, if as Naomi reflected, we are not encouraged in, but rather discouraged from being 'real' in church, and pain must be hidden for the benefit of those who do not want to experience Presence in *all* of life, where is the community spiritual praxis that I have suggested Paul was urging as the basis for ministry in Philippi and which Job's nascent Epilogue community revealed? There *are* examples of good practice as in Tamar's and Esther's cases, and of course there are dangers, not least in the problem recounted by some interviewees of priests and counsellors who prey on the vulnerable because they have not tested their own boundaries. This relates back to the second point I have made above.

---

10 See n. 16, p. 32.

11 Schermer (2003), p. 24.

12 This is the word mentioned in Job 3.14 meaning 'waste, desolation, ruin'.

13 Muers (2004), p. 79.

There are some very important issues at stake. For if survivors are viewed only as receivers of ministry and not givers; if spiritual discipline as espoused in Porete's *Mirror*, which shows there is a path to 'annihilation' without having to suffer abuse, is disregarded in favour of self-enhancing charismatic experience and emphasis on good works (seen as proof of, rather than as result of faith); and if communities of justice and equality and 'kenotic' surrender that are completely open to God, as hinted at by Job's Epilogue and Paul's letter to the Philippians, are deemed too risky, then we may be ill-equipped to deal with our society's spiritual requirements. The present 'boundary-holders' who occupy the threshold of the Church need to be challenged. The little voices are trying to get a word in; the vulnerable are knocking on the door; those who have faced the abyss of lost identity are before the threshold. Exposure to an authentic spirituality that reminds us that we do not have all the 'right' answers is indeed terrifying, for it constantly compels us to allow that ultimately we live in nothingness. This nevertheless is the place where resurrection happens, where we rest in the transformative presence of the God of Love who is timeless, and who loves us for no other reason but that we are, and God is.

Epilogue

Since I completed the empirical research for this book, I have contacted all the participants from time to time in order to request various permissions to publish, and to keep abreast of their news. As this book is about them, I offer some of that news to the reader in this short Epilogue

Deborah was turned down a second time for ordained ministry. She is endeavouring to contribute to ministry in her local cathedral but is encountering some obstacles there. Nevertheless, she continues faithfully as a lay woman in her parish church and community.

Two of Esther's children have continued to draw closer to her and listen to her story, but one of her children has sadly cut ties with her. Mourning the loss, her approach is to pray and 'to let it go and let God deal with it'.

There have been striking developments for Joanna, who finally plucked up the courage to inform the authorities, that over 40 years ago, she had been sexually assaulted as a child by a priest who was teaching at her school. With the support of her female curate and healing ministry team, she has made a statement to the police and has been interviewed by a diocesan investigator. She learnt that the priest in question was a known offender against other children. MACSAS continues to give Joanna support in her search for justice.

Lydia, a decade on from her husband's conviction, has been looking back over these years. She says that on the anniversary, her 'rip off' calendar coincidentally had the scripture Gal 2.20, 'I have been crucified with Christ and I no longer live, but Christ lives in me.' It was accompanied by a quote by Alan Redpath: 'God saves a man, not by improving his old life, but by crucifying it, and by raising him up to walk in newness of life with Christ.' Lydia asked me to include this quote because she believes this is relevant to her, her husband and her family, and sums up where she is today, for which she is grateful.

Miriam has continued the struggle to have her voice heard by church authorities. She has written many letters, only some of which have been answered, and usually only months later. More than three years after being forced to leave her church community, she was finally made party to that Church's new ethical policy on clergy discipline and has been invited to comment on the draft, which she is working on at present. She has still received no pastoral care or contributions towards her counselling. Her spiritual journey is now expressed in a commitment to Christian arts productions and she still worships with the Quakers. On reading the original thesis which she found helpful, Miriam gave me some important feedback for which I am indebted to her.

Naomi has been severely ill. Nevertheless on completion of the research she took time to send me God's blessings on my work and ministry.

Priscilla wrote to say that on reading her interview transcript again recently, she feels exactly the same about God and her experiences, if not more strongly than ever. She has left the church where she had been worshipping and has joined a different denomination where she is following her vocation to train as a lay preacher. She says she feels 'so blessed'.

Sarah has sadly had a diagnosis of MS. Her focus on her health has taken precedence over her struggle for reconciliation with the Church, with which she no longer has any contact.

Tamar continues in her life of service despite having had a battle with cancer over the past year. She still works as a teacher, and is a youth leader at her church.

Bibliography

Acker, J., Barry, K. and Esseveld, J., 'Objectivity and Truth: Problems in Doing Feminist Research', in Fonow, M.M. and Cook, J.A. (eds), *Beyond Methodology: Feminist Scholarship as Lived Research* (Bloomington, IN: Indiana University Press, 1991), pp. 133–53.

Addelson, K.P., 'Knower/Doers and Their Moral Problems', in Alcoff, L. and Potter, E. (eds), *Feminist Epistemologies* (London: Routledge, 1993), pp. 265–94.

Ainscough, C. and Toon, K., *Breaking Free* (London: Sheldon Press, 1993).

Alcoff, L. and Potter, E. (eds), *Feminist Epistemologies* (London: Routledge, 1993).

Allan, G., 'A Critique of Using Grounded Theory as a Research Method', *Electronic Journal of Business Research Methods*, 2/1 (2003): 1–10.

Ancient Hebrew Poetry (2005), 'Regularities in Ancient Hebrew Verse: An Overview'. Available at: http://www.ancienthebrewpoetry.typepad.com/ (accessed 5 July 2010).

Anderson, J., 'Sexual Assault and Substance Abuse', *Research and Advocacy Digest*, 8/1 (2005): 7.

Anderson, K. and Jack, D.C., 'Learning to Listen: Interview Techniques and Analyses', in Gluck, S.B. and Patai, D. (eds), *Women's Words: The Feminist Practice of Oral History* (New York: Routledge, 1991), pp. 11–26.

Arms, M.F., 'When Forgiveness Is Not the Issue in Forgiveness: Religious Complicity in Abuse and Privatized Forgiveness', *Journal of Religion and Abuse*, 4/4 (2002): 107–28.

Aune, K., 'The Significance of Gender for Congregational Studies', in Guest, M., Tusting, K. and Woodhead, L. (eds), *Congregational Studies in the UK: Christianity in a Post-Christian Context* (Aldershot: Ashgate, 2004), pp. 185–202.

Babinsky, E.L., 'The Use of Courtly Language in Le Mirouer des simples ames anienties', *Essays in Medieval Studies*, 4 (1987): 91–106.

——, 'Christological Transformation in *The Mirror of Souls* by Marguerite Porete', *Theology Today*, 60 (2003): 34–48.

Banyard, K., *The Equality Illusion: The Truth about Women and Men Today* (London: Faber & Faber, 2010).

Barnes, L.P., 'Forgiveness, the Moral Law and Education: A Reply to Patricia White', *Journal of Philosophy of Education*, 36/4 (2002): 529–44.

——, 'Talking Politics, Talking Forgiveness', *Scottish Journal of Theology*, 64/1 (2011): 64–79.

Barton, S. (ed.), *'Where Shall Wisdom Be Found?' Wisdom in the Bible, the Church and the Contemporary World* (Edinburgh: T&T Clark, 1999).

Beaudoin, M.N., 'Agency and Choice in the Face of Trauma: A Narrative Therapy Map', *Journal of Systemic Therapies*, 24/4 (2005): 32–50.

Belenky, M.F., Clinchy, B.V., Goldberger, N.R. and Tarule, J.M., *Women's Ways of Knowing: The Development of Self, Voice and Mind*, tenth anniversary edition (New York: Basic Books, 1997).

Birchard, T., 'Clergy Sexual Misconduct: Frequency and Causation', *Sexual and Relationship Therapy*, 15/2 (2000): 127–39.

Blamires, A., 'Women and Preaching in Medieval Orthodoxy', *Viator*, 26 (1995): 135–53.

Bolton, B.M., 'Mulieres Sanctae', in Stuard, Susan Mosher (ed.), *Women in Medieval Society* (Pennsylvania, PA: University of Pennsylvania Press, 1976), pp. 141–58.

Børresen, K.E. and Vogt, K., *Women's Studies of the Christian and Islamic Traditions: Ancient, Medieval, and Renaissance Foremothers* (Boston, MA: Kluwer, 1993).

Bradley, R., SFCC, 'Background of the Title Speculum in Medieval Literature', *Speculum*, 29 (1954): 100–115.

Brady, J.L., Guy, J.D., Poelstra, P.L. and Brokaw, B.F., 'Vicarious Traumatization, Spirituality and the Treatment of Sexual Abuse Survivors: A National Survey of Women Psychotherapists', *Professional Psychology: Research and Practice*, 30/4 (1999): 386–93.

Brock, R.N. and Parker, R.A., *Proverbs of Ashes: Violence, Redemption and the Search for What Saves Us* (Boston, MA: Beacon Press, 2001).

——, *Saving Paradise: How Christianity Traded Love of This World for Crucifixion and Empire* (Boston, MA: Beacon Press, 2008).

Brown, F., Driver, S. and Briggs, C., *The Brown-Driver-Briggs Hebrew and English Lexicon* (Peabody, MA: Hendrickson, 1996).

Bruce, F.F., *Philippians*, New International Bible Commentary (Exeter: Paternoster, 1995).

Brueggemann, W., *Theology of the Old Testament: Testimony, Dispute, Advocacy* (Minneapolis, MN: Fortress Press, 1997).

Bryant, G., 'The French Heretic Beguine: Marguerite Porete', in Wilson, K.M. (ed.), *Medieval Women Writers* (Manchester: Manchester University Press, 1984), pp. 204–26.

Bryman, A., 'The Debate about Quantitative and Qualitative Research', in Bryman, A. and Burgess, R.G. (eds), *Qualitative Research* (4 vols, London: Sage, 1999), vol. 1, pp. 35–69.

Burrus, V., *Begotten Not Made: Conceiving Manhood in Late Antiquity* (Stanford, CA: Stanford University Press, 2000).

Bussey, F.C., 'The World on the End of a Reed: Marguerite Porete and the Annihilation of an Identity in Medieval and Modern Representations – A Reassessment' (Phd Thesis: University of Sydney, 2007).

Bynum, C.W., *Holy Feast and Holy Fast: The Religious Significance of Food to Medieval Women* (Berkeley, CA: University of California Press, 1988).

——, *Fragmentation and Redemption* (New York: Zone, 1991).
Carlson Brown, J. and Bohn, C., *Christianity, Patriarchy and Abuse: A Feminist Critique* (Cleveland, OH: Pilgrim, 1989).
Carson, A., 'Decreation: How Women Like Sappho, Marguerite Porete, and Simone Weil Tell God', *Common Knowledge*, 8/1 (2002): 188–201.
Cashman, H., *Christianity and Child Sexual Abuse* (London: SPCK, 1993).
Chance, J., 'Speaking *in propria persona*: Authorizing the Subject as a Political Act in Late Medieval Feminine Spirituality', in Dor, J., Johnson, L. and Wogan-Browne, J. (eds), *New Trends in Feminine Spirituality: The Holy Women of Liège and Their Impact* (Turnhout: Brepols, 1999), pp. 269–94.
Chanfrault-Duchet, M.F., 'Narrative Structures, Social Models, and Symbolic Representation in the Life Story', in Gluck, S.B. and Patai, D. (eds), *Women's Words: The Feminist Practice of Oral History* (New York: Routledge, 1991), pp. 77–92.
Churches Together in Britain and Ireland, *Time for Action: Sexual Abuse, the Churches and a New Dawn for Survivors* (London: Church House Publishing, 2002).
Clines, D., *Job 1–20*, World Bible Commentary 17 (Dallas: World Books, 1989).
——, 'Job's God', in van Wolde, E. (ed.), *Job's God* (London: SCM, 2004), pp. 39–51.
Coakley, J., 'Gender and Authority and the Friars', *Church History*, 60 (1991): 445–60.
Coakley, S., 'Kenosis and Subversion', in Hampson, D. (ed.), *Swallowing a Fishbone?* (London: SPCK, 1996), pp. 82–111.
——, *Powers and Submissions: Spirituality, Philosophy, and Gender* (Oxford: Blackwell, 2002).
Code, L., 'Taking Subjectivity into Account', in Alcoff, L. and Potter, E. (eds), *Feminist Epistemologies* (London: Routledge, 1993), pp. 15–48.
Cohen, F.S. and Densen-Gerber, J., 'A Study of the Relationship between Child Abuse and Drug Addiction in 178 Patients: Preliminary Results', *Child Abuse and Neglect*, 6/4 (1982): 383–7.
Cohen, L., Manion, L. and Morrison, K., *Research Methods in Education*, 5th edition (London: Routledge, 2000).
Coll, R., 'Power, Powerlessness and Empowerment', *Religious Education*, 81/3 (1986): 412–23.
Cooper-White, P., *The Cry of Tamar: Violence against Women and the Church's Response* (Minneapolis, MN: Augsburg Fortress Press, 1995).
——, 'Opening the Eyes: Understanding the Impact of Trauma on Development', in Stevenson-Moessner, J. (ed.), *In Her Own Time: Women and Developmental Issues in Pastoral Care* (Minneapolis, MN: Augsburg Fortress Press, 2000), pp. 87–102.
Corduan, W., 'The Gospel According to Margaret', *Journal of the Evangelical Theological Society*, 35/4 (1992): 515–30.
Cotter, J., 'You Can't Be Serious!', *Theology and Sexuality*, 13 (2000): 55–61.

Cottrell, R.D., 'Marguerite Porete's Heretical Discourse; or, Deviating from the Model', *Modern Language Studies*, 21 (1991): 16–21.

Council of Vienne (1311–1312), *Introduction and Translation Taken from Decrees of the Ecumenical Councils*, ed. Tanner, N.P. Available at: http://www.ewtn.com/library/councils/ vienne.htm (accessed 1 May 2010).

Cox, D., *The Triumph of Impotence: Job and the Tradition of the Absurd* (Rome: Universita Gregoriana, 1978).

——, *Man's Anger and God's Silence: The Book of Job* (Slough: St Paul, 1990).

Cré, M., 'Women in the Charterhouse? Julian of Norwich's *Revelations of Divine Love* and Marguerite Porete's *Mirror of Simple Souls* in British Library, MS Additional 37790', in Renevey, D. and Whitehead, C. (eds), *Writing Religious Women: Female Spiritual and Textual Practices in Late Medieval England* (Toronto: University of Toronto Press, 2000), pp. 43–62.

Cresswell, J., *Research Design: Qualitative, Quantitative and Mixed Methods Approaches*, 2nd edition (London: Sage, 2003).

Crisp, B.R., 'Reading Scripture from a Hermeneutic of Rape', *Theology and Sexuality*, 14 (2001): 7–23.

——, 'Spiritual Direction and Survivors of Sexual Abuse', *The Way*, 43/2 (2004): 7–17.

——, 'Spirituality and Sexual Abuse: Issues and Dilemmas for Survivors', *Theology and Sexuality*, 13 (2007): 301–14.

Davie, G., *Religion in Britain since 1945* (Oxford; Cambridge, MA: Blackwell, 1994).

Davis, P.H., 'Horror and the Development of Girl's Spiritual Voices', in Stevenson-Moessner, J. (ed.), *In Her Own Time: Women and Developmental Issues in Pastoral Care* (Minneapolis, MN: Augsburg Fortress Press, 2000), pp. 103–14.

D'Costa, G., *Sexing the Trinity: Gender, Culture and the Divine* (London: SCM, 2000).

DeVault, M.L., 'Talking and Listening from Women's Standpoint: Feminist Strategies for Interviewing and Analysis', in Bryman, A. and Burgess, R.G. (eds), *Qualitative Research* (4 vols, London: Sage, 1999), vol. 4, pp. 86–111.

Devlin, D., 'Feminine Lay Piety in the High Middle Ages: The Beguines', in Nichols, J.A. and Shank, L.T. (eds), *Distant Echoes: Medieval Religious Women I* (Kalamazoo, MI: Cistercian, 1984), pp. 183–96.

Douglas, D., 'Inductive Theory Generation: A Grounded Approach to Business Inquiry', *Electronic Journal of Business Research Methods*, 2/1 (2003): 47–54.

Doward, J., 'Catholic Church's Plea Could Rule Out Damages for Priests' Abuse', *The Observer* (2011). Available at: http://www.guardian.co.uk/world/2011/jul/24/ (accessed 1 September 2011).

Dronke, P., *Women Writers of the Middle Ages: A Critical Study of Texts from Perpetua to Marguerite Porete* (Cambridge: Cambridge University Press, 1984).

Dussell, E., 'The People of El Salvador: The Communal Sufferings of Job', *Concilium*, 189 (1983): 61–8.

Epiney-Burgard, G. and Zum Brunn, E., *Femmes troubadours de Dieu* (Turnhout: Brepols, 1988).

Evinger, J.S. and Yoder, D.L., 'Sexual Abuse, Forgiveness and Justice: A Journey in Faith', *Journal of Religion and Abuse*, 4/4 (2003): 71–88.

Falvay, D., 'Felfedeztek mint Korai Előzményt ... aki Női Vallásossággal Foglalkozott: Beszélgetés Romana Guarnieri-vel' ('Discovered as an Early Pioneer Who Researched Women's Religiosity: A Conversation with Romana Guarnieri'), *Aetas: Történettudományi folyóirat*, 4 (2002a): 140–43.

——, 'Marguerite Porete, az Egyszerű lelkek tükre és annak magyar vonatkozásai' ('the *Mirror of Simple Souls* and Its Hungarian Connections'), *Aetas: Történettudományi folyóirat*, 4 (2002b): 148–51.

Fawcettsociety (2012). Homepage. Available at: http://www.fawcettsociety.org.uk/ (accessed 10 January 2012).

Fee, G.D., *Paul's Letter to the Philippians*, the New International Commentary on the New Testament (Grand Rapids, MI: Eerdmans, 1995).

Field, S.L., *The Beguine, the Angel and the Inquisitor: The Trials of Marguerite Porete and Guiard de Cressonessart* (Indiana: Notre Dame University Press, 2012)

Finch, J., '"It's Great to Have Someone to Talk to": The Ethics and Politics of Interviewing Women', in Bryman, A. and Burgess, R.G. (eds), *Qualitative Research* (4 vols, London: Sage, 1999), vol. 2, pp. 68–80.

Finkelhor, D., Hotaling, G.T., Lewis, I.A. and Smith, C., 'Sexual Abuse and Its Relationship to Later Sexual Satisfaction, Marital Status, Religion and Attitudes', *Journal of Interpersonal Violence*, 4/4 (1989): 379–99.

Flaherty, S.M., *Woman, Why Do You Weep?: Spirituality for Survivors of Childhood Sexual Abuse* (Mahwah, NJ: Paulist Press, 1992).

Fonow, M.M. and Cook, J.A., 'Back to the Future: A Look at the Second Wave of Feminist Epistemology and Methodology', in Fonow, M.M. and Cook, J.A. (eds), *Beyond Methodology: Feminist Scholarship as Lived Research* (Bloomington, IN: Indiana University Press, 1991), pp. 1–15.

Fortune, M.M., *Keeping the Faith: Guidance for Christian Women Facing Abuse* (New York: Harper One, 1987).

——, *Is Nothing Sacred?* (Cleveland, OH: United Church Press, 1999).

——, 'Pastoral Responses to Sexual Assault and Abuse: Laying a Foundation', *Journal of Religion and Abuse*, 3/3 (2002): 91–112.

Fulkerson, M.M., *Changing the Subject: Women's Discourses and Feminist Theology* (Minneapolis, MN: Fortress Press, 1994).

Ganje-Fling, M.A. and McCarthy, P., 'Impact of Childhood Sexual Abuse on Client Spiritual Development: Counselling Implications', *Journal of Counselling and Development*, 74/1 (1996): 253–58.

Gilligan, C., *In a Different Voice: Psychological Theory and Women's Development* (London: Harvard University Press, 1993).

Girard, R., *Job the Victim of His People*, trans. Freccero, Y. (London: The Athlone Press, 1987).

Glaser, B.G., *Theoretical Sensitivity: Advances in the Methodology of Grounded Theory* (Mill Valley, CA: Sociology Press, 1978).
——, *Emergence vs Forcing: Basics of Grounded Theory Analysis* (Mill Valley, CA: Sociology Press, 1992).
Glaser, B.G. and Strauss, A.L., *The Discovery of Grounded Theory*, 4th edition (New Brunswick, NJ: Aldine Transaction, 2009).
Gluck, S.B. and Armitage, S., 'Reflections on Women's Oral History: An Exchange', *Frontiers: A Journal of Women Studies*, 19/3 (1998): 1–11.
Gluck, S.B. and Patai, D., *Women's Words: The Feminist Practice of Oral History* (New York: Routledge, 1991).
Gordis, R., *The Book of God and Man: A Study of Job* (Chicago, IL: Chicago University Press, 1965).
Gosney, J., *Surviving Child Sexual Abuse: Supporting Adults in the Church* (Cambridge: Grove Books, 2002).
Graham, E., *Making the Difference: Personhood, Gender and Theology* (London: Mowbray, 1995).
Griffin, L. and Griffin, P., *Hope and Healing for the Abused* (Lancaster: Sovereign World, 2007).
Groupe d'anthropologie scolastique (2010), 'Colloque international Marguerite Porete'. Available at: http://actualites.ehess.fr/nouvelle3904.html (accessed 10 May 2010).
Grundmann, H., 'Ketzerverhöre des Spätmittelalters II–III', in *Ausgewählte Aufsätze 1: Religiöse Bewegungen: Monumenta Germaniae Historica Schriften* (Stuttgart: Hiersemann, 1976), pp. 368–403.
Guest, M., Tusting, K. and Woodhead, L., *Congregational Studies in the UK: Christianity in a Post-Christian Context* (Aldershot: Ashgate, 2004).
Gunton, C., 'Proteus and Procustes: A Study in the Dialectic of Language in Disagreement with Sallie McFague', in Kimel, A.F. (ed.), *Speaking the Christian God: The Holy Trinity and the Challenge of Feminism* (Grand Rapids, MI: Eerdmans, 1992), pp. 65–80.
Gutiérrez, G., *On Job: God-talk and the Suffering of the Innocent*, trans. from the Spanish by O'Connell, M.J. (Maryknoll, NY: Orbis, 1987).
Habel, N., 'Only the Jackal Is My Friend: On Friends and Redeemers in Job', *Int*, 31 (1977): 227–36.
——, *The Book of Job: A Commentary*, The Old Testament Library (London: SCM, 1985).
——, 'The Verdict on/of God at the End of Job', in van Wolde, E. (ed.), *Job's God* (London: SCM, 2004), pp. 27–38.
Hall, T.A., 'Spiritual Effects of Childhood Sexual Abuse in Adult Christian Women', *Journal of Psychology and Theology*, 23/2 (1995): 129–34.
Hampson, D., *After Christianity* (London: SCM, 1996a).
—— (ed.), *Swallowing a Fishbone?* (London: SPCK, 1996b).
Harding, S. (ed.), *Feminism and Methodology: Social Science Issues* (Bloomington, IN: Indiana University Press, 1987).

——, *Whose Science? Whose Knowledge?: Thinking from Women's Lives* (Milton Keynes: Open University Press, 1991).

Häring, H., 'Who Is Responsible?', in van Wolde, E. (ed.), *Job's God* (London: SCM, 2004), pp. 67–82.

Harrison, B.W., 'The Power of Anger in the Work of Love: Christian Ethics for Women and Other Strangers', in Loades, A. (ed.), *Feminist Theology: A Reader* (London: SPCK, 1990), pp. 194–214.

Hawthorne, G.F., *Philippians*, Word Biblical Commentary 43 (Waco, TX: Word Books, 1983).

Hedges-Goettl, L., *Sexual Abuse: Pastoral Responses* (Nashville, TN: Abingdon, 2004).

Herman, J.L., *Trauma and Recovery* (London: Pandora, 1994).

Higgins, G. O'Connell, *Resilient Adults: Overcoming a Cruel Past* (San Francisco, CA: Jossey-Bass, 1994).

Hillerbrand, H.J., 'On Book Burnings and Book Burners: Reflections on the Power (and Powerlessness) of Ideas', *Journal of the American Academy of Religion*, 74/3 (2006): 593–614.

Hollywood, A., 'Suffering Transformed: Marguerite Porete, Meister Eckhart, and the Problem of Women's Spirituality', in McGinn, B. (ed.), *Meister Eckhart and the Beguine Mystics* (New York: Continuum, 1994), pp. 87–113.

——, *The Soul as Virgin Wife: Mechtehild of Magdeburg, Meister Eckhart and Marguerite Porete* (Notre Dame, IN: University of Notre Dame Press, 1995).

——, 'Bataille and Mysticism: A "Dazzling Dissolution"', *Diacritics*, 26/2 (1996): 74–85.

——, 'Who Does She Think She Is? Christian Women's Mysticism', *Theology Today*, 60 (2003): 5–15.

——, 'Sexual Desire, Divine Desire: Or Queering the Beguines', in Burrus, V. and Keller, C. (eds), *Toward a Theology of Eros: Transfiguring Passion at the Limits of Discipline* (New York: Fordham University Press, 2006), pp. 119–33.

Hopkins, J., 'Radical Passion', in Hampson, D. (ed.), *Swallowing a Fishbone?* (London: SPCK, 1996), pp. 66–81.

House of Bishops, *Women Bishops in the Church of England?* (London: Church House Publishing, 2004).

——, *Responding Well to Those Who Have Been Sexually Abused* (London: Church House Publishing, 2011).

Hughes, G., *God of Surprises* (London: DLT, 1985).

Humphreys, J., 'Spirituality and Distress in Sheltered Battered Women', *Journal of Nursing Scholarship*, 32/3 (2000): 273–8.

Insdorf, A., 'The Night Porter' (2000). Available at http://www.criterion.com (accessed 18 October 2011).

Jackson, L.A., *Child Sexual Abuse in Victorian England* (London: Routledge, 2000).

Jans, J., 'Neither Punishment nor Reward: Divine Gratuitousness and Moral Order', in van Wolde, E. (ed.), *Job's God* (London: SCM, 2004), pp. 83–92.

Jantzen, G.M., 'Disrupting the Sacred: Religion and Gender in the City', in Ruffing, J.K. (ed.), *Mysticism and Social Transformation* (Syracuse, NY: Syracuse University Press, 2001), pp. 29–44.
Jarvis, P., *The Practitioner-Researcher: Developing Theory from Practice* (San Francisco, CA: Jossey-Bass, 1999).
Jayaratne, T.E. and Stewart, A.J., 'Quantitative and Qualitative Methods in the Social Sciences: Current Feminist Issues and Practical Strategies', in Fonow, M.M. and Cook, J.A. (eds), *Beyond Methodology: Feminist Scholarship as Lived Research* (Bloomington, IN: Indiana University Press, 1991), pp. 85–106.
Johnson, E., CSJ, 'The Incomprehensibility of God and the Image of God Male and Female', *Theological Studies*, 45/3 (1984): 441–65.
Kahn, J., *Job's Illness: Loss, Grief and Integration, A Psychological Interpretation*, with Hester Solomon (Oxford: Pergamon Press, 1975).
Kamp, A., 'With or Without a Cause: Images of God and Man in Job 1–3', in van Wolde, E. (ed.), *Job's God* (London: SCM, 2004), pp. 9–17.
Kane, D., Cheston, S.D. and Greer, J., 'Perceptions of God by Survivors of Childhood Sexual Abuse: An Exploratory Study in an Under-researched Area', *Journal of Psychology and Theology*, 21/3 (1993): 228–37.
Keller, C., 'Power Lines', *Theology Today*, 55/2 (1995): 188–203.
——, '"She Talks Too Much": Magdalene Meditations', in Burrus, V. and Keller, C. (eds), *Toward a Theology of Eros: Transfiguring Passion at the Limits of Discipline* (New York: Fordham University Press, 2006), pp. 234–54.
Kendall, J., 'Axial Coding and the Grounded Theory Controversy', *Western Journal of Nursing Research*, 21/6 (1999): 743–57.
Kennedy, H., *Eve Was Framed*, revised edition (London: Vintage, 2005).
Kennedy, M., *The Courage to Tell* (London: CTBI, 1999).
——, 'Sexual Abuse of Women by Priests and Ministers to Whom They Go for Pastoral Care and Support', *Feminist Theology Continuum*, 11 (2003): 226–35.
Kliewer, S., 'Allowing Spirituality into the Healing Process', *Journal of Family Practice*, 53/8 (2004): 616–24.
Kocher, S.A., 'Marguerite de Navarre's Portrait of Marguerite Porete: A Renaissance Queen Constructs a Medieval Woman Mystic', *Medieval Feminist Newsletter*, 26 (1998): 17–23.
Kvale, S., *Interviews: An Introduction to Qualitative Research Interviewing* (London: Sage, 1996).
Lambert, M., *Medieval Heresy: Popular Movements from the Gregorian Reform to the Reformation*, 2nd edition (Oxford: Blackwell, 1992).
Lawless, E., 'Women's Life Stories and Reciprocal Ethnography as Feminist and Emergent', *Journal of Folklore Research*, 28/1 (1991): 35–60.
Layton, L., 'Trauma, Gender Identity and Sexuality: Discourses of Fragmentation', *American Imago*, 52/1 (1995): 107–25.
Lea, H.C., *A History of the Middle Ages*, vol. 2 (London: Sampson/Rivington, 1887).

Leicht, I., *Marguerite Porete – eine fromme Intellektuelle und die Inquisition* (Freiburg: Herder, 1998).

Lerner, R.E., 'Late Medieval Mysticism Image of Mixed Liquids', *Church History*, 40 (1971): 397–411.

——, *The Heresy of the Free Spirit in the Later Middle Ages* (Berkeley, CA; London: University of California Press, 1972).

Levenson, J.D., *Resurrection and the Restoration of Israel: The Ultimate Victory of the God of Life* (New Haven, CT; London: Yale University Press, 2006).

Leyden-Rubenstein, L., 'Treating Child Survivors of Clergy Sexual Abuse (Spirituality)', *Annals of the American Psychotherapy Association*, 5/4 (2002): 32+.

Lichtmann, M., 'Marguerite Porete and Meister Eckhart: *The Mirror of Simple Souls* Mirrored', in McGinn, B. (ed.), *Meister Eckhart and the Beguine Mystics* (New York: Continuum, 1994), pp. 65–86.

——, 'Marguerite Porete's Mirror for Simple Souls: Inverted Reflection of Self, Society and God', *Studia Mystica*, 16 (1995): 4–29.

——, 'Negative Theology in Marguerite Porete and J Derrida', *Christianity and Literature*, 47/2 (1998): 213–27.

Loades, A., *Feminist Theology: Voices from the Past* (Cambridge: Polity, 2001).

Loftus, J.A., SJ, 'Victims of Abuse as Candidates', *Review for Religious*, 45 (1986): 724–38.

MACSAS (2006), 'Betrayed or Supported? Clergy Abuse Survivors' Experiences of the Catholic Church's Response to Clergy Sexual Abuse: Survey Conducted for Cumberlege Commission'. Available at: http://www.macsas.org.uk (accessed 28 May 2009).

—— (2009), 'Clergy or Minister Sexual Exploitation of Adults in the Pastoral Relationship' (Leaflet). Available at: http://www.macsas.org.uk (accessed 28 May 2009).

—— (2010), *Out Loud*, 6/1. Available at: http://www.macsas.org.uk (accessed 1 October 2010).

Maguire, E., *Princesses and Pornstars. Sex, Power, Identity* (Melbourne: Text Publishing, 2008).

Makowski, C., 'Mulieres Religiosae Strictly Speaking: Some Fourteenth-Century Canonical Opinions', *The Catholic Historical Review*, 85/1 (1999): 1–14.

Malone, M.T., *Women and Christianity Vol. II: The Medieval Period AD 1000–1500* (Blackrock, Co. Dublin: Columba Press, 2001).

Martin, R.R., *The Epistle of Paul to the Philippians: An Introduction and Commentary*, Tyndale New Testament Commentaries (London: IVP, 1974).

——, *Philippians*, New Century Bible Commentary (Grand Rapids, MI: Eerdmans, 1976).

McFadyen, A., *Bound to Sin: Abuse, Holocaust and the Christian Doctrine of Sin* (Cambridge; New York: Cambridge University Press, 2000).

McFague, S., *Models of God* (London: SCM, 1987).

McGinn, B. (ed.), *Meister Eckhart and the Beguine Mystics* (New York: Continuum, 1994).

——, *The Flowering of Mysticism: Men and Women in the New Mysticism, 1200–1350*, The Presence of God: A History of Western Christian Mysticism, vol. 3 (New York: Crossroad, 1998).

——, 'Evil-sounding, Rash, and Suspect of Heresy: Tensions between Mysterium and Magisterium in the History of the Church', *The Catholic Historical Review*, 90/2 (2004): 193–212.

McLaughlin, E., 'The Heresy of the Free Spirit and Late Medieval Mysticism', *Medievalia et Humanistica*, 4 (1973): 37–54.

McRobbie, A., *The Aftermath of Feminism: Gender, Culture and Social Change* (London: Sage, 2009).

Meyer, R., *Through the Fire: Spiritual Restoration for Adult Victims of Childhood Sexual Abuse* (Minneapolis, MN: Augsburg Fortress Press, 2005).

Mies, M., 'Towards a Methodology for Feminist Research', in Bryman, A. and Burgess, R.G. (eds), *Qualitative Research* (4 vols, London: Sage, 1999), vol. 4, pp. 67–85.

Miles, J.A., 'Gagging on Job, or the Comedy of Religious Exhaustion', in Robertson, D.A. and Polzin, R. (eds), *Semeia 7: Studies in the Book of Job* (Missoula, MT: Scholars Press, 1977), pp. 71–126.

Miles, M.B. and Huberman, A.M., *Qualitative Data Analysis: An Expanded Sourcebook*, 2nd edition (London: Sage, 1994).

Miles, M.R., 'A Sea of Love: Marguerite Porete's Mirror for Simple Souls', *Christian Century*, 110/4 (1993): 115–22.

Miller, T.S., 'What's in a Name? Clerical Representations of Parisian Beguines (1200–1328)', *Journal of Medieval History*, 33/1 (2007): 60–86.

Minister, K., 'A Feminist Frame for the Oral History Interview', in Gluck, S.B. and Patai, D. (eds), *Women's Words: The Feminist Practice of Oral History* (New York: Routledge, 1991), pp. 27–42.

Muers, R., *Keeping God's Silence* (London: Blackwell, 2004).

Murray-Swank, N.A. and Pargament, K.I., 'God, Where Are You?: Evaluating a Spiritually Integrated Intervention for Sexual Abuse', *Mental Health, Religion and Culture*, 8/3 (2005): 191–203.

Neel, C., 'The Origins of the Beguines', *Working Together in the Middle Ages: Perspectives on Women's Communities*, *Signs*, 14/2 (1989): 321–41.

Neuger, C.C., 'Narratives of Harm: Setting the Developmental Context for Intimate Violence', in Stevenson-Moessner, J. (ed.), *In Her Own Time: Women and Developmental Issues in Pastoral Care* (Minneapolis, MN: Fortress Augsburg, 2000), pp. 65–86.

Newman, B., *From Virile Woman to WomanChrist*, *Studies in Medieval Religion and Literature* (Philadelphia, PA: University of Pennsylvania Press, c.1995).

——, 'The Mirror and the Rose: Marguerite Porete's Encounter with the *Dieu d'Amours*', in Blumenfeld-Kosinski, R., Robertson, D. and Warren, N. (eds),

The Vernacular Spirit: Essays on Medieval Religious Literature (New York: Palgrave, 2002), pp. 105–22.
Ngwa, K.N., *The Hermeneutics of the 'Happy' Ending in Job 42:7–17* (Berlin; New York: de Gruyter, 2005).
Oakley, A., 'Interviewing Women: A Contradiction in Terms', in Roberts, H. (ed.), *Doing Feminist Research* (London: Routledge & Keegan Paul, 1981), pp. 30–61.
Ong, W.J., *Orality and Literacy*, 2nd edition (London: Routledge, 2002).
Opie, A., 'Qualitative Research, Appropriation of the 'Other' and Empowerment', *Feminist Review*, 40 (1992): 52–69.
Orbach, S., *Bodies* (London: Profile, 2010).
Orcibal, J., 'Le "Miroir des simples *âmes*" et la "secte" du Libre Esprit', *Revue de l'histoire des religions*, 175 (1969): 35–60.
Ormerod, N. and Ormerod T., *When Ministers Sin: Sexual Abuse and the Churches* (Alexandria, Australia: Millennium Books, 1995).
Ormerod, P. and Roach, A.P., 'The Medieval Inquisition: Scale-free Networks and the Suppression of Heresy', *Physica A*, 339 (2004): 645–52.
O'Sullivan, R.A., 'The School of Love: Marguerite Porete's Mirror of Simple Souls', *Journal of Medieval History*, 32/2 (2006): 143–62.
Petroff, E.A. (ed.), *Medieval Women's Visionary Literature* (Oxford: Oxford University Press, 1986).
Poling, J., *The Abuse of Power: A Theological Problem* (Nashville, TN: Abingdon, 1991).
——, 'God, Sex and Power', *Theology and Sexuality*, 11/2 (2005): 55–70.
Polzin, R., 'John A. Miles on the Book of Job: A Response', in Robertson, D.A. and Polzin, R. (eds), *Semeia 7: Studies in the Book of Job* (Missoula, MT: Scholars Press, 1977), pp. 127–33.
Pope, M., *Job: Introduction, Translation and Notes*, The Anchor Bible (New York: Doubleday, 1965).
Porete, M., *The Mirror of Simple Souls*, trans. and introduced by Babinsky, E.L. (Mahwah, NJ: Paulist Press, 1993).
——, *The Mirror of Simple Souls/Margaret Porette*, trans. from the French with introductory interpretative essay by Colledge, E., Marler, J.C. and Grant, J. (Notre Dame, IN: University of Notre Dame Press, c.1999).
Punch, K., *Introduction to Social Research: Quantitative and Qualitative Approaches* (London: Sage, 2005).
Randall, C., 'Changing Places: Marguerite Porete, Meister Eckhard and the Question of Perspective', *The Romantic Review*, 85 (1994): 341–60.
——, 'Person, Place, Perception: A Proposal for the Reading of Porete's Miroir des âmes simples et anéanties', *Journal of Medieval and Renaissance Studies*, 25 (1995): 229–44.
Ribbens, J., 'Interviewing: An "Unnatural Situation"?' *Women's Studies International Forum*, 12 (1989): 579–92.

Ridpath, P., 'Life of Boethius', in his translation of *Consolations of Philosophy* (London, 1785).

Riessman, C.K., 'When Gender Is Not Enough: Women Interviewing Women', *Gender and Society*, 1 (1987): 172–207.

Robinson, J.M., *Nobility and Annihilation in Marguerite Porete's Mirror of Simple Souls* (Albany, NY: State University of New York Press, 2001).

Ronan, M., 'Reclaiming Women's Experience: A Reading of Selected Christian Feminist Theologies', *Cross Currents*, 48/2 (1998). Available at http://www.crosscurrents. org/ronan.htm (accessed 8 January 2012).

Rosetti, S.J., 'Attitudes toward God and the Catholic Church', *Child Abuse and Neglect*, 19/12 (1995): 1469–81.

Rubin, M., 'Choosing Death? Experiences of Martyrdom in Late Medieval Europe', in Wood, D. (ed.), *Martyrs and Martyrologies*, Studies in Church History 30 (Oxford: Blackwell, 1993), pp. 153–83.

Ruh, K., 'Beginenmystik: Hadewijch, Mechthild von Magdeburg, Marguerite Porete', *Zeitschrift für Deutsches Altertum und deutsche Literatur*, 106 (1977): 265–77.

Sargent, M.G., 'The Annihilation of Margaret Porete', *Viator*, 28 (1997): 253–79.

Sargent, N.M., 'Spirituality and Adult Survivors of Child Sexual Abuse: Some Treatment Issues', in Sgroi, S.M. (ed.), *Sexual Abuse Treatment for Children, Adult Survivors, Offenders, and Persons with Mental Retardation: Vulnerable Populations, vol. 2* (New York: Lexington, 1989), pp. 167–202.

Schermer, V.L., *Spirit and Psyche: A New Paradigm for Psychology, Psychoanalysis, and Psychotherapy* (London: Jessica Kingsley, 2003).

Scherr, R., 'The Uses of Memory and the Abuses of Fiction: Sexuality in Holocaust Fiction and Memoir, *Other Voices*, 2/1 (2000). Available at: http://www.othervoices.org/ 2.1/scherr/sexuality.php (accessed 14 October 2011).

Schreiner, S.E., *Where Shall Wisdom Be Found? Calvin's Exegesis of Job from Medieval and Modern Perspectives* (London: University of Chicago Press, 1994).

Schweiker, W., 'Power and the Agency of God', *Theology Today*, 55/2 (1995): 204–24.

Sells, M.A., *Mystical Languages of Unsaying* (Chicago, IL; London: University of Chicago Press, 1994).

Sgroi, S.M. (ed.), *Sexual Abuse Treatment for Children, Adult Survivors, Offenders, and Persons with Mental Retardation: Vulnerable Populations, vol. 2* (New York: Lexington, 1989).

Shaw, J., 'Women, Rationality and Theology', in Hampson, D. (ed.), *Swallowing a Fishbone?* (London: SPCK, 1996), pp. 50–65.

Sherwood, Y., 'Passion – Binding – Passion', in Burrus, V. and Keller, C. (eds), *Toward a Theology of Eros: Transfiguring Passion at the Limits of Discipline* (New York: Fordham University Press, 2006), pp. 169–93.

Shields, V.R. and Dervin, B., 'Sense-making in Feminist Social Science Research: A Call to Enlarge the Methodological Options of Feminist Studies', *Women's Studies International Forum*, 16 (1993): 65–81.

Shooter, S., 'How Feminine Participation in the Divine Might Renew the Church and Its Leadership', *Feminist Theology* (2013).

Skårup, P., 'La Langue du Miroir des simples âmes attribué à Marguerite Porete', *Studia Neophilologica*, 60 (1988): 231–6.

Slee, N., 'The Power to Re-member', in Hampson, D. (ed.), *Swallowing a Fishbone?* (London: SPCK, 1996), pp. 33–49.

——, *Women's Faith Development: Patterns and Processes* (Aldershot: Ashgate, 2004).

SlutWalk London! (2011) Homepage. Available at: http://slutmeansspeakup.org.uk/ (accessed 1 January 2012).

Smith, A., 'Spiritual Appropriation as Sexual Violence', *Wicazo Sa Review*, 20/1 (2005): 97–111.

Smith, C.E., Reinert, D.F., Horne, M., Greer, J.M. and Wicks, R., 'Childhood Abuse and Spiritual Development among Women Religious', *Journal of Religion and Health*, 34/2 (1995): 127–33.

Smith, S., 'Exploring the Interaction of Trauma and Spirituality', *Traumatology*, 10/4 (2004): 231–43.

Soskice, J.M., 'Turning the Symbols', in Hampson, D. (ed.), *Swallowing a Fishbone?* (London: SPCK, 1996), pp. 17–32.

Souillac, G., 'Charisme et prophétisme féminins: Marguerite Porete et le miroir des simples âmes', *Australian Journal of French Studies*, 35 (1998): 261–78.

Stanford Encyclopaedia of Philosophy (2005), 'Anicius Manlius Severinus Boethius'. Available at: http://plato.stanford.edu/entries/boethius (accessed 1 June 2010).

Stogdon, K., *Can Self-Surrender Ever Be a Good Idea? Feminist Suspicions of Surrender and Whether It Is Worth Taking the Risk*, Roehampton Research Seminar on Religion and Gender (2007).

Strauss, A.L. and Corbin, J.M., *Basics of Qualitative Research: Techniques and Procedures for Developing Grounded Theory*, 2nd edition (London: Sage, 1998).

Strimple, R.B., 'Philippians 2.5–11 in Recent Studies: Some Exegetical Conclusions', *Westminster Theological Journal*, 41/2 (1979): 247–68.

Suddaby, R., 'What Grounded Theory Is Not', *Academy of Management Journal*, 49/4 (2006): 633–43.

Sullivan, M.G., 'Spiritualized Therapy May Lessen Symptoms in Sex Abuse Survivors', *Clinical Psychiatry News*, 33/3 (2005): 18.

Tamez, E., 'From Father of the Needy to Brother of Jackals and Companion of Ostriches: Meditation on Job', in van Wolde, E. (ed.), *Job's God* (London: SCM, 2004), pp. 103–11.

Ticciati, S., 'Does Job Fear God for Naught?', *Modern Theology*, 21/3 (2005a): 353–66.

——, *Job and the Disruption of Identity: Reading beyond Barth* (London; New York: T&T Clark International, 2005b).
Trible, P., *Texts of Terror* (London: SCM, 2002).
Trombley, J.L., 'The Master and the Mirror: The Influence of Marguerite Porete on Meister Eckhart', *Magistra*, 16 (2010). Available at: http://www.highbeam.com/ doc/1P3-2122721481.html (accessed 30 September 2011).
Turner, D., *The Darkness of God: Negativity in Christian Mysticism* (Cambridge: Cambridge University Press, 1995).
——, 'The Art of Unknowing: Negative Theology in Late Medieval Mysticism', *Modern Theology*, 14/4 (1998): 473–88.
Valentine, L. and Feinauer, L.L., 'Resilience Factors Associated with Female Survivors of Childhood Sexual Abuse', *American Journal of Family Therapy*, 21/3 (1993): 216–24.
Van Hecke, P., 'But I, I Would Converse with the Almighty (Job 13.3): Job and His Friends on God', in van Wolde, E. (ed.), *Job's God* (London: SCM, 2004), pp. 18–26.
Van Wolde, E., *Mr and Mrs Job*, trans. Bowden, J. (London: SCM, 1997).
—— (ed.), *Job's God* (London: SCM, 2004).
Verdeyen, P., 'Le procès d'inquisition contre Marguerite Porete et Guiard de Cressonessart (1309–1310)', *Revue d'histoire ecclésiastique*, 81 (1986): 47–94.
Ward, P., *Liquid Church* (Peabody, MA: Hendrickson Paternoster Press, 2002).
Watson, N., 'Melting into God the English Way: Deification in the Middle English Version of Marguerite Porete's Mirouer des simples âmes anienties', in Voaden, R. (ed.), *Prophets Abroad: The Reception of Continental Holy Women in Late Medieval England* (Woodbridge: Brewer, 1996), pp. 19–50.
Weinandy, T.G., *The Father's Spirit of Sonship: Reconceiving the Trinity* (Edinburgh: T&T Clark 1995).
Wendel, S., 'We Cannot Fathom the Almighty: The Relationship between Transcendence and Immanence in the Light of Job's God', in van Wolde, E. (ed.), *Job's God* (London: SCM, 2004), pp. 52–66.
West, G. with Bongi Zengele, 'Reading Job "Positively" in the Context of HIV/AIDS in South Africa', in van Wolde, E. (ed.), *Job's God* (London: SCM, 2004), pp. 112–24.
Whedbee, J.W., 'The Comedy of Job', in Robertson, D.A. and Polzin, R. (eds), *Semeia 7: Studies in the Book of Job* (Missoula, MT: Scholars Press, 1977), pp. 1–39.
Wheeler, E., *Men of Power: Court Intrigue in the Life of Catherine Howard* (Glastonbury: Martin Wheeler, 2008).
Williams, J.G., 'Comedy, Irony, Intercession: A Few Notes in Response', in Robertson, D.A. and Polzin, R. (eds), *Semeia 7: Studies in the Book of Job* (Missoula, MT: Scholars Press, 1977), pp. 135–45.
Williams, R., *On Christian Theology* (Oxford: Blackwell, 2000).

Wogan-Browne, J. and Henneau, M.E., 'Introduction: Liège, the Medieval "Woman Question", and the Question of Medieval Women', in Dor, J., Johnson, L. and Wogan-Browne, J. (eds.), *New Trends in Feminine Spirituality: The Holy Women of Liège and Their Impact* (Turnhout: Brepols, 1999), pp. 1–32.

Wolfers, D., *Deep Things out of Darkness: The Book of Job: Essays and a New Translation* (Grand Rapids, MI: Eerdmans, 1995).

Woods, R., OP, 'Conclusion: Women and Men in the Development of Late Medieval Mysticism', in McGinn, B. (ed.), *Meister Eckhart and the Beguine Mystics* (New York: Continuum, 1994), pp. 147–64.

Wright, T., *Paul for Everyone: The Prison Letters – Ephesians, Philippians, Colossians and Philemon* (London: SPCK, 2004).

Author Index

Addelson, K.P. 36
Ainscough, C. 14, 91
Allan, G. 48
Anderson, J. 165
Anderson, K. 39
Arms, M.F. 16–17, 19, 25

Babinsky, E.L. 7, 114, 116, 124, 127, 134, 137
Banyard, K. 3, 4, 13
Barnes, L.P. 17
Baumann, Z. 170
Beaudoin, M.N. 15
Bohn, C. 19
Bolton, B.M. 116
Bonhoeffer, D. 161, 171
Briggs, C. 98
Brock, R.N. 16, 21–3, 26, 27, 37, 164, 166
Brown, F. 98
Brueggemann, W. 99, 100, 129
Bryman, 39
Burrus, V. 5, 155
Bussey, F.C. 115, 118, 120–21

Carlson Brown, J. 19
Cashman, H. 2, 16, 27
Cavani, L. 151
Coakley, S. 153, 158–9, 162
Cohen, F.S. 165
Colledge, E. 115, 117, 121
Cooper-White, P. 1, 2, 5, 10, 16, 17. 21, 24, 27, 30, 34, 86
Corbin, J.M. 46–8
Corduan, W. 138, 157
Cotter, J. 4
Cox, D. 83–4, 86, 92–3, 99–100
Crawford, C. 115
Cré, M. 115, 149
Crisp, B.R. 16, 26–7

Davie, G. 44
Davis, P.H. 29–30, 170
D'Costa, G. 135
Densen-Gerber, J. 165
Devault, M.L. 38
Douglas, D. 41
Doward, J. 1
Driver, S. 98
Dussell, E. 11

Edmondson, M. 29
Epiney-Burgard, G. 134, 144

Falvay, D. 115
Fawcettsociety 3
Feinauer, L.L. 1, 32
Field, S.L. 115, 117
Flaherty, S.M. 16, 18, 20, 23–4, 26, 92
Fortune, M.M. 2, 16–18, 22
Fulkerson, M.M. 33–4

Ganje-Fling, M.A. 10, 31–2
Gilligan, C. 37
Girard, R. 83, 92, 98
Glaser, B.G. 6–7, 39–42, 45–9, 60
Gordis, R. 83, 87, 89, 98
Gosney, J. 1, 16, 26
Graham, E. 37–8
Griffin, L. 16, 18–19, 23, 25
Griffin, P. 16, 18–19, 23, 25
Grovijahn, J. 34
Guarnieri, R. 114, 116, 143
Gunton, C. 4–5, 136
Gutiérrez, G. 82, 106, 107

Habel, N. 82, 84, 86, 87, 94, 97–8, 102, 104, 106–8
Hall, T.A. 1, 10, 31
Hampson, D. 154–5, 158–9
Harding, S. 37, 40

Harrison, B.W. 30
Hawthorne, G.F. 159
Hedges-Goettl, L. 1, 16
Henneau, M.E. 116
Herman, J.L. 1, 3, 10–14, 32
Herman, M. 29
Higgins, G.O. 24, 32, 163, 169
Hollywood, A. 118, 121–2, 136
House of Bishops 4, 15
Huberman, A.M. 46
Hughes, G. 55, 155
Humphreys, J. 31

Jack, D.C. 39
Jackson, L.A. 10
Jayaratne, T.E. 39
Johnson, E., C.S.J. 109

Kahn, J. 84, 87, 90–91, 102
Käsemann, E. 162
Kendall, J. 48
Kennedy, H. 1, 13
Kennedy, M. 2, 16–19, 21, 23, 26–7, 51, 88, 131–2
Kirchberger, C. 116
Kliewer, S. 10
Kocher, S.A. 115

Lawless, E. 44–5
Leclercq, J. 122
Leicht, I. 117, 122
Lerner, R.E. 114–15, 117
Lichtmann, M. 136
Loades, A. ix, xi, 1, 5, 10, 16
Loftus, J.A., S.J. 170
Lohmeyer, E. 159
Longchamp, H. de 121–2

MACSAS xi, xiii, 16–17, 21–2, 73, 78, 131, 173
Maguire, E. 4
Martin, R.R. 159–60
McCarthy, P. 10, 31–2
McDonnell, E. 117
McFadyen, A. 11, 155–8, 164
McFague, S. 5, 155
McGinn, B. 116–18, 122
McLaughlin, E. 120
McRobbie, A. 4
Meyer, R. 16, 20–21, 23
Miles, M.B. 46
Minister, K. 44
Morton, N. 30
Moosbach, C. 113
Muers, R. 160–62, 169, 171
Murray-Swank, N.A. 31

Neuger, C.C. 30
Newman, B. 118, 136
Ngwa, K.N. 106, 109

Oakley, A. 38, 44
O'Connor, S. 9
O'Mahoney, G. 132
Ong, W.J. 113
Opie, A. 39, 41
Orbach, S. 4
Orcibal, J. 134
Ormerod, N. 2, 63
Ormerod, P. 120
Ormerod, T. 2, 63
O'Sullivan, R.A. 116, 118

Pargament, K.I. 31
Parker, R.A. 16, 21–3, 26–7, 37, 163–6
Phillips, A. xi–xii, 31
Poling, J. 1, 3–5, 16–22, 24–6, 28, 37, 44, 86–8, 157
Pope, M. 82–3, 87, 93, 98, 104
Porete, M. ix, xi, xii, 7, 49, 52, 79, 113–49, 153, 155–7, 160, 163–7, 172
Porter, F. 31
Punch, K. 31, 35, 44, 46–9

Randall, C. 134–6
Roach, A.P. 120
Robinson, J.M. 117–18, 123, 136
Ronan, M. 34
Rosetti, S.J. 1
Rubin, M. 120, 149
Ruh, K. 114–15

Sargent, M.G. 118
Sargent, N. 10, 31
Schermer, V.L. 10, 32, 171
Scherr, R. 151

Schreiner 104
Schweiker, W. 154
Sells, M.A. 117, 143
Sgroi, S.M. 12–15, 32, 91
Shengold, L. 2
Shooter, S. 4
Slee, N. xi, 31–4, 37–8, 40, 44–5, 133
Souillac, G. 118–19, 125, 148–9
Stewart, A.J. 39
Stogdon, K. 158
Strauss, A.L. 7, 40, 45–9
St Thierry, W. 144

Ticciati, S. xi, 85, 94–8, 102–3, 107, 138
Toon, K. 14, 91
Trible, P. 5, 19, 81, 155
Trombley, J. 119
Turner, D. 119

Valentine, L. 1, 32
Verdeyen, P. 114, 116, 143–4

Ward, P. 154, 170
Weinandy, T.G. 135
Wheeler, E. 9
Williams, R. 164–7
Wogan-Browne, J. 116
Wolde, E. van 84–7, 92, 94, 102, 106–7, 111
Wolfers, D. 83, 87, 91, 93–4, 98, 102, 110

Zemeckis, R. 2
Zum Brunn, E. 134, 144

Scripture Index

Genesis
16.8–9 9

Numbers
27.1–11 109
36.1–12 109

Deuteronomy
28 93

Judges
19 9

2 Samuel
13 5

Psalms
131.2 97

Job
1.1 86
1.3 86, 110
1.4 101
1.5 86–7, 94, 101
1.6–12 93
1.8 94, 104–5
1.9 84
1.10 87–8, 103, 111
1.12 112
1.21–2 101
2.1–6 93
2.3 94, 104–5
2.4–5 90
2.6 112
2.7 104
2.8 89, 106
2.9 110–11
2.10 90, 102
3 84, 95–7
3.1–26 90
3.14 171
3.23 111
5.17 104
6 107
6.4 91
6.7 91
6.14 107
7.5 90
7.13–16 90
7.17–19 95
8.13 95
9.11 95
9.16–17 96
9.17 97
9.33 107–8
13.4–7 89
15.20 110
15.29 87
16.1–6 89
16.6 89
16.9 95
16.13 110
16.19 107–8
19 108
19.13 110
19.13ff. 107
19.25 107
19.26 82
19.28 108
22.4–11 88
22.6–9 88
22.11 97–8
22.27 84
22.30 84
28 102
28–31 84
28.3 102
29.2–4 94
29.5–6 88
29.5–11 86

29.14 86
29.12–14 88
29.22 88
29.24–5 86
29.25 88
30.1–2 87
30.1–8 88, 97
30.8 88
32–37 82
33.19 104
33.23 108
38 102
38–41 93
38–42.8 93
38.4–6 96
38.7 97
38.8–11 100
38.13 109
38.16 8, 97, 109
38.16–17 97
38.17 97
38.18 100
38.19–20 97
38.22 97
38.26–7 97
38.28–9 97
38.34 97
39.1–2 97
39.1 110
39.3 110
39.5–8 98
39.9–12 98
39.13–30 98
40.4 98
40.4–5 88, 97–8
40.9 99
40.11–14 99
40.16 98
40.19 99
40.23 98
41.3 99
41.8 99
41.9 98
41.12 99
41.13 99
41.33 99
42.3 105
42.5 105
42.6 83, 106
42.7 105
42.7–8 93, 105, 107
42.7–9 103
42.8 84, 92, 106
42.8–10 107
42.10 105, 107
42.11 103, 105, 107, 110
42.15 110

Isaiah
42.2 51
43.2 141
45 102–3
45.3 62, 102
45.5 102
45.8 102

Matthew
15.13–14 170

Luke
2.22–35 51
11.13 68
16.9–31 77
17.3–4 18

John
13.3–17 159

1 Corinthians
13.3 163

Philippians
1.5 159
1.7 160
1.27 160
2 159–62
2.5–11 153, 158
2.5 161
2.6–8 161–2
2.6 162
2.7 158–9, 162
2.8 162
2.12 159
2.13 160
2.25 160
3.2–7 160

3.10 160
3.20 162
4.2 160
4.3 160
4.14–15 159
4.18 160

Hebrews
13.8 54

Subject Index

AA 32, 171
abuse *see also* recovery from; sexual abuse; violence
child 2–3, 22, 28, 42, 78
divine 19, 155
by clergy 1–2, 18, 24–5, 42, 64, 75
definition of 4, 41
effects of 3–5, 11–15, 17, 23, 25–7, 88–91, 152, 156–7, 164–6
spiritual 17, 64, 72–3
as test 63–4, 104, 166
theology of 63–4
abyss 8, 85, 97–8, 100, 109, 126, 128, 131, 133, 167, 172
addiction 32, 164–5, 171
adultery 77, 100
agency *see also* surrendering agency
lack of 19, 25, 154
of survivors ix, 11, 15, 21, 143, 147–8, 157
ambiguity 24–5, 76, 164
in Job 7, 86–92, 102, 108
annihilated soul
authentic spirituality of 151–68
as divested/naked 137–40
as exemplar 130, 139, 145
at home with God 129
nobility of 121, 123, 130, 136, 139
at rest/repose 122, 133, 138, 145, 147
willing nothing 128, 138
and works 118, 123–6, 128–31, 135, 137, 141, 166, 172
of Charity 132, 140
of the Virtues 132, 143–7
and wretchedness 123, 126, 130, 139–40, 145, 147, 167
annihilation
concept of 123, 130–31, 133, 138, 152
of desire 131–2, 139, 142–5
process of 7, 114, 121, 123–9, 139–40, 143, 153, 172
of will 126, 136–40, 145, 149
apophaticism *see Mirror of Simple Souls*
atonement theologies 6, 10, 16, 18–23, 27, 63–4, 152
incarnational 20–23
penal substitution 19–20
violence in 21–3, 28, 155 n.12, 166
attentive listening
of God 8, 97–8, 107–8, 160–62
of interviewees 147–8
of Job 7, 98, 109, 148, 161
in Philippians 159–62
in therapy 15
Augustine of Hippo 11, 134, 156
authenticity xi, 8, 23–4, 51–2, 143–4, 152–3, 159–60, 170–72
authority 40, 74, 111, 124, 130
of the Church ix, 4, 117–19
autonomy 5, 7–8, 153
female 154–5

Babylonian exile 83, 102
Baptism 4, 23, 123, 129
beguines 116–18, 134
beguinage/beguine community 116, 118, 124 n.66, 135
Behemoth 98–9, 110
Bible 16, 147 *see also* Scripture
study 66–7, 71, 81–2
birth 37, 89–90, 97, 110, 164
Bishop of Cambrai 115
body/bodies 10, 15, 73
church 16, 26–8
female 2, 4–5, 9, 22, 28–9, 151
image 4, 26
Job's 90–91
male 22, 28
in the *Mirror* 122–3, 129, 135, 140

mortification of 118, 124, 163
Boethius 121
boundaries ix, 14, 25–6, 79, 81, 96, 115, 119, 135, 152, 154
as analytical concept 52, 74, 76–9, 82, 93, 108–12
gender 81, 109–10, 119
of interviewee 76–9, 111, 140, 152, 157, 163–5
invasion of 25, 77–8, 87–8, 90, 108, 152, 163–4
of Job 7, 87, 90, 93, 96, 108–11
of justice and equality 7, 93, 106, 108–12, 146
and liminality 76–7, 108–9, 111, 165
and ministry 152, 160
boundary-less-ness 165–7

calling *see also* vocation
sense of 66–73
Cassia 109
charity 124, 135
as power 88
Charity 132, 136, 140, 143–9
peace of 146–8
choice 4, 21, 57–9, 62–3, 85, 131, 140, 142–3, 151–4, 159, 166, 169–71
Christian
community 26–8, 33, 65, 71–2, 78, 82, 120, 152, 159–60, 162
survivors ix, 3, 6, 10, 16–17, 20, 23, 26–7, 30, 34, 41–4, 51–79, 149, 169
Christianity 2–4, 7, 10–11, 16–17, 19–20, 27–8, 34–5, 63, 114, 120–21, 123, 129, 154
Christology 158–9
Church, the 1–2, 17, 21, 25–6, 28–9, 33, 71, 76–8, 101, 113, 115–17, 147, 152, 169–70
action of 25, 73–5, 103
based on Mary 67–8
Catholic 1–2, 66, 115
denominations 42–3
of England 4, 35, 71
as healing 70, 153, 162
leadership of 17, 25, 64, 71, 74–5, 78, 132 n.14, 147, 172
liquid 170
medieval 113–15, 117, 135
in the *Mirror* 7, 127, 136, 148
and patriarchy 4, 7, 33, 35
purpose/vocation of 17, 74–6, 171
as refuge/security/safe place 70, 170
and silence about abuse 1–2, 27, 44, 71, 171
clergy *see also* abuse
action of 68, 71, 74–5, 130
codes *see* data analysis
compassion 69, 108, 147, 163
concubine 5, 9
concentration camp 53, 59, 151–2
confidentiality 41, 75
conscience 128, 144
consolation 105, 124, 130, 132
constant comparative method 45–6, 48, 52
contemplation 93, 96, 122, 124–5, 127–8, 159
core category *see* data analysis
Council of Chalcedon 135, 158–9, 161
Council of Vienne 117
creation 16, 24, 26, 85, 97, 109–10, 153, 167 *see also* universe*ex nihilo* 26, 164
and God 22, 24, 84–5, 94, 96, 98–100, 102, 105, 108, 110, 112, 114, 125–6, 137, 139, 163
pre- 126, 144
Creative Media Source 44
CSSA xiii, 17
culture 1, 3–5, 9, 13–14, 27, 30, 37, 81, 115
sexualization in 1, 4
Western 5, 29, 136, 153, 158, 170
Cursillo 67–8
Cyrus 102

data analysis 45–9
coding 41, 45–9, 52–3, 55–8, 65
axial coding 46–7
open coding 46–8, 52–3, 57, 59, 65
selective coding 48–9, 52, 76–9, 82, 93
theoretical coding 47–8, 52
core category 7, 46, 48–9, 51–2, 76, 79, 92, 114

saturation of theory 7, 34, 49, 52, 79, 93–112
theoretical sampling 7, 49, 79
variable 43, 46 n.72, 48, 53–5
death 4, 9, 25–6, 60, 77, 90, 97, 108, 121–2, 152, 163–4, 166 *see also* Jesus Christ
of nature 123
of spirit 123, 125
dependence 164–5
on God 75–6, 98, 130, 140–41, 147, 152–5, 158
desire 27, 124, 127, 132, 142–3, 146, 154 n.6, 166, 170 *see also* annihilated Soul; annihilation
for God 93, 95, 170
God's 137, 139
to serve 66, 70–72, 131
desolation 5, 97, 171
disclosure 41–2, 51, 88, 170
dispossessed, the 88, 97, 109–10
Dives and Lazarus 77, 109
doctrine *see also* atonement
Christian 11, 16, 19, 24, 28, 134–6, 164
effects of 65–6
of original sin 11, 156
of retribution 83, 86

ecclesiology 65, 74–6
empathy 33, 69, 109–10
lack of 25
entitlement
of daughters 109–10
male 3, 5, 24, 86, 153–4
of wealthy 87
Epaphroditus 160
epistemology
feminist 35–8
mystical 118
patriarchal 36
and social science 39–40
standpoint 36–7
equality 78, 93, 111–12, 139, 142, 146–7, 156, 161–2, 171–2
gender 1–3, 109–11
lack of 14, 21, 88, 107
eroticism 128, 137, 151
eternity 97, 123, 126, 129, 135, 137–40, 143, 146, 149 *see also* timelessness
Eucharist 26–7, 118
Euodia 160
Europe 113–16, 136
Evagrius Ponticus 169
evangelicalism 43, 116, 123, 129
evangelism 145, 147–8, 170
evil 14, 21, 24–9, 57, 63, 68, 99, 108–9, 131 *see also* God allowing; transformation of

faith 29–30, 35, 120, 125, 136, 143, 157–8, 160, 172
'chinam' 84–5, 107, 126
of Job 7, 82–5, 93, 101, 103
justification by 125
practices 65–6, 68, 94, 161
of survivors xi, 3, 6–8, 16, 30–32, 41, 44, 52–3, 55–8, 60, 70–71, 95, 101–4, 129, 131, 140, 147, 153, 157, 162, 164, 169
women's 31–2, 35, 37, 41, 133 n.120
family 3–4, 19, 24, 30, 62, 89, 101–3, 105, 107, 157
fear 12–13, 54, 87–8, 138, 141, 146–8, 159, 167
fellowship *see* koinonia
feminism 1, 4, 32–3, 35–40, 48, 81, 115–17, 154–5, 158–9
and academy 6, 33–4
postmodern 4, 37
and social science 36–40, 43
and theology 5, 16, 19, 30–31, 33–5, 116, 136, 153–9
films
Forrest Gump 29, 170
Little Voice 29
Night Porter 151–2
What Lies Beneath 2
flood 97–8, 165
forgiveness ix, 6, 10, 16–20, 47
and power dynamics 16–18, 28
and reconciliation 17–18
of self 13–17, 106, 156
free will 7, 52, 67, 114, 126, 138–9, 142, 145, 149
gift of 126 n.78, 138–9, 142

Freud, S. 9–10, 29
Friends of Job 85–6, 103, 127
Bildad 95, 107–8
as denouncers 88, 92, 108
Elihu 82, 101, 104, 108
Eliphaz 84, 87–8, 97–8, 104–5, 107–8
as God's defenders 84, 97, 108–9
incompetence of 84, 104–6
not listening 88–9
Zophar 107–8

gender 4, 30, 43–4, 72, 74, 81, 123, 136, 155 *see also* equality
bias 35–6, 43, 81
discourses of 30, 117, 119
essentialism 36–7, 40
socialization 4, 37, 81, 110
girls 1, 4, 9, 29–31, 109, 170
God *see also* God's Holding Company; Holy Trinity; Theophany; Yahweh
absence of 30, 55, 95
action of 55, 58, 60, 62, 76, 107 n.113, 126, 135, 140, 160, 163
allowing abuse/evil 55–8, 61–3, 70, 91, 98, 155
healing 54, 69–70, 76, 111
responding to Job 84–5, 92–3, 96–8, 103–4, 106, 110
saving 22, 70, 123, 146, 164
taking initiative 62, 106, 126, 128, 133, 144
transforming bad to good 57, 59, 62–5, 69, 76
attributes of
generosity/largesse 124–6, 128, 136–8, 142–3, 165
goodness 11, 24, 125–6, 128, 130, 133, 139–40, 143, 145, 167
grace 18, 123, 137, 145–6
immanence 35, 53, 78, 94, 96, 104, 106, 109, 111
permissiveness 57, 96, 108
power 21, 26, 73, 96, 98, 133, 152–3, 155, 166
sufficiency 125, 127, 138, 141
timelessness 8, 53–7, 172
transcendence 96, 104, 106, 154, 156
Being of 125, 127–8, 133, 138, 154
communion/union with 118, 121, 123, 125, 127–8, 135–8, 140, 142, 144, 158, 160, 162
gender of 123, 136
images of 23–4, 94, 109
Creator 84, 96–100, 102, 109, 111, 125–6, 139
Far-nearness 128, 134
Father 4–5, 19–20, 22–3, 55, 63, 95, 97, 109, 111, 135
Mother 23, 97, 109
Other 8, 85, 152–4, 161, 165
Judge 84, 96, 106
Lady Love 121, 136
Spouse 132, 134
nature of 6, 10, 16, 23–8, 30, 155–6, 165
as abusive 21, 155, 157
as all-powerful/almighty 18–19, 21, 23, 74, 85
as angry/wrathful 19, 55, 95
as constant/faithful/same 54, 60, 69, 74, 98, 139
for interviewees 55–8, 60, 64
as intimate 94, 135
in Job 84, 94, 100
as loving/love 23, 55–6, 60, 64, 71, 95, 98–9, 108, 114, 123, 126–47, 149, 155, 157, 165–7, 171–2
as male 4–5, 9, 23, 142, 155
in the *Mirror* 126, 135–7
as patriarchal 4–5, 111, 155
as remote 55–6, 157
as violent 92–3, 95, 104
non-intervention of 55–8, 60, 70, 73, 98
presence of 3, 26, 52, 103, 105–7, 130, 134, 138–40, 145, 152–4, 159–61, 163–7, 170–71 *see also* God's timeless presence;
God's Holding Company 8, 153, 163–7
God's timeless presence ix, 6–8, 52–7, 82, 93–100, 114, 136, 140–43, 153–4, 163
grace xi, 18, 122–3, 137, 145–6, 155–6, 163, 171
fall from 82, 92

grass roots, from 6, 36–9, 41
Guarnieri, Romana 114 n.5, 116, 143

Hadewijch of Antwerp 118
Hagar 5, 9, 160
Hainaut 116
healing 2, 10 n.10, 11, 17–19, 21, 26–7, 31–2, 53–4, 58, 61–3, 66, 69, 74, 77–8, 91–3, 101, 104, 130, 132, 141 *see also* recovery process
heaven 68, 83, 107–8, 122, 128, 133, 162
heavenly court 93, 136
Hegel 36
heresy 117, 120
  of Free Spirit 117
  in Job 83
  of Meister Eckhart 119
  of Porete 115–19, 143
history 9–10, 37, 51, 54, 85, 113, 115
  Church 35, 82, 115–21, 151, 158, 161
Holocaust, the 11, 28, 151
  Holy Spirit 4, 56, 68, 130, 135, 137, 140–41 *see also* Holy Trinityas actor/agent 69, 101, 135, 156
  empowering 147, 156
  gifts of 103
  in prayer 54, 69, 101, 103
  presence of 130
Holy Trinity 4, 118, 126 n.77, 128–30, 133–7, 145–6
Horeb 171
hospitality 7, 9, 103, 109 *see also* Theophany
  of interviewees 8, 70, 103, 157
humanity 10, 21, 23–8, 51, 84–5, 98–9, 110, 126–7, 129, 131–2, 135, 137–40, 152–3, 155–7, 164–5
  of Christ 158–9, 161–2
  freedom of 57–9, 62, 85, 100, 108, 160
humility 128, 133, 148, 158, 162
Huot de Longchamp 121

illness 69–70, 90–91
  mental
    depression 13, 26, 58, 60, 70, 75, 90–91
    eating disorders 12–13, 26, 91
    stigma of 91

incest 9, 13, 18–20, 23–4, 56, 71, 91, 166
Inquisition 7, 116–17, 119–20, 144, 149
interviewees *see also* survivors
  age of 42
  denominational adherence of 43
  and forgiveness 47, 75
  experiences of abuse 42
  feelings of
    anger 55–8, 70, 74–5, 77
    empathy 69
    guilt 47
    hurt/pain 54, 56, 61–5, 69–70
    love 56, 60
    passion 69
    suicidal 70, 90
    upset 89
  and loss 61, 72–3, 77
  revising view of God 58–65
  scepticism of 68
  self-worth 60, 70
  spiritual preparation of 54
  struggle of 51, 55–7, 60, 63, 75
  as witnesses 51
interviews 44–5
  sampling 36, 40–44

Jean d'Outremeuse 116
Jean Leclercq 122 n.56
Jemimah 109
Jesus Christ 24–5, 72, 132, 144
  2nd person of Trinity 4, 63, 130, 135
  action of 21–2, 64
  death of 20–23, 47, 59, 61, 63–4,130, 162, 166
  as example 123, 130, 160
  images of 20, 23
  as intimate 68, 75, 130, 132
  kenosis of 64, 158–9, 161–2
  as Lord 4
  love of 56
  as lover 68, 132, 142
  nature of 158–9, 161
  Presentation of 51
  resurrection of 26, 153, 15–61, 166
  and Samaritan woman 75
  as scapegoat 92
  significance of 63–4
  teaching of 18, 64, 170

with interviewee 54–6, 58, 90, 130, 134
Job, the Book of
approaches to 82–92
and Deuteronomy 83, 85, 91, 93, 105
genres
folk-tale 83
legal framework 104
mashal 84
poetry 82–5, 96–7, 102, 110
prose framework 82–3
heavenly wager 83, 93–4
integrity of 82–6, 112
as lay theology 83
and nature of God 84–5
plot of 82–4, 92
sections
Dialogue 82 n.6, 83–4, 86, 89–90, 92–4, 97, 102, 104, 107–8
Elihu's speech 82, 104, 108 n.363
Epilogue 83–5, 92–3, 96, 100, 102–3, 105–8, 110, 172
Job's monologues 84, 95, 97, 102
Prologue 7, 83–6, 93–4, 100–101, 103–5, 109–10, 112, 130, 154, 164
Whirlwind speeches 84–5, 97 *see also* Theophany
as spiritual resource 86
tempest in 96, 104–5
Job, the character *see also* faith; silence
as abuser/perpetrator 86–8, 92, 102, 112
as agent of change 85, 107–8
ambiguity of 86–92, 94, 102
anger of 84, 89, 91–2, 97
as arbiter/friend 107–8, 112
and boundaries 82, 87, 90, 93, 96, 106, 108–112
daughters of 109–10
and election by God 98, 103, 106
and Epilogue community 85, 103, 105, 107–10, 146, 161–2, 171–2
and equality 93, 106, 108–12
exclusion/isolation of 82, 89, 101, 107–8, 110–12
family of 101–3, 105, 107, 109–10
as God's servant 93, 103, 105–8
healing of 89, 91, 93
identifying with vulnerable 92, 105, 109–10
identity of 85–6, 106
illness of 90–91
integrity/righteousness/uprightness of 86–7, 94 n.308, 102, 104
as intercessor 84–5, 103, 105–8, 112
and loss 89, 94, 106
obsessiveness of 87, 94, 101
as Patriarch/powerful 83, 86–8, 106, 109, 167
piety of
in Epilogue 85, 93, 103, 105–8, 146, 148, 153, 161
in Prologue 85, 93–4, 101, 103, 106, 130
questioning/rebellion of 84, 102
repentance of 83, 106
restoration of blessings to 83, 92, 105, 107
as scapegoat/persecuted 88–9, 92, 108–9
and self-examination 85, 106
sin of 88, 102
skin of 90, 108
spiritual journey of 84–5, 91–2, 97, 105, 121
struggle of 84–6, 88
as survivor/victim 82, 86, 88–93, 102, 105–12, 167
John the Baptist 121
Judaism 166
Julian of Norwich 70, 148
justice 17, 93, 104, 108, 112, 142, 146, 157, 172
retributive 88, 93–4, 106, 111, 167

kenosis 64, 153, 158–62
Keren-Heppuch 109
Knowing ministry 6–7, 65–76, 82, 93, 105–8, 147–8
koinonia 159–60

language 25, 38, 110, 113–15, 161
Leviathan 98–9, 110
liminality 77–9, 108–12, 165
listening *see also* attentive listening

lack of 3, 6, 9, 29–30, 44, 75, 88–9
with the Other 7–8, 153, 158–62
to survivors ix, 2, 6, 11, 28, 33, 49, 51, 169
liturgy 4, 26–8, 65, 159
love
Fine Love 123–5, 132
loyal 98, 107–8
romantic 142
unconditional 23–4, 137, 146

MACSAS xi, 17, 21, 22, 73, 78, 131
male
academia 5, 36, 81, 113, 118
alpha 81–2
entitlement 5, 24, 86, 154
experience 44
identity 5
puberty rites 113
Marguerite of Navarre 115 n. 13
martyrdom 121–2, 124, 131, 146
Marxism 36
Mary Magdalene 121
Mary of Nazareth 51, 67, 121
Mechtehild of Magdeburg 118
Meister Eckhart 119
memory/remembering 12–13, 15, 54, 58, 151
Middle Ages 113–21
ministry 8, 18, 20, 23, 64, 66 *see also* Knowing ministry
to the abused 15–16, 18, 20, 23, 76
of annihilated Soul 143–7
authentic 152, 160
of deliverance 19, 25
healing 8, 75, 153, 167
of interviewees
educational 147
evangelistic 71, 147
exclusion from 71–4
formal 65, 72–6
informal 65, 67–72
prayer 67–71, 74–5, 148
of Job 93, 96, 103, 105–9, 112, 153
ordained 66–7, 72–3
prayer 54, 67, 69, 74–5, 103, 105, 130, 148
preparation for 106, 160, 171
quality of 171
helpful 54, 74, 89, 162
reflecting God 64, 69, 76, 106, 148, 152
unhelpful 18–19, 55, 93
suitability for 76, 171
women's 33, 67–8
Mirror of Simple Souls
apophaticism in 129, 133, 145
as antinomian 116, 117, 144
authorship of 115–16
as didactic 120, 145–6
Dialogue in 121, 127, 136, 146
and divine/human union 114, 118, 121, 123, 125, 128, 136–9, 142
indictments extracted from 116, 144
genres of 121
history of 114–21, 144, 148–9
manuscripts 114–15
metaphors in 127, 136, 141–2
and neo-platonism 118, 135
paradox in 127, 138–9, 146, 149
personifications in 121, 127, 136–7
Reason in 127, 136, 144, 146, 148
and quietism 135
satire in 143
schemata/structure of 121–2
soteriology in 135, 145
Souls 122 *see also* annihilated Soul
active 123
contemplative 124
lost 124
merchant 143
sad 124–5, 130 n.103
unencumbered 129, 138, 143, 146
stages in 114, 121–9, 147
first 123, 129
second 123, 129
third 123–4
fourth 123–5
fifth 121, 123, 125–9
sixth 125, 128–9, 133
seventh 123, 128–9
translations of 114–16, 121 n.51
Moses 171
mother *see also* God as
silent 19, 24, 54
tongue 113–14, 149

Mrs Job 110–11
mutuality 14–15, 21, 56, 155
mysticism 7, 34
of the Cross 23
medieval 114–15, 118–21, 128

narratives of harm 30, 35
nothingness 8, 25–6, 165, 167, 172
in the *Mirror* 122, 126, 138, 144, 149, 165
NVIVO*8 45

original sin *see* doctrine

paradise 23 n.64, 122, 136, 146
Paris 7, 115, 117 n.23, 119 n.43
pastoral *see also* theology
care ix, 31, 73, 146, 148, 161
as response to abused 15–16, 30, 76
relationship 69
abuse within 1–2, 21–2, 72–3
patriarchy 40, 88, 156, 159 *see also* God; Job
and academy 31, 35
and power 5, 28, 86
and social science 38–40
and theology 3–6, 16, 19–22, 28, 30, 86, 135, 154–5, 160
patriarchal
Church 4, 33, 35
society 4–5, 7, 9–10, 36f., 81, 86
values 2–5, 10, 22–3, 44, 100, 153
virtue 7
Paul
letter to the Philippians 153, 158–62, 171–2
peace 64, 77, 101, 132, 142
in the *Mirror* 122, 124–6, 128, 130, 132, 137–42, 146–8
perpetrators *see also* Job; sexual abusers
freedom of 57
healing of 88, 92, 112, 167
intransigence of 17, 23, 86
Philippians *see* Paul
Porete, Marguerite ix, 7, 113–49
as anomaly 118–21
as beguine 116–18, 124 n.66, 134
as elitist 123, 136, 164 n.49
as esoteric 123
execution of 7, 115, 117 n.23, 119, 148–9
and gender 115–19
as prophet 114, 125 n.76, 148–9
power 5, 39, 96, 153, 158
abuse of 3, 5, 8, 24, 39, 87–8, 100, 110–11
institutional 17, 64, 111, 119
as theological problem 5, 24
dynamics/relations
abusive 2–3, 13, 21, 28, 140, 155–7
in forgiveness 17
in knowledge/research 33–5, 40–41
inequalities of 3, 36, 111
in atonement theology 21
patriarchal/male 9, 23–4, 28, 86–7, 163
personal/individual 8, 154, 169
political 5, 119
of speech 160
powerlessness 5–6, 8, 12, 15, 18, 30, 111
practical theology *see* theology
prayer 17, 67–8, 70–71, 78, 144, 169 *see also* ministry
as context for abuse 17, 66
of Julian of Norwich 70
wordless 159
psychological
abuse 42, 70, 77–8, 152
interpretation of Job 83–4
psychology 10–15 *see also* Freud
child 1, 29
developmental theory 37
research in 31
men as normative in 37
and spirituality 10, 31–2

Quakers 43, 78, 132 n.119, 147

rape *see* sexual violence
reasoning, moral 36–7
reconciliation *see* forgiveness
recovery from abuse
process of 6, 10–15, 19, 23, 25, 70, 89, 141, 164, 166

research, social scientific
on abuse and spirituality 11, 31–3
scarcity of 10, 31–2
design 6, 30, 32, 36, 40–49
ethical 6, 34, 41
methodology 35–40, 43, 46, 129
congregational studies 31–4
discourse analysis 33
ethnography 33–4, 40
feminist 32–3, 36, 38–40
Glaserian grounded theory 6, 30–31, 40–49
grounded theory 7, 26, 30–34, 39, 52, 55, 79, 81, 85, 92–3, 114, 152–3, 169
and the marginalized 35–41, 43
oral life history 38–40
patriarchal 35, 38
qualitative 32–4, 39
quantitative 31, 39
and reflexivity 34–5, 38, 40
and theology 6, 11, 16, 30, 33–4
and women 32, 37–8
on women's faith 31–4
resurrection *see* Jesus Christ

sacrifice
ritual 87, 93–4, 101, 105–6, 108
of self 19–24, 123, 152, 161
Christ's 153
salvation 22, 122, 163
Satan, the 87, 90, 93–4, 101–2, 104, 107, 112
scholasticism *see* theology
Scripture ix, 17–18, 62, 71, 78, 81, 121
see also Bible
effects of 65–8, 77
images from 54, 109
as metaphor 64,
reading of 7, 33, 64, 122 n.56, 159
use/misuse of 64, 77, 127
victims of abuse in 5, 9, 19, 81
women in 9, 41, 71
silence of 5, 9, 81
service *see also* Knowing ministry; ministry
of God and others 52, 62, 65–70, 76
sexual
abuse 1–2, 16, 23, 30, 41, 63, 70, 151
see also incest
child 1, 9–15, 18, 21, 25–7, 31–2, 42–3, 101, 152, 163, 166, 169
clergy 1–2, 5, 13, 21–2, 42, 54–5, 57, 65–6, 72–4, 77–8, 100, 131 n.110, 142, 152
statistics 1, 24, 43
abusers/perpetrators 1, 5, 7, 13, 17, 23–6, 57–8, 61, 88 n.41, 102, 140, 151, 155–7, 164, 167 *see also* Job
intensity 100
violence 2–4, 9–10, 20, 27, 29–30, 42
pornography 4, 9, 27
rape 1, 3, 5, 9, 11–13, 18, 24, 26, 41–2, 58, 166
silence
about abuse 1–2, 17
of annihilated Soul 146
of dispossessed 88, 151
of God 5, 8, 97, 160, 162, 169
of Jesus 20, 22
of Job 7, 88, 90, 93, 97–8, 107, 109, 154
opening up 5–8
in pastoral care 146, 148
of Porete 113, 119–20
of Quakers 147
in spirituality 38, 78, 159, 161–2
of women 1, 19 *see also* Scripture
silencing of victims 13, 21, 27, 30, 161
sin *see* Job; original sin
slave(s) 9, 28, 36, 122–3, 160, 161–2
social science *see* research
special experience
of interviewees 53, 68, 70, 77, 130, 132–4
of Job 93, 96, 112
of Paul 160
spiritual
awakening 33, 57, 59–60, 68, 77
discipline 152, 154, 163–4, 170–72
illumination ix, 163
maturity 23, 85, 93, 143, 170–71
process 7, 49, 114
spirituality
and abuse 6, 10, 31–2, 91
authentic 3, 8, 10, 76, 172
beguine 118, 134
community 160

of girls 29
kenotic 153, 158–9
men's 37 n.40
and psychotherapy 10, 31–3
somatic 118, 121, 124
of survivors ix, xi, 7, 28, 42–3, 51, 76, 140, 152–3, 169
vernacular 114
of women 7, 31–3, 35, 118, 121 n.51, 133, 154
sublation 138, 157
suffering
of God 21–3, 145
of Jesus 19–21, 159–60, 166
of Job 81, 88–91, 93, 96, 104, 107, 110, 112
of women 110
suicide 13, 60, 70, 89–90
surrendering agency 7, 153–7
survivors
resilience of 24, 32
stories of
Abigail 13
Deborah 66–8, 72, 78–9, 94, 173
Esther 43, 47, 53, 58, 61, 67–8, 70, 74–5, 77, 89, 94, 96, 140–42, 148, 152, 171, 173
Joanna 54–5, 58, 60, 67, 70–72, 75, 88–91, 95–6, 133–4, 147, 152, 173
Karen 16, 18, 24, 26, 44
Lydia 35, 54, 56, 60–62, 67, 69–70, 72, 74–5, 101–3, 130–31, 134, 141, 148, 152, 166–7, 173
Miriam 43, 47, 55, 63–4, 67–9, 72–3, 75–6, 77–8, 89, 94–6, 100, 109, 111, 131–2, 142, 147, 173
Naomi 43, 54, 60, 67, 71–2, 90–91, 133, 142, 147, 169, 171, 173
Priscilla 47, 55–6, 62–3, 65, 67, 69, 72, 75, 91, 95, 99, 104–5, 148, 159, 166, 174
Sarah 43, 54, 63–4, 67, 72, 75–6, 78, 91, 140, 147–8, 171, 174
Tamar 47, 57, 66–7, 72–5, 77, 171, 174
symbiosis 24–5, 152–3, 155–7, 164–6
Syntyche 160

Tamar, daughter of David 5
terror 4, 22, 25–6, 51, 163
of God 91
Texts of 81, 155 n.12
theology *see also* annihilation; atonement; doctrine
of abuse 63–4
academic 4, 6, 31, 33, 119
Augustinian 11, 156
biblical 7, 16, 81
conservative 18
distorted 3, 6, 24
dominating/patriarchal 2–6, 10–11, 16, 28, 30–31, 113ff., 135, 155
feminist 4–5, 16, 19, 153, 155, 158
feminist pastoral theology 30–34
'grass roots' 41
lay 83, 115
medieval 113–20
mystical 7, 34, 118–19
pastoral/practical 6, 10–11, 15–28, 30–31, 76, 86
and praxis model 33–4
and power abuse 5, 18–23, 110–11
scholastic 118–19
simplistic 16–18
speculative 93 n.63
survivor 6, 16, 24–8, 31, 104, 111, 147, 169
dearth of 24, 34, 76
traditional 2, 16, 21–3, 28, 51, 64, 95, 135
Trinitarian 118, 130, 134–7
vernacular 118–19
women's 5, 35, 114–16, 119
exclusion/lack of 30–31, 35, 114, 119
Theophany 7, 84–5, 93, 96–100, 104, 126, 129
dialectic aspects of 106
hospitality/visitation 97–8
permissiveness/limit-setting 98–100
transcendence/immanence 96–7
equality in 109–11
and Isaiah 102–3

theoretical memos *see* data analysis
timelessness 53–5, 62, 76, 157, 166–7, 172
see also God's timeless presence
transcription 44–6
Transformation, as higher concept 6–8, 52, 57–66, 69, 75, 77, 82, 93–4, 101–5, 112, 114, 129–34, 137, 141, 156
transformation 33, 76, 85, 120, 156, 160, 162–3
of annihilated Soul 121, 123, 126–9, 137, 141–2, 144, 156
of community 8, 33, 82, 108
of culture 37
of evil into good 57, 59, 65, 69
of interviewees ix, 7, 57–9, 65, 68–70, 76, 157, 162
of Job 82, 85, 91–3, 101–5, 111–12
of survivors 26, 152, 163
of theology 24
trial 60–62, 74, 102–3
of Eckhart 119 n.43
in Job 95
of Marguerite Porete 116–17, 120–21
of the will 130–32, 156

underclass 87–8
union *see* God
universe 96, 100, 102, 109, 112, 125, 165

violence 12, 41, 140, 165, 169 *see also* atonement theologies; sexual violence
of creation 98
domestic 4–5, 10, 16, 41–3, 53
exposure of 27
intimate 22, 27–8
in Job 92, 96–7, 106
male experience of 44
political 42
vocation
of interviewees 62, 66–73
of Job 85, 91, 102, 106
in Paul 161
preparation for 171
of survivors 169
vulnerability 21, 29, 103, 131, 153–4, 158–9
of interviewees 54, 72–5
of Job 88, 92–3, 109
of survivors 13–15, 20, 142–3
vulnerable, the 5–6, 17, 30, 74, 87 n.35, 111, 153, 161, 170–72
as voiceless 2, 5–6, 16, 29–30, 88

warfare 3, 22–3, 128, 139
Second World War 75, 151
Western culture *see* culture
will *see also* annihilation of will; free will; trial of will
as analytical concept 52, 114
of annihilated Soul 114, 124, 126–8, 136, 138–9, 144, 160
conscripted 156
dissolution of 133–4, 139–40
God's 22–3, 58, 63–5, 77, 106, 124–7, 131, 134, 138–40, 142–3, 152, 157, 160, 163
not willing abuse 63, 65, 166
as unchanging 127, 142, 157
human 98, 100, 108, 126, 128, 135, 139, 142–3, 146, 152, 156
as alterable 127, 132, 139, 157
of perpetrator 19
of the Son 135
(sur)rendering to God 126–7, 139, 142, 149, 152–5, 166
of survivor/victim 18, 130–32, 140, 142–3, 153–6, 166
William Humbert 116, 119 n.43
William of St Thierry 144
women *see also* equality; silence; spirituality
abuse of 4–5, 10, 21–2
as abusers 24 n.70
bishops 4
blaming of 3, 9, 20
control of 3, 117
exclusion of 4, 35, 37–8
mystics 118, 124
submission/subordination of 4–5, 154, 156, 158
survivors 6, 13, 32, 43, 51
women's *see also* bodies; research; spirituality; theology
development 37–9

experience/issues 33, 35–9, 110, 121 n.51
movement 1, 5, 10
work 37
works *see* annihilated Soul
wretchedness *see* annihilated Soul

Yahweh 93–4, 99–100, 103–6, 110, 164
reliability of 83

24237390R00129

Printed in Great Britain
by Amazon